A SPREADING AND ABIDING HOPE

THEOPOLITICAL VISIONS

SERIES EDITORS:

Thomas Heilke
D. Stephen Long
and C. C. Pecknold

Theopolitical Visions seeks to open up new vistas on public life, hosting fresh conversations between theology and political theory. This series assembles writers who wish to revive theopolitical imagination for the sake of our common good.

Theopolitical Visions hopes to re-source modern imaginations with those ancient traditions in which political theorists were often also theologians. Whether it was Jeremiah's prophetic vision of exiles "seeking the peace of the city," Plato's illuminations on piety and the civic virtues in the Republic, St. Paul's call to "a common life worthy of the Gospel," St. Augustine's beatific vision of the City of God, or the gothic heights of medieval political theology, much of Western thought has found it necessary to think theologically about politics, and to think politically about theology. This series is founded in the hope that the renewal of such mutual illumination might make a genuine contribution to the peace of our cities.

FORTHCOMING VOLUMES:

Charles K. Bellinger
Jesus v. Abortion: They Know Not What They Do

David Deane
The Matter of the Spirit: How Soteriology Shapes the Moral Life

A Spreading and

ABIDING HOPE

A Vision for Evangelical Theopolitics

JACOB SHATZER
Foreword by D. Stephen Long

CASCADE *Books* • Eugene, Oregon

A SPREADING AND ABIDING HOPE
A Vision for Evangelical Theopolitics

Theopolitcal Visions 18

Cascade Books
An Imprint of Wipf and Stock Publishers
199 W. 8th Ave., Suite 3
Eugene, OR 97401

www.wipfandstock.com

ISBN 13: 978-1-62564-875-4

Cataloging-in-Publication data:

Shatzer, Jacob

    A spreading and abiding hope : a vision for evangelical theopolitics / Jacob Shatzer ; foreword by D. Stephen Long.

    xiv + 202 p. ; 23 cm. —Includes bibliographical references and index.

    Theopolitical Visions 18

    ISBN 13: 978-1-62564-875-4

    1. Conyers, A. J., 1944–. 2. Theology, Doctrinal. 3. Christianity and culture. I. Long, D. Stephen, 1960–. II. Title. III. Series

BR1642.U5 S44 2015

Manufactured in the U.S.A.

For Keshia

Contents

Foreword

A. J. Conyers may not be well known among theologians outside the Baptist tradition. Born during the tumultuous end of World War II, 1944, Conyers grew up in rural Georgia and recognized early on that the political reality in the United States was not as it should be. An active Baptist and evangelical, Conyers attended Southeastern Baptist Theological Seminary in North Carolina before the conservative takeover. He then pursued his doctorate at the Southern Baptist Theological Seminary, where he was influenced by an unlikely cadre of political and theological thinkers. A founding member of George W. Truett Theological Seminary at Baylor University in 1994, Conyers was poised to make major contributions to a theopolitical vision, identifying and naming what was not as it should be and how it might be addressed. Diagnosed with cancer in 2002, Conyers died in 2004. Although his life was cut short, Conyers nonetheless made some significant interventions into theology and politics, including *The Long Truce: How Toleration Made the World Safe for Power and Profit* (2001) and *The Listening Heart: Vocation and the Crisis of Modern Culture* (posthumously published, 2006).

In *A Spreading and Abiding Hope*, Jacob Shatzer takes up Conyers's mantle. He accomplishes at least three important goals in making his own significant contribution to theopolitics. First, he interprets Conyers for those unacquainted with his work, carefully positioning him within the theological and political milieu out of which he worked. Not only does he know Conyers's work, but even more importantly, he knows the work Conyers knew. From the Reformed jurist Althusius to the Southern Agrarians Richard Weaver and (briefly) Wendell Berry to Dale Moody and Jürgen Moltmann, Shatzer renders intelligible Conyers's work and its importance. Long before critiques of "modernity" were fashionable, A. J. Conyers recognized that modern political arrangements were too often founded upon pure power, and he traced that error to medieval metaphysics, especially nominalism. But Shatzer, following Conyers, does not find the remedy to those errors in organic, romantic medieval communities. Instead, he finds resources in the Reformed tradition, especially the Baptist and evangelical traditions, to move beyond modern political misalignments.

Shatzer's second contribution is to move from Conyers to an evangelical political theology that is neither fundamentalist nor liberal. This is where he sees Conyers's work leading before it was cut short by his death. Shatzer offers an evangelical theopolitics that draws upon the resources present in the Reformed and Baptist traditions to address the common errors whose identification are often associated with Catholic and Anglican theologians. Shatzer draws on Conyers's work to address the question, is there such a thing as an evangelical theopolitical imagination? He concludes that there is but that it is underrepresented in the political positions presented by evangelical theologians. He is not shy in identifying the "weaknesses" in evangelical politics; his work is by no means triumphalistic about the future of evangelicalism. Rather, it is a warning about the consequences intrinsic to the evangelical "embrace" of democratic and free-market institutions— consequences Conyers identified. Neither fundamentalism nor liberal Protestantism move us beyond those consequences. Shatzer's work is not, however, reactive. It is not determined by what it opposes but by what it affirms. What he offers here is a constructive evangelical political theology.

This constructive proposal provides a third contribution. Much of contemporary political theology turns to the Eucharist or the liturgy in order to illumine a way forward, but this is not a readily available option for a Baptist or evangelical theologian. So what is a theologian to do who identifies similar errors as those political theologies but cannot follow their constructive proposals without leaving his or her Baptist/evangelical tradition behind? Without dismissing those more Catholic and Anglican proposals and thereby replaying the sixteenth century, Shatzer complements them by showing what the Baptist tradition has to contribute.

Shatzer's three contributions noted above are not the only contributions this work makes. He also offers illuminating insights and interpretations of current theologians and political theorists, especially as they seek to bring those two discourses together. He listens generously to those outside his own tradition while remaining indebted to it. He does not merely repeat Conyers but raises questions about the racism present in some of those involved in the Southern Agrarian movement, and he questions aspects of

Conyers's deep commitments to Moltman's theology. Shatzer offers a theo-politics that draws on the communion of saints. Conyers may no longer be with us, but that does not mean his voice should not be heard and engaged. This book is a tribute to Conyers, a fascinating proposal that evangelicals would benefit from if they take it to heart, and a profound reflection on a theopolitical vision.

D. Stephen Long

Acknowledgments

I must begin by thanking God for calling me to and equipping me for such work. Looking back over years of formal academic preparation, God's guidance and provision are particularly evident.

This work would not have seen completion without the guidance of my dissertation board: D. Stephen Long, Joseph Ogbonnaya, and Michael Duffey. Steve Long's truly incredible work ethic, editing skills, and kindness made this whole process much more enjoyable than it might have been. In addition, Brad Green's personal and academic knowledge of A. J. Conyers proved vital.

I would not have pursued graduate theological work if it were not for the influence of three men. John Wojtowicz, my high school Academic Decathlon coach, was the first person outside of my family both to see my academic potential and to encourage me to develop it further. Greg Thornbury, my first college professor, has always pushed me to serve God with my academic gifts and to love the church. C. Ben Mitchell has kindly allowed me to steal him as a mentor. Though we've never lived in the same city, Ben has always taken my calls, given me advice, and reminded me how exciting it is to do theology and ethics faithfully and well. All three of these men have believed in me more than I believe in myself.

Matthew Crawford and Nathan Willowby both read numerous drafts of this book and spent hours talking to me about it. While I thank them for their editorial prowess, I am more grateful that they took the years necessary to teach me about lasting friendship.

Numerous other individuals have provided support along my journey: Emmanuel and Camille Kampouris, Brian Pinney, Michael McClenahan, Al Mohler, Russ Moore, and Jay Sanders, to name a few. Special thanks to Deb Conyers and Robert Sloan for talking with me about A. J. Conyers and his legacy. My Sterling College colleagues have made my first semesters teaching enjoyable. Thanks especially to Tom Bronleewe, Daniel Julich, Roy Millhouse, and Felicia Squires. I also appreciate Jeremy Labosier, librarian extraordinaire, for helping me compile the index.

I also thank the editorial team at Cascade. Charlie Collier has been quick to answer my questions. Jacob Martin proved an expert copy editor, saving me from murky wording and bibliographical errors. It is a privilege to publish in such a great series: I've benefited from other installments in Theopolitical Visions and hope my work will be a worthy addition to it.

Finally, I would like to thank my family. My mother taught me to love Jesus and books—in that order—from a very young age. My father taught me to work hard, to sacrifice, and to read the Bible. My grandparents, siblings, and in-laws have all been appropriately curious about my academic work—and supportive of it as well. My children have been very welcome diversions: Ezekiel has reminded me of the need to take time to play; Jackson has reminded me of the excitement of discovering books for the first time; and Ramona has reminded me of the joyful interruption that new life can be—her birth was a welcome diversion in the final stages of this work!

My wife, Keshia, deserves more thanks than I can give. Her love and joy have fueled me through this work and all the preparation that has led up to it. I dedicate this book to her.

Evangelical Theology and Political Formation

Now is the time for evangelicals to declare themselves in a very intentional way for the recovery of the intellectual aims that are unapologetically catholic—not as a way of losing their distinctiveness, but as a way of recovering the task that made the separation necessary in the first place: the safeguarding of a truly catholic vision of the world and its redemption.[1]

Evangelicalism suffers from an underdeveloped theopolitical imagination. Evangelicals excel—at least as portrayed by the media—at adopting and promoting political stances on specific issues, but less reflection occurs on the level of *imagination* and how it influences such choices. The imagination seems like a slippery concept because in its most popular usage it refers to thinking about what does not exist, or to pretending or inventing something.

But what exactly is "evangelical theopolitical imagination"? On one hand, I simply mean imagination in the sense of "moral imagination": the ability to think about what the world should be like and how to work for it to be so. This ability includes moral vision, commitment to creative moral

---

1. Conyers, "Protestant Principle, Catholic Substance," 17.

action, and the relevant habits, practices, and reasoning.[2] On the other hand, I mean imagination in the sense that William Cavanaugh has used it in recent political theology. Cavanaugh, relying on the work of Benedict Anderson,[3] argues that politics is a practice of the imagination that organizes bodies according to stories of human nature and human destiny that are ultimately theological in nature.[4] He relies on the concept of the "social imaginary," which refers to the unavoidable background beliefs that are the context for social theory and analysis,[5] or in this case, theopolitical analysis. The social imaginary has to do with how people understand themselves, what they expect of each other, and what background practices inform social behavior.[6]

In my use, the imagination includes both practice and theory. One recent scholar using the idea of imagination theologically would disagree: James K. A. Smith separates imagination from intellect. Relying on the work of Charles Taylor, Smith argues, "The imaginary is more a kind of noncognitive *understanding* than a cognitive *knowledge* or set of beliefs."[7] In a footnote, he admits to drawing the difference between practices and

2. James K. A. Smith's recent work on imagination in Christian discipleship is very helpful in broadening the way intellect and practices come together to form people. He defines imagination as "a quasi-faculty whereby we construe the world on a precognitive level, on a register that is fundamentally *aesthetic* precisely because it is so closely tied to the body." Smith, *Imagining the Kingdom*, 17.

3. See Anderson, *Imagined Communities*. Anderson argues that the rise of vernacular languages and the printing press combined to influence the way people thought about themselves in relation to others. He explains the rise of nationalism by turning to changes that made the imagination of such communities possible. A nation is "an imagined political community—and imagined as both inherently limited and sovereign" (6). It is imagined because the members of even the smallest nation will never know everyone else. It is limited because no nation sees itself as coterminous with all mankind. It is imagined as a community because the nation is conceived of as a deep comradeship, and this fraternity makes it possible that people would be willing to die for the nation. He traces how changes in religious community and the dynastic realm left a need for a larger frame of reference, which nationality rose to fulfill. Changing notions of time also influenced these changes, as the novel made it possible to think about homogenous, empty time (36). Print-languages laid the basis for national consciousness in three ways. Print languages (1) created unified fields of exchange and communication, (2) gave a new fixity to language, and (3) created languages of power of a kind different than older administrative vernaculars (44–45).

4. Cavanaugh, *Theopolitical Imagination*, 1–2.

5. Lyon, "Being Post-Secular," 649.

6. This description is drawn from Charles Taylor.

7. Smith, *Desiring the Kingdom*, 65.

understanding more sharply than Taylor does,[8] but the body of Smith's text maintains that a sharp distinction between imagination and intellect is necessary to the social imaginary. Taylor, on the other hand, draws a picture of a dynamic relationship between theory and practice, such that each informs the other in the social imaginary—though such influence is not always readily apparent or translatable into propositions.[9] The sense of "imagination" that I employ depends more on this dynamic relationship between theory and practice that Taylor expounds.

Like any group, evangelicals exhibit weaknesses, and some weaknesses flow directly out of our distinguishing marks and strengths. Four tendencies—which exist in evangelicalism to varying degrees—contribute to evangelicalism's underdeveloped theopolitical imagination. In short, we tend to rely on binary rhetoric and polarization; we often (somewhat ironically, as I will explain below) take certain aspects of modernity for granted and even champion them; we sometimes read Scripture in an oversimplified manner; and we often fail to incorporate the insights of political theology into our theopolitical imagination. Such weaknesses contribute to a growing exodus of believers from evangelical churches to more historically substantive Christian traditions, such as Anglicanism and Roman Catholicism.

But does evangelicalism itself have resources for strengthening these weaknesses? I think so, and one potential resource is the work of the late Baptist theologian A. J. Conyers, whose theological vision of the modern world provides both content and a method for overcoming evangelical weaknesses and developing a more critical, biblical, evangelical theopolitical imagination. In what follows, we will look more closely at the weaknesses I have identified in evangelical political theology, and then introduce Conyers in more detail before turning to the overall shape of this work.

Weaknesses of Evangelical Political Theology

Defining evangelicalism has never been easy or without controversy. David Bebbington's popular "Quadrilateral" identifies four distinct marks of

---

8. Ibid., 67 n. 53.

9. For example, Taylor states, "What we see in human history is ranges of human practices that are both at once, that is, material practices carried out by human beings in space and time, and very often coercively maintained, and at the same time, self-conceptions, modes of understanding." Taylor, *Modern Social Imaginaries*, 31.

evangelicalism: conversionism (the belief that lives need to be changed), activism (the expression of the gospel in effort), biblicism (a particular regard for the Bible), and crucicentrism (a stress on the sacrifice of Christ on the cross).[10] More recently, Timothy Larsen has provided a more expansive set of distinguishing marks: an evangelical is (1) an orthodox Protestant (2) who stands in the tradition of the global Christian networks arising from the eighteenth-century revival movements associated with John Wesley and George Whitefield, (3) who gives preeminent place to the Bible in her Christian life as the divinely inspired, final authority in matters of faith and practice, (4) who stresses reconciliation with God through the atoning work of Jesus Christ on the cross, and (5) who stresses the work of the Holy Spirit in the life of an individual to bring about conversion and an ongoing life of fellowship with God and service to God and others, including the duty of all believers to participate in the task of proclaiming the gospel to all people.[11] Christians marked by such commitments generally fit with the designation "evangelical" as it is used culturally and theologically today.

The common story of American evangelicals in politics is a simple one: emerging out of the fundamentalist entrenchment of the early twentieth century, evangelicals such as Carl F. H. Henry called conservative Christians into cultural and political engagement in the name of the gospel. The tale since Henry's 1947 jeremiad, *The Uneasy Conscience of Modern Fundamentalism*, is one of increasing influence into the Ronald Reagan and George W. Bush presidencies—and even into the Tea Party movement.

Yet various tendencies cause evangelical theopolitical imagination to suffer. These tendencies are related to distortions that stem from evangelical identity markers, like those formulated by Bebbington. In what follows I highlight four weaknesses that occur to varying degrees: first, a tendency to reduce everything to a binary, us-versus-them rhetoric, which stems in part from an evangelical emphasis on conversionism (a focus on conversion contributes to viewing people in two opposing camps, which can then fuel an us-versus-them rhetoric). Second, evangelicals uncritically embrace certain aspects of the modern world. This is especially true about democratic and free-market institutions. Evangelicals try to promote the ways in which such institutions can cooperate with the advance of the gospel without being as aware of how these institutions can be harmful. This weakness

10. Bebbington, *Evangelicalism in Modern Britain*, 3.

11. See Larsen, "Defining and Locating Evangelicalism," 1. For recent evaluation of "the Bebbington thesis," see Haykin and Stewart, *Emergence of Evangelicalism*.

is related to evangelical activism, and specifically with the desire to leave fundamentalist isolationism behind. Third, in seeking to be biblical, evangelicals sometimes revert to an oversimplified reading of Scripture, despite our commitment to the Bible as authority. This oversimplified reading reduces the text and makes it serve ideological ends, often related to modern institutions. This weakness is a perversion of evangelical biblicism (though many outside evangelicalism identify this perversion with biblicism itself). Fourth, evangelicals often fail to incorporate the theological work of other Christian traditions, even when that work would strengthen evangelical priorities. In the case of political theology, more could be done to connect the thinking of evangelicals to that of other Christians. This weakness correlates (at least in part) to a focus on the Bible as the primary authority. Such a focus can lead to a neglect of other sources for consideration, such as the work of Christians from other traditions.

These individual tendencies—related to the very marks of strength that define evangelicalism—weaken evangelical political thought and witness. In the following sections, I draw on various examples to illustrate (though not conclusively prove) these tendencies. Every great tradition develops certain flaws, and attempting to address them helps strengthen that tradition.

Weakness One: Binary, "Us-versus-Them" Rhetoric

The first weakness is a consistent reversion to a binary, "us-versus-them" rhetoric. The "us" and the "them" change depending on the topic, with the distinction being drawn even among evangelicals. This tendency occurs at least in part because "evangelical identity has its origins in strongly particularist senses of Christian self-identity, and has tended to form its own social culture over and against that of the world around (as witnessed to in its Puritan and Pietist past)."[12] These particularist senses of self-identity play positive roles, but they can lead theopolitical imagination to conceive of everything using such binaries. These constructed binaries artificially deform debates and conversations. The circles of acceptability become increasingly narrow, with certain issues and attitudes framed as essential. Even when evangelicals seek to be charitable, "our conversation frequently revolves around where we place that binary dividing line."[13]

12. Greggs, "Beyond the Binary," 153.
13. Ibid.

Weakness Two: Taking Modernity and Its Institutions for Granted

Evangelicals often take modernity and its institutions—such as democracy, the nation-state, and free-market capitalism—for granted.[14] This second weakness also grows out of one of evangelicalism's strengths: while fundamentalism refused to capitulate to modernity but instead reacted strongly against it and developed an isolationist "bunker mentality," evangelicalism defines itself against this isolationism. But reacting against isolationism has led many evangelicals to take modernity for granted. This "taking modernity for granted" appears in two forms: in some cases, evangelicals do not think critically about how modernity and its institutions form us as individuals and communities, and in other cases, evangelical theologians find a stake in modern institutions and promote and defend them, while at the same time neglecting or downplaying their negative aspects.

This tension can also be seen when considering the relationship of Christianity to Western civilization.[15] In his book tracing the concept of the sacredness of human life, David Gushee notes that Christianity itself is divided on the question of the relationship of Christianity to the West. As Gushee observes, "It seems most of the highly regarded thinkers in progressive Christianity attack the history of the church, at least after the conversion of Constantine, as at best a detour from the church's originally peaceable and liberating vision, and at worst a grotesque moral capitulation to violence and imperialism."[16] On the other hand, more culturally conservative Christians tend to celebrate the achievements of Christendom and its positive legacy to Western civilization. The issue is not whether this particular issue is on people's minds when they consider issues like economics, but instead that it lies in the background to a degree, influencing a positive or negative posture toward the West and its heritage from the outset and setting up this tension.

Two modern institutions that often receive evangelical support are democracy and free-market economics. Evangelicals tend to champion both of these institutions without seriously considering how they are formative and not simply neutral. I will discuss both of these examples in the next weakness, which will illustrate that an emphasis on the Bible as final

14. As with the other weaknesses, there are exceptions and points of hopeful change. For example, Peter Leithart begins to critique what he calls "Americanism." See Leithart, *Between Babel and Beast.*

15. See Gushee, *Sacredness of Human Life.*

16. Ibid., 116.

authority can lead to an oversimplified use of the Bible. The point in view, however, is not whether one can be a Christian and a capitalist,[17] for instance, but rather how finding a stake in defending certain institutions can contribute to a social imaginary that is then blind to the negative formation that even the best of human institutions can provide.

Weakness Three: Oversimplified Reading of Scripture

Evangelicals often rely on oversimplified readings of Scripture. In the evangelical quest to be rooted in the Bible, it is easy to enlist biblical proof texts to support positions that one has already arrived at without taking into account other positions or the exegetical and theological contexts of the texts being used. Oversimplified readings of Scripture can also emphasize a surface-level interpretation of key texts while neglecting the broader canonical context and the scriptural themes that speak to similar issues. Further, evangelical readings of Scripture can become oversimplified not because they lack sophistication but because they bring ideological concerns to the text without adequately realizing it and accounting for it. In this instance, the oversimplification stems from failing to analyze complex factors such as ideological motives or preferences. When the evangelical theopolitical imagination is blind to problems in modern capitalism, for instance, evangelicals are less likely to hear the biblical text speak against such realities and are more likely to use historical context or other arguments to explain what the text says. I will illustrate this weakness by briefly turning to two different conservative evangelical treatments of economic and political issues. In both cases, the scholars are rightly concerned with the evangelical priority of recognizing the Bible as the ultimate authority, but their interpretations are open to criticism for not incorporating the biblical witness more broadly.

Economist John Lunn's work serves as a representative example of evangelical engagement with economics, shown both by his general affirmation of capitalism and also the inclusion of his essay in *The Oxford*

---

17. This is the question asked in Richards, *Money, Greed, and God*. Richards does an exemplary job of explaining some "myths" regarding capitalism in order to argue that Christianity and capitalism are not necessarily opponents. He admits that capitalism is not perfect and that sin is present, but in defending capitalism so strongly he makes it more difficult to recognize that capitalist practices can form the social imagination in a way that goes against Christianity.

Handbook of Evangelical Theology.[18] His reading of Scripture is not over-simplified because he neglects historical context or fails to give careful attention to the text; instead, he seems to come to the text with the desire to defend a certain form of economics, which then drives—at least to a degree—his exegesis and argument.

Lunn addresses a concern that many Christians have about affluence in modern industrial and postindustrial societies and how that concern relates to the Bible's views on wealth and poverty. He constructs an apology for modern capitalism by setting up a difference between biblical economies and market economies and applying those differences to how Christians interpret the language of rich and poor and concepts of greed.

The economy of Israel and Scripture is significantly different from market economies. While this claim is not controversial, the way that Lunn substantiates it provides the foundation for the ethical arguments he constructs. Two elements of biblical-era economies are the most important. First, "most people in biblical times perceived all goods to be limited in supply, including land, wealth, prestige, power, status, honor, and security. There was a zero-sum mentality concerning any of these goods."[19] In such a system, it makes more sense to consider that the rich and the poor are two poles; for the rich to have more the poor must necessarily have less in a zero-sum game. Second, Lunn problematizes the terms *rich* and *poor* as they are used in the Bible (and therefore as they are used in authoritative ethical statements). *Rich* and *poor* were not economic descriptions but descriptions of attitudes or behavior. *Rich* did not refer simply to someone with material wealth; instead, it almost always referred to someone who came upon that wealth in a dishonorable way, because he would have had to ignore and break biblical laws to obtain more land. The "poor," on the other hand, were not people with few resources but "those who cannot maintain their inherited status due to circumstances that befall them and their families, such as debt, being in a foreign land, sickness, death of a husband, or some personal physical accident."[20] Thus, Lunn concludes,

> in the perception of people in [a] limited-good society, the majority of people are neither rich nor poor, but equal in that each has a status to maintain in some honorable way. Personal assessment is not economic but a matter of lineage. In this context, the

18. Lunn, "Economics," 402–17.

19. Ibid., 404.

20. Ibid.

designations rich and poor really refer to the greedy and the socially ill-fated. The terms do not characterize two poles of society
as much as two minority categories, the one based on the shame-
less desire to expand one's wealth, the other based on the inability
to maintain one's inherited status of any rank.[21]

By resituating the biblical descriptions, Lunn is able to make a more nuanced shift between the Bible and its ethical standards with regard to the
rich and the poor in modern market economies.

Modern market economies differ in key respects from the economies
of biblical times. These differences inform the way the ethical prescrip-
tions translate. In Palestine, exchange was personal, but modern market
economies operate with impersonal transactions. Also, in biblical times
intentions were very important, whereas in market economies it is more
important to abide by the "rules of the game." And a difference in attitudes
and basic beliefs of people alters our understanding: people no longer view
life as a zero-sum game but see that market economies operate on the idea
that all parties can benefit from transactions. Christians must keep certain
guidelines in mind. First, an appropriate ethic must emphasize the rules
of the game, such as contracts and regulations, because of the impersonal
nature of transactions. Second, Christians should develop a separate ethic
to govern personal relationships. Third, "effort should be made to define
the boundaries between the world of personal relationships and the world
of impersonal relationships."[22] Finally, Christians must recognize that they
have an obligation to the poor. It remains unclear whether this is a third
ethic, or if it is a subset of the impersonal or personal ethic Lunn points out
in previous responses. Yet, Christians must be careful in applying the Bible's
statements on economics.[23]

Lunn turns to issues of greed and materialism, the primary ethical
concerns for Christians in market societies. He briefly argues that greed
is not necessary in order for market societies to function and insists that
markets require virtue for their operation (he names trust as an example).
In fact, "markets *can* make us better. As people are more affluent and have
more choices, they can become either greedy and materialistic—or generous and caring."[24] Wealth can be associated with exploitation, but it can

21. Ibid., 404–5.
22. Ibid., 408.
23. Ibid.
24. Ibid., 414.

also be directed at providing people with better lives. In Lunn's eyes, the morality of the market economy emerges purely from the direction that individual moral agents direct it. It is neutral at worst, and morally superior at best because of its ability to lift people out of poverty.

Lunn serves as an excellent example of the evangelical desire to recognize the Bible's authority over all of life. And he takes the Bible seriously, providing a careful reading that considers context and other important issues. However, his emphasis on the amount of change between biblical times and today can serve to undercut the very biblical authority that he wants to uphold. This emphasis can also condition us evangelicals to be so accepting of the free-market system that we neglect the critical faculties necessary for serving God and not money in a materialistic society. Evangelicals at least have to be willing to question whether enthusiasm for the free market and its strengths leads to reading and categorizing biblical texts in a certain way, one that unnecessarily limits evangelical theopolitical imagination. An imagination that sees capitalism and the free market as the best possible scenario can be blind to warnings in the biblical text, and reading the text this way further reinforces evangelical theopolitical imagination regarding capitalism.

A brief example from Baptist theologian Chad Brand offers a more blatant instance of how placing an emphasis on Scripture's authority may lead to an oversimplified reading. In seeking to address the size of government and the extent of taxation in the United States, Brand turns to the Old Testament for insight. He argues that Solomon's and Rehoboam's taxation policies led to the separation of Israel into the northern and southern kingdoms. The kings had great wealth, which they did not create through commerce but rather took from others. This decision led to the collapse. Therefore, since heavy taxation led to the collapse of that civilization, limited government and low taxation are the wise course of action for today.[25] And Brand's work is not a small, idiosyncratic contribution: his book *Flourishing Faith* is published by the Acton Institute for the Study of Religion and Liberty, an influential conservative research institution devoted to integrating Judeo-Christian truths with free-market economics.[26] My interest here is not to rule rule on the validity of the Acton Institute or its various projects but to note that a reading such as Brand's fails to advance issues of

---

25. See Brand, *Flourishing Faith*, 46–53.

26. See the Acton Institute website: http://www.acton.org. Lunn is likewise associated with the Acton Institute.

evangelical politics or economics and in fact weakens them, no matter what conclusions are reached.

Another aspect of this weakness deals not only with the way Scripture is used but the context in which arguments are made. In an article on evangelicalism and the political, Andi Smith argues that evangelicals too often translate Scripture into ideology without allowing the narrative to form us. Evangelicals also fail to question how the way we are formed by the narrative might challenge ideas that we think we agree with, such as the free market. "The evangelical *use* of Scripture has consistently failed to recognize the church as that community of narrative by which the truthfulness of our discipleship *is* the appropriation of an alternative politics," Smith writes.[27] This piece points more toward the idea of witness, and how embodying the Scripture's narrative is a politics because it locates the present within God's time. This is a limited place to be, but we must grow more comfortable with such limitation, for it is a reminder of God's grace.

The problem is not that these evangelicals are being "too biblical." My argument is the opposite: we evangelicals are not being biblical enough, because our readings can desensitize us from broader, relevant biblical themes and can encourage us to accept modern institutions to such a degree that we neglect the critical faculties necessary to identify the evil that comes with the good in any human institution. Such readings oversimplify matters because they tend to neglect the negative aspects of even the best of human systems. In addition, ideological readings meant to support current systems limit the ability of Christians to imagine anything different. The problem with many evangelical thinkers' treatments of the Bible and politics is not that they turn to Scripture too often but that they rely on surface-level interpretations that ignore broader themes and that they often bring concerns to the text that frame the reading to confirm previously held positions.

Weakness Four: Isolated from Broader Political Theology

Evangelicals rightly turn to the Bible and biblical arguments as the highest authority. However, this emphasis can lead to a neglect of other sources for consideration, including Christian scholarship from other traditions. A fourth weakness of evangelical political theology is a lack of connection to and interaction with the political theology being done by other Christian

27. Smith, "Evangelicalism and the Political," 171.

thinkers. Political theology has enjoyed a resurgence of interest in the last decade, and evangelicals could benefit from theologians working in this field because the resurgence in political theology connects to issues that evangelicals have historically considered important: how social orderings and political activities relate to God.

Not long ago, conventional wisdom took for granted that God had disappeared from public life. Few today believe this to be the case. Intellectual historian Mark Lilla claims that God disappeared for a short time in a "Great Separation," but modern insecurities brought him back into the equation, leading to the tumultuous twentieth century. Peace and order demand that God again be jettisoned.[28] According to William Cavanaugh, Jeffrey Bailey, and Craig Hovey, theology did not in fact vanish: "theology, despite the hopes of some, never really went away; it simply masqueraded in other guises throughout modernity."[29] Michael Allen Gillespie agrees with this assessment. He traces out the way various theological notions were translated into other, secularized ideas.[30]

Today, the time of God's supposed disappearance has passed. Political theology seeks to understand how theology can "speak to the public realm in its own voice again."[31] This subfield of theology "asks how what we believe about God (theology) orders our life together in the world (politics)."[32] It is an exercise in vision, both seeing what really is and what could be.[33] Cavanaugh looms large on the contemporary landscape of political theology. His theopolitical vision—seeing what really is and what could be—has grown in popularity and significance. In particular, Cavanaugh's work has challenged accepted views of the advent of the nation-state (and its relation to religious violence), of economics, and of globalization. In each area, he seeks to expose the problems with accepted views and demonstrate how a more faithful theological analysis yields a different posture and way forward in the modern world. He focuses particularly on the implications of the Eucharist for imagining space and time and for resisting modern problems.

Must evangelicals return to more historically substantive traditions to overcome our weaknesses? Does evangelicalism lack the resources for

28. Lilla, *Stillborn God.*
29. Cavanaugh et al., "Introduction," xviii.
30. Gillespie, *Theological Origins of Modernity.*
31. Cavanaugh et al., "Introduction," xviii.
32. Fitch, *End of Evangelicalism?*, xv–xvi.
33. Cavanaugh et al., "Introduction," xxi.

overcoming our own problematic tendencies—tendencies that stem, at least to a certain degree, from the very strengths that mark evangelicals as evangelical? Must younger evangelicals turn away from their tradition in order to be true to their sense of Christ's rule over political and economic life? I do not think so, and this work is one step in the direction of overcoming some of the weaknesses within evangelicalism by turning to a neglected evangelical theologian. I am not arguing that there is *no* hope—we could point to other good examples of evangelical political theology—but that A. J. Conyers is one such source that merits attention and emulation. Turning to his work serves as a helpful starting point for constructing an evangelical theopolitical imagination that can aid in navigating these weaknesses within the movement.

A. J. Conyers (1944–2004)

Abda Johnson ("Chip") Conyers III was born on May 29, 1944.[34] In 1957, Chip's father moved the family from suburban Atlanta to a farm in rural Georgia. Chip spent his high school years in a small school among rural people who valued relationships with their neighbors. His family joined a small church that was the center of community life, and Chip became involved in teaching Sunday school. He was an honor student and the president of the local chapter of Future Farmers of America. During this time Chip began to read widely and to make connections between American history and culture, particularly in relation to the Civil War. He had family connections to the war, and its memory was a very real influence on him.

> Mostly he read about science, Karl Marx, and was an avid reader of Civil War history, which was often discussed in the family and the classical writings of Bruce Catton and Douglas Southall Freeman were readily available in the beautiful handmade plantation desk that had been rescued during Sherman's fiery march through Georgia. He told me once that he had seen *Gone With the Wind* countless times, went to the Cyclorama in Grant Park (not Ulysses S.), and spent hours walking around the many battle scenes in the area looking for artifacts. In Cartersville, GA, there were some famous old Indian mounds, and he and his brother loved to visit there and pick up arrowheads and other trophies. At some point, he set up a "Civil War Museum" on the front porch of his home

34. The information in this biography, unless otherwise noted, is found in Conyers and Conyers, "Biography of A. J. 'Chip' Conyers."

and invited all the neighbors to come for a tour. The family was steeped in this history, which didn't seem so far in the past then. They had letters sent between his great grandmother and his great grandfather who was off fighting in the war. They knew many of the places he had been, including Vicksburg, Mississippi.[35]

Chip attended junior college at Young Harris College and was active in social and political organizations on campus. He met his wife, Debby Anderson, at Young Harris, and the two married on December 26, 1964,[36] after graduating and moving to Athens to attend the University of Georgia. There, Chip studied political science and planned a career in public office or law. He continued to be influenced by conservatism and subscribed to *National Review*.[37]

After graduation, four experiences influenced Chip's direction. First, Debby and he began attending a Baptist church. Chip had grown up Methodist but became disenchanted with that denomination due to some bad experiences in the Methodist campus student organization. Second, after graduating from Georgia, Chip taught school for a year. During this year, he decided to pursue seminary rather than law school due to a growing sense of a call to ministry. He believed that he could be a better influence on people through the church than through politics.[38] These two experiences combined to lead Chip to enroll in Southeastern Baptist Theological Seminary in Wake Forest, North Carolina, the closest Southern Baptist seminary. Seminary at Southeastern became the third significant experience. At the time, Southeastern was the most liberal seminary in the Southern Baptist Convention (which, at an institutional level, was much more liberal in the 1970s than it is today),[39] and this atmosphere drove him to study, research, and think about the connection between theology and various philosophies and worldviews. The fourth significant experience was Chip and Debby's church ministry. Chip was pastor of Good Hope and Mt. Carmel Christian Churches in Youngsville, North Carolina, from 1967 until graduation in 1971. After graduating with a master of divinity

35. D. Conyers, e-mail message to author, July 25, 2013.

36. Conyers, "Moltmann's Concept of History," vita.

37. D. Conyers, e-mail message to author, July 25, 2013.

38. D. Conyers, phone conversation with author, July 19, 2013.

39. For more information on Southern Baptist conservatives and the shift in denominational control from the "moderates" to the "conservatives," see Hankins, *Uneasy in Babylon*.

degree, he served as pastor at Maple Spring Baptist Church in Louisburg, North Carolina (two years) and a church in the small town of Ila, Georgia (two years).[40] On the whole, Chip enjoyed these ministry experiences, but he also grew to miss the more academic and scholarly pursuits of seminary. It was becoming more obvious that his gifts were in writing, teaching, and speaking; therefore, he decided to pursue a doctorate in theology in order to have more opportunities to exercise these gifts.

Chip began the PhD program in systematic theology at The Southern Baptist Theological Seminary in 1975. He learned from scholars in theology and politics not only through reading but also through direct influence. Three thinkers in particular were important sources for his growth and development. First was Dale Moody,[41] who had taught theology at Southern for almost thirty years by the time Chip arrived. Moody found Chip interested in theology, history, and politics, and suggested that he focus his dissertation on the writings of Jürgen Moltmann. This suggestion influenced more than just Chip's dissertation, as Moltmann's influence can be clearly seen in his major writings. Chip also worked as a graduate assistant to Moody from 1976 to 1977.[42]

The second influence was political scientist, philosopher, historian, and theologian Gerhart Niemeyer of the University of Notre Dame. In the spring of 1976, Chip had classes with Niemeyer and was influenced by his traditionalism, which gave Chip the chance to examine political ideologies and gain a deeper understanding of the gospel in the modern world. Niemeyer served as one of Conyers's most significant connections to a strand of "conservatism" that I explore later in this work.

Third was Moltmann. Chip and Debby spent six months in Germany, mostly at the University of Tübingen. Chip had conversations with Moltmann that became the basis for his dissertation, later revised and published as *God, Hope, and History: Jürgen Moltmann and the Christian Concept of History*.[43] Studying Moltmann's view of history opened the way for Conyers's later critiques of the modern world from a Christian perspective.

---

40. Conyers, "Moltmann's Concept of History," vita. Chip also served as pastor of English Baptist Church in Carrollton, Kentucky, from 1975 until the completion of his degree.

41. Moody studied with Emil Brunner and Karl Barth.

42. Conyers, "Moltmann's Concept of History," vita.

43. Conyers, *God, Hope, and History*.

Chip defended his dissertation the day that his daughter, Emily Mc-Call Conyers, was born: July 12, 1979. By the time his degree was conferred in December 1979, he had already finished his first semester teaching at Central Missouri State University (CMSU) as Baptist Chair of Bible. While at CMSU, Chip organized a series of symposia on subjects such as bioethics, the arts, and other topics, reflecting his broad interests. During these years, Chip and Debby also welcomed a son into their family, Abda Johnson Conyers IV ("John").

In 1987 Chip accepted an invitation to teach at the Baptist College of Charleston, which was later renamed Charleston Southern University—a name Chip proposed.[44] The family spent seven years there, and Chip continued to publish and speak. In the summer of 1994, he moved to Waco, Texas, in order to become one of the founding faculty members of Baylor University's George W. Truett Theological Seminary (his family joined him in Waco shortly thereafter). The chance to be a part of something new and his friendship with Dean Robert Sloan were the main factors that drew him to Truett.[45] As a founding member of the faculty, he was able to influence the curriculum, advocating, for instance, the use of primary texts in the study of theology. He went on to become a beloved faculty member, twice voted by the graduating class as "Professor of Choice." There is now a Conyers Scholars Program at Baylor in his honor.

Chip struggled with his health while transitioning to Waco. At his wife's urging, he visited a doctor, and a biopsy revealed that he was in the early stages of chronic lymphocytic leukemia (CLL). Chip continued in good health for the next three years; because the disease was at such an early stage, the doctors decided close monitoring was the best way forward. However, in the summer of 1997, his oncologist noticed an elevation in the number of white blood cells and began to talk about chemotherapy. Chip hoped to make it to Christmas before starting treatment, but by mid-November his condition and symptoms returned. He woke up one morning with dizziness and blurred vision, too weak to stand. At the hospital he began to slip into a coma, and he was transferred to a hospital in Dallas. Though he was released in late January, his health never completely recovered from this prolonged illness: "From that time until the end of his life

---

44. D. Conyers, phone conversation with the author, July 19, 2013.
45. Ibid.

six years later, he was in and out of hospitals, periodically receiving blood transfusions, and regularly receiving chemotherapy."[46]

Chip continued to fulfill his duties at the seminary, and he still found time to write. He did not mention his sickness but responded gladly to questions and expressions of sympathy. During this time he wrote his final two books: *The Long Truce: How Toleration Made the World Safe for Power and Profit* (2001) and *The Listening Heart: Vocation and the Crisis of Modern Culture* (posthumously published, 2006). By 2002 he was diagnosed with an aggressive skin cancer, requiring painful surgeries and skin grafts. When preparing for a bone marrow transplant, he slipped on a wet floor. This accident required x-rays, which revealed a small mass in his right lung. This finding led to a diagnosis of small-cell carcinoma, a very aggressive and untreatable form of cancer. The doctors said he had only a few months to live.

Chip lived nearly two more years, continuing to teach, write, and speak. He finished his last book, *The Listening Heart*, shortly before his death on July 18, 2004.

Outline of Book

In this work I argue that A. J. Conyers provides a promising way for countering various weaknesses in evangelical theopolitical imagination. I make this argument in two ways. First, I provide a critical reading of Conyers's overall scholarly project, seeking to understand it in its own context and in conversation with other scholars. I focus on Conyers's political theology, exploring how he diagnoses the modern world and what he proposes as remedies. Second, I provide a reading of Conyers's political theology while bringing it into conversation with prominent political theologian William Cavanaugh. As noted above, Cavanaugh serves as a leading representative of contemporary political theology, and he provides a position that many people find compelling. His work also proves useful in understanding Conyers, because the two read modernity in overlapping and mutually reinforcing ways, with a few important differences. Identifying these differences will situate Conyers as a helpful political theologian and also contribute to some current debates in political theology. In my conclusion, I utilize the insights from Conyers to begin building an evangelical political

---

46. Conyers and Conyers, "Biography of A. J. 'Chip' Conyers," xxxiii.

theology that points the way forward for overcoming the typical evangelical weaknesses highlighted above.

In each chapter, I explore an aspect of Conyers's work that helps counterbalance each of the four problematic tendencies that I earlier identified in evangelical political theology. I begin in chapter 1 with an intellectual biography of Conyers in order to understand the foundation from which he engages the questions of theology and the modern world. I argue that he incorporates "conservative" political influences and his interest in Jürgen Moltmann's eschatology to forge a point of view by which he understands the modern world in his mature work. I look at Conyers's early work to gain a sense of his understanding and critique of Moltmann and then provide important background and context on the "conservative" political tradition that influenced him. In the second chapter, I explore Conyers's body of work to show the trajectory that led to his focus on theology and modernity. Together, these two chapters set up the context of Conyers as a theologian while also pointing a way beyond the simple "conservative or liberal," "us-versus-them" binary that often characterizes evangelical theology (Weakness One).

I turn to Conyers's mature work on political theology in the third and fourth chapters in order to highlight his contribution to a theological diagnosis of modern problems and his theological remedies for those problems. In chapter 3, I argue that Conyers diagnoses modernity in a way that both harmonizes with other treatments and adds descriptive precision. He does this by charting the use of a changing term (*toleration*) and related conceptual shifts and disorders. This chapter begins to correct the evangelical tendency to take modernity and its institutions for granted (Weakness Two). In chapter 4, I argue that Conyers confronts modern disorders with a recovery of the theological concept of vocation,[47] which reopens a proper Christian worldview and reestablishes important Christian practices for resisting sin and being the church. Thus his work aids in the reimagination of space and time. His work on vocation demonstrates how evangelicals can remain robustly biblical while moving into more nuanced and careful readings of Scripture that can help overcome the oversimplified readings that evangelicals too often offer (Weakness Three).

---

47. Conyers's work on vocation was part of a project funded by the Lilly Endowment to design and implement programs on vocation for students and others associated with universities. See Conyers, *Listening Heart*, 15–16.

In the fifth chapter, I turn to William Cavanaugh, one of the dominant voices in contemporary political theology. I seek to understand his diagnosis of the modern world, as well as his remedies for the problems he identifies. Throughout this treatment, I draw Conyers into the conversation to demonstrate how each can strengthen the other. This chapter begins to show the relevance of Conyers to the field of political theology, and it shows how his work can serve as a bridge for evangelicals to engage in the political theology being done in other traditions (Weakness Four).

In my conclusion, I attempt to make plain what an evangelical political theology might look like that draws positively and critically on Conyers's work. In the end, this book not only places Conyers among political theologians and evaluates the fruitfulness of his work as a resource for evangelical theology; it also serves to test whether Conyers's work achieved the goals he set for evangelical thought in the quotation that opened this introduction: "recovering the task . . . [of] safeguarding . . . a truly catholic vision of the world and its redemption."

CHAPTER 1

The Theology and Politics That Influenced Conyers

INTRODUCTION

Conyers incorporates various theological and political influences in a constructive manner that points a way beyond the typical "conservative versus liberal" rhetoric that colors the evangelical social imaginary. While I laid out the general shape of Conyers's career and interests in the brief biography above, in this chapter I focus on Conyers's intellectual biography and what it tells us about his formation. Conyers's interaction with Jürgen Moltmann's eschatology, which he refines by his own interaction with a specific brand of conservative social thought, forges his early theological foundation. He incorporates "conservative" political influences and his interest in Moltmann's eschatology to forge a unique theological point of view that he focuses on understanding the modern world in his mature work. I make this argument in two basic moves: I explain the major influences on Conyers's thought and then follow with a chapter explaining and categorizing his work. Taken together, these two moves provide a basic understanding of Conyers as a theologian and lay the foundation for analyzing his treatment of modernity in chapters 3 and 4. These first two chapters prepare us to understand how Conyers shapes a social imaginary for navigating the modern world.

In this chapter, I explain the major influences on Conyers's political theology in three steps that seek to highlight the way Conyers incorporated diverse influences in his creative framework, using the tendencies from one group to counteract perceived weaknesses in the others. First, I demonstrate how the eschatology of Jürgen Moltmann influenced Conyers early in his theological career, as evidenced in Conyers's dissertation. Second, I show how Conyers drew on three particular examples of "conservative" social-political thought. I pay particular attention to the way that he incorporates an older form of conservatism than that commonly referenced today.[1] Third, I return to his treatment of Moltmann. I move from Moltmann to conservative social thought then back to Moltmann in order to demonstrate how Conyers uses his conservative framework to critique Moltmann and vice versa. Conyers on Moltmann in the 1980s is different than Conyers on Moltmann in the late 1970s because of the influence of conservative social thought. This intellectual biography shows how Conyers critiqued both Moltmann and a form of "conservative" tradition in order to lay his own foundation for approaching theopolitical questions, a foundation on which he would build in his two monographs on political theology. In this chapter and the next, I am primarily concerned with understanding this

---

1. The story of Conyers's connection to an older form of political conservatism (what some call "paleoconservatism"—see below) is complicated to tell. This complication stems from at least two roots. On one hand, nowhere in his work on modernity does Conyers explicitly spell out his main influences. On the other hand, conservatism as a movement in the American political scene has changed dramatically over the last seventy years, due to the fusionist conservatism of William F. Buckley Jr. that brought several types of conservatism together and ultimately dulled the emphases of some of these groups. Thus the associations that modern audiences have with the term *conservative* do not necessarily do justice to earlier forms. For just one example, some earlier conservatives maintained a critique of capitalism that is no longer part of the "platform" of today's conservatives. Conyers was more influenced by an older form of conservatism than this fusionist conservatism, a term associated with Frank Meyer, an associate editor for the *National Review* in its early years. Meyer was a main figure in the effort to fuse libertarianism with traditional conservatism. For a helpful overview of the conservative intellectual movement from 1945 to the mid-1970s, see Nash, *Conservative Intellectual Movement*. Nash identifies three sources of the postwar intellectual movement: the classical liberals or libertarians (who resisted the threat of the expanding state to liberty, private enterprise, and individualism), the new conservatives (traditionalists who resisted totalitarianism, total war, and the development of mass society), and a militant anti-Communism. In fact, Nash argues that by the end of Reagan's second term, conservatism encompassed five impulses: "libertarianism, traditionalism, anti-Communism, neoconservatism, and the Religious Right" (332). Also see Nash, *Reappraising the Right*. In that work, Nash provides further scholarship on conservatism, considering key figures and assessing the future of conservatism. For a more recent evaluation of the current American political landscape with reference to types of conservatism, see Mitchell, *Eight Ways to Run the Country*.

foundation, while the specific connections between these influences and his political theology will become more apparent later.

Jürgen Moltmann and Eschatology

Jürgen Moltmann is the most prominent theological influence on Conyers. He was the subject of his dissertation (1979) and his second book, *God, Hope, and History* (1988)—a revision of the dissertation with a few added chapters. In what follows, I first analyze the way Moltmann influences Conyers's views on eschatology and history as evidenced in the dissertation and as demonstrated by Conyers's critique of Moltmann in that work. Understanding the influence of Moltmann elucidates Conyers's early theological vision and trajectory and prepares us for evaluating his mature work on political theology.

Through his work on Moltmann, Conyers became convinced of the importance of eschatology for orienting both the understanding and experience of history, opening it to the future. Conyers turned to Moltmann for his dissertation work at the suggestion of Dale Moody, Conyers's doctoral supervisor at Southern Seminary. For one semester, Conyers studied with Moltmann at the University of Tübingen.[2] His dissertation pursued three goals: "(1) to state the main features of Jürgen Moltmann's concept of history as these come to light in an examination of his theological writings; (2) to determine how he has perceived the problems related to the formulation of a theological concept of history, particularly as these problems are evidenced in contemporary theology; and (3) to offer an estimate of his contribution to the resolution of these problems."[3] The work focused primarily on three of Moltmann's books: *Theology of Hope, The Crucified God*, and *The Church in the Power of the Spirit*.

According to Conyers, Moltmann poses one central question: "How does a promise work in history?"[4] Scripture speaks of a God of history, but it uses words of temporal significance like "hope," "promise," "covenant," and other images of a God who is coming and who goes before. Conyers notes, "Therefore Moltmann considers it fundamental that 'Christian

2. Conyers, "Jürgen Moltmann's Concept of History," ix. Conyers maintained a relationship with Moltmann, as evidenced by pieces such as his interview of Moltmann for *Christianity Today*. See Conyers, "*Christianity Today* Talks to Moltmann," 67.

3. Conyers, "Jürgen Moltmann's Concept of History," abstract, 1.

4. Ibid., 1.

theology speaks of God historically and history eschatologically."[5] God is known from the category of promise, which points ahead to the eschatological coming of God.[6]

Conyers provides a brief review of how Christian theology has treated history in order to set up his treatment of Moltmann on history. He divides his treatment into three possibilities for understanding history, categorized as the "Augustinian heritage," the "Hegelian heritage," and the "Kierkegaardian heritage."[7] According to this schema, the Augustinian heritage believes "that history can be seen as a movement toward a goal, and that both the movement and the goal are the work of a Providence or of that which is outside of history."[8] The Hegelian heritage holds "that history moves toward a goal, but that movement and goal are of the nature of history itself and are thus understood from within history." And the Kierkegaardian heritage holds the view "that history which moves toward some provident goal is unknowable and can neither be seen by faith nor by reason."[9] These labels make clear the alternatives available for contemporary theology.[10] The Augustinian heritage places the weight of history's purposeful movement on the transcendent; the Hegelian heritage, on the immanent;[11] the Kierkegaardian, on a strong historical dualism.[12]

The twentieth century occasioned a general revolt in theology against assurances of meaning in history. Two convictions grounded this revolt: the general progressive improvement of the human situation was no longer easily supported, and the "dénouement of Life of Jesus research with its heightened emphasis upon the eschatological character of primitive Christian consciousness provided little, if any, textual support for historical optimism as a theological premise."[13] Recognizing these two convictions,

5. Ibid., 1–2.

6. Ibid., 2.

7. Ibid., 17.

8. Ibid., 16.

9. Ibid., 17.

10. Conyers acknowledges that "while to state such views in quite these terms involves us necessarily in an exaggeration from the point of view of the individual thinker, I believe we are justified in saying that this is broadly speaking the way their thought is received in our century" (ibid.).

11. In a way, the Hegelian heritage inverted the Augustinian's "history-within-salvation" perspective to make a "salvation-within-history" perspective (ibid., 19).

12. Ibid., 17.

13. Ibid., 50–51.

Moltmann is part of a group of theologians seeking to relate Christian theological findings to historical experience in a way that provides witness to its eschatological outlook. For Moltmann, revelation "proceeds from the identity of God's promise with the fulfillment of his promise"; it determines to effect a future reality in terms of God's promise.[14] While the perceived present seems to contradict the promised future, God demonstrates his faithfulness through his promise. Through this treatment of theories of history and their impact on theology, Conyers begins to set the stage for his analysis of Moltmann's views on theology in the future tense and its promise for political theology. He moves on to investigate the nature and development of the concept of history as God's open future.[15]

Conyers explains three perspectives, or stages, from which Moltmann's dialogue with modern theology and philosophy has brought him into the discussion of history. These three perspectives arise out of the fact that "[Christian theology] must inevitably relate ancient events and promises to a modern context and mission. . . . But if it is to be more than a 'fossil theology,' sealed up in a dead past, or a 'chameleon theology,' colored by its contemporary environment, then it must demonstrate a contemporary faith that opens the past to its own universal future."[16] The three perspectives correspond to the three main works with which Conyers engages, as noted above.

The first stage comes into focus in Moltmann's *Theology of Hope*. Here he argues that Christian hope provides history with a "promissory structure that remains eschatologically open to a universal future," with the emphasis on the resurrection, the eschaton, and the future of Christ. It provides a view of history that is not closed off in irrelevant or inflexible dogma.[17] Conyers makes several interrelated points with regard to this stage. He shows that Moltmann rejects any concept of history that sees it as a metaphysic of being, rendering history unhistorical by seeking to escape the insecurity of thinking with the contexts of risks, dangers, and promises that make up real history.[18] Moltmann instead turns to the biblical category of promise, which

14. Ibid., 54.

15. By "open future" here I mean the idea that God is drawing creation toward its future consummation, as I will draw out below. It should not be confused with open theism, which is a different matter.

16. Conyers, "Jürgen Moltmann's Concept of History," 56.

17. Ibid., 56–57.

18. Ibid., 59–74.

he sees as the key to thinking of history in terms of genuine experience.[19] At its core, history must be understood via Christology.[20] Moltmann's understanding of history focuses on three developments in the history of Jesus Christ: "the death and resurrection of Jesus has an eschatological focus and gives rise to an eschatological Christology . . . it is an *anticipation* of God's future. . . . The future of God in his kingdom has a Christological focus and calls forth a Christological eschatology. In this sense it is an *incarnation* of the future of God's kingdom. . . . The structure that history takes, in anticipation of God's future, and the mode of Christ's present in history are viewed in terms of mission."[21] Thus the Old Testament provides Moltmann with the concept of promise, and the New Testament expands it by adding the ideas of anticipation, incarnation, and mission.

This Christian view of history expands to the horizons of universal concern because it is rooted in the ultimate border of death in light of resurrection.[22] The promises of the future are not drawn out of the possibilities of the present order but are anticipated in light of the new possibilities of the new creation.[23] Mission, transformation, and openness to God's future are key concepts: "The point, in light of the suffering of this world and the promise of the new, is not only to interpret things as they are but to transform them by faithful obedience in anticipation of the future of God."[24] This

19. Ibid., 76–85. Conyers notes, "Here he finds that the movement of Israel's worldview is directed toward future goals, the remembered future of God's promise. While this world-view is reminiscent of their migratory heritage, it is here retained in the community cultus and in the theological heritage of a settled agrarian society" (104).

20. Moltmann: "A Christian understanding of history at its core must . . . be developed out of Christology" (quoted in ibid., 85).

21. Ibid.

22. Conyers explains, "The resurrection which pointed beyond the horizons of the experienced cosmos and of death was not the resurrection in abstract, but it was the resurrection specifically of the crucified one. This resurrection therefore does not bypass the terrors of history, but releases the promise of God from the very midst of history and its suffering. The concept of history which this involves, therefore, speaks of a dialectic of the crucifixion and the resurrection, or promise and experience, of the universality of God's future and the particularity of the presence of his future" (ibid., 105). Conyers deals more with the concept of dialectic, noting that "the experience of anticipation and that of incarnation must, therefore, mutually interpret one another. The one stretches forward to the future of a God who is 'ahead of us' yet without becoming lost in utopian dreams. The other grounds that hope in the concrete suffering of a God who is 'for us' yet without becoming lost in despair" (ibid., 96).

23. Ibid., 92.

24. Ibid., 105. Other comments in the chapter expound on this: "The character of

promissory structure of history itself points to this universal future that God has opened via the resurrection of Christ.

Conyers identifies Moltmann's second stage in the book *The Crucified God*. Here, Moltmann argues "for a theology of the cross that gives identity to, and determines the form of, the historical mission of Christianity." Moltmann emphasizes hope in the form of remembering the death of Jesus and in the solidarity of the God of hope with mankind's suffering in history.[25] A truly Christian concept of history centers "in the death and resurrection of Christ—it means an eschatologically open history, one in which new possibilities are appearing in history and are made possible by the history-making acts of God."[26] In Moltmann's thought, the eschatological process has an inner identity with Jesus's mission, life, and death. Thus, "whereas Moltmann began with a view of the anticipations that Christian faith engenders in the context of experienced history, now he intends to show how that very history, with its struggles and suffering, is taken up into the life of God. For Moltmann this is the proper second step in understanding God's promise in the resurrection of the crucified Christ."[27] A proper understanding of history must share the same focus: the cross.

The cross—a concrete historical event—grounds the history of God as a history of suffering.[28] God reveals himself via a negative dialectic,[29] in the cross of Christ, as the one who is abandoned by God.[30] The transcendent

---

Christian thinking about history does not call for theory, or an inquiry into the essence of things, but practice and an inquiry into the transformation of things" (ibid., 93); "At this point in Moltmann's thought we begin to see that a Christian concept of history takes the form of mission. . . . This is why Moltman speaks of the resurrection as a 'history-making' event. Its historical character does not lie within the realm of theory, as if it could be proved on the grounds of an underlying foundation of existence, but it belongs also to the realm of mission which brings forth its as-yet unrealized reality" (ibid., 98).

25. Ibid., 57.

26. Ibid., 106.

27. Ibid., 107.

28. "Moltmann's concept of history cannot, as we have seen again and again, be understood apart from the concrete reality of historical events; and it is marked as Christian only when it springs from the Christ event" (ibid., 121).

29. However, Moltmann does not entirely reject the analogical principle; rather, he insists that the cross must define the basis of the analogy. See ibid., 149.

30. "For Moltmann, therefore, as we have already seen, the negation of the negative lies in the historical reality of the cross. Here, in the cross, is reflected a continual tendency in the biblical experience of God: God is made known to the outcasts, to the unrighteous, and to the slaves. This makes it possible to understand both the biblical presentation of Jesus and the Pauline theology of the cross" (ibid., 148–49).

aspect of the Trinity, however, reminds us that the future must not be conceived as more of the same, a continuation of the present, but as a new future, a new creation.[31] When the resurrected one is identified with the crucified one, then Christian theology becomes not about handing on something preserved but about summoning the dead and godless to life. This means that Jesus's death "opens history toward its eschatological future precisely by offering hope to those most hopeless. . . . Thereby human suffering is taken up into the history of God; in its cry of pain it participates in his trinitarian history, which in the Sonlessness of the Father, and in the Fatherlessness of the Son, is united in the suffering, thus hoping love, of the Spirit."[32] The Christian concept of history is a Christian concept because of its openness to the future of God, who has demonstrated himself in the cross and resurrection of Jesus.

Moltmann's third stage comes into focus in *The Church in the Power of the Spirit*. Here Conyers sees that Moltmann "relates the trinitarian structure of God's history to the history-making mission of the church."[33] He draws on the Spirit's presence (mediation of eschatology in history) and power (eschatological promise in terms of mission).[34] The Spirit is the power of futurity as well, drawing power from the pain of suffering and historical reality but connecting believers to God's open future.[35] In Moltmann's thinking, history is an open history with new possibilities.[36] Creation itself does not stand outside of this dynamic as something static and established. Creation opens to the processes of history; it opens to the future.[37] Molt-

31. Ibid., 134.

32. Ibid., 150.

33. Ibid., 57.

34. Ibid., 152.

35. "Like Bultmann, only without the ahistorical 'Eternal Now,' Moltmann can call the Spirit the power of futurity, a power that is manifested in the fact that 'it gives the believer freedom' to be 'open for the genuine future, letting oneself be determined by the future.' Yet here the eschatological dimension does not forget historical reality and the pain of suffering, but draws power from it" (ibid., 162).

36. "Therefore God's mystery is not a closed and perfect order above us, that which is eternally unchanging and stands in contrast to the changes of temporal existence. It is open to the future, and as the 'sending' suggests, is itself changed by the suffering, hopes, expectations, and possibilities of human history" (ibid., 170). Conyers also notes, "Thus the concept of God inferred from 'sending' is one of change, of process. This would mean that the Trinity has a future and a fullness that is not to be conceived at the beginning" (ibid., 171).

37. Conyers, "Jürgen Moltmann's Concept of History," 183–84. "The openness of

mann refrains from a vision or a theory of the kingdom of God, because "what is proposed in this respect is not one final possibility, but the openness to infinite possibilities. Thus to conceive of such an existence would mean to conceive of its limit. . . . For these reasons Moltmann's discussion of the kingdom of God necessarily relates the infinitely open possibilities of God's future to the relatively open possibilities of human history."[38]

Conyers organizes Moltmann's messianic mediation of the kingdom of God in three "mediating categories": anticipation (an attitude toward the future),[39] resistance (resisting whatever resists change, whatever is closed off against the future), and representation (self-giving, giving oneself to risks for the sake of others).[40] These categories, especially anticipation, are not divorced from willing suffering in the present.[41] Conyers summarizes his thinking on the importance of the Trinity as follows:

> The trinitarian process of God provides an inclusive symbol for the ideas of God's promise and God's suffering that came forth in Moltmann's first two major volumes of theology. It is important here that one recognize the place of pneumatology, which makes the death and resurrection of Christ, as an inner-trinitarian event, more than an evocative symbol, but reveals it as an event opening up the tendency of the resurrection to the universal possibilities of a new creation. . . . These possibilities for the future . . . are nevertheless aspects of the present. Because, in that they are possibilities—and not inevitable realities of some unavoidable future—they hold the present accountable, thus calling forth into mission.[42]

---

creation is seen as openness to the creative possibilities of the future. It is a willingness to endure the suffering and crises of history in anticipation of the consummation of creation in God. It is not yet the establishment of order, it is not yet the establishment of safety, for the promise of order comes not from the integrity of the beginning but out of the anticipation of the future. . . . Openness to the creative possibilities of history, therefore, means accepting the risks of history in order to live by faith in hope of the new creation" (ibid., 186).

38. Ibid., 191.

39. Anticipating the kingdom of God points toward an unlimited freedom, which Moltmann calls "indeterminate behavior" (ibid., 187).

40. Ibid., 192.

41. Ibid., 194.

42. Ibid.

For Moltmann, the Spirit draws believers into the dynamism of the inner-trinitarian experience with history, opening up the new possibilities of God's future for humans.

These three perspectives or stages in Moltmann's work provide the shape for his theology of history, as Conyers understands it. It is "a way to *conceive* history, to conceive it in terms of *Christian* theology, and to conceive it in terms of a *contemporary* Christian theology."[43] Conyers summarizes Moltmann's contribution in his closing chapter: "History is then seen as a dialectic of promise and experience, acted out in mission within the conditions of history and directed toward world transforming goals whose ultimate horizon is universal liberation and reconciliation with God. This dialectic of reconciliation presupposes that history is open and capable of yielding new creative possibilities. Thus the very experience of history as crisis, risk, and open possibilities provides the way for meaningful action."[44] The cross is central, and it allows Moltmann to be sensitive to the historical pessimism evident in his time. History is not reduced to some predetermined vision or order, and it does not rely on anything immanent within the world itself.

Conyers also highlights some difficulties that he sees in Moltmann's work. These criticisms provide an important area of comparison with Conyers's book on Moltmann published nine years later (a comparison I take up below). In the final chapter of the dissertation, Conyers levels one main criticism against Moltmann's theology of history: "Moltmann's categories of promise and suffering, by which God is known in the world, necessarily involve him in a radical critique of existence."[45] In other words, openness and new possibilities in Moltmann's thought make the connection to any present positive mediation difficult to maintain. He has too severely restricted the mediation of the kingdom of God to negative categories. This comes out in his treatment of messianic mediation, which as "anticipation," "resistance," and "self-giving" is entirely negative, related to the absence of the future's newness in the present. Conyers turns to the concept of the kingdom of God in the teaching of Jesus to emphasize that while there are elements that are waited for, Jesus seems clear that there are positive ways that the kingdom is present now.[46] While he acknowledges

43. Ibid., 57. Emphasis original.

44. Ibid., 197.

45. Ibid., 212.

46. For his treatment of Jesus's teaching, see ibid., 212–35. He also says, "The Kingdom

the strengths of Moltmann's treatment in connecting God as revealed in Scripture (especially with themes of promise) to the experience of history now (with its crises and risks) in a way that communicates the open future that God is drawing people toward, Conyers worries that Moltmann leaves little room for positive categories. Conyers does, however, acknowledge the danger of such positive categories: "For mediating categories, which are essentially symbols of order, have a way of becoming petrified and claiming to be absolute embodiment[s] of truth."[47] Thus his criticism of Moltmann does not serve to devastate Moltmann's system or position. Instead, Conyers points cautiously to a way to overcome Moltmann's reliance on negative concepts—like absence and anticipation—by connecting to more positive categories.

An overall positive reception characterizes Moltmann's influence at this stage. Conyers approves of Moltmann's emphasis on the cross and the idea that history must be understood as God's working reconciliation. New creative possibilities exist, and God summons people to new life, not to some static element of the past. However, despite broad agreement with Moltmann, Conyers begins to raise questions. He critiques Moltmann for failing to acknowledge anything positive in the present. And in the wording of this basic critique—using the language of "symbols of order"—we begin to see the evidence of the next major influence on Conyers's thought.

Braiding Three Strands of "Conservatism": Conyers and Social-Political Thought

Conyers "braids" three strands of "conservative" political thought together in his work. I begin by explaining who these figures were and how they influenced Conyers specifically, moving from lesser to greater in terms of influence. First, I turn to Conyers's use of Johannes Althusius as an example of a political path not taken by modernity, one that offers hope that conditions could be different. Second, I explain the work of Eric Voegelin, who provided Conyers with both particular philosophical interpretations and

---

is not only hidden in terms of its futurity (which speaks of its absence from the present) and in suffering and oppression (which speaks of its negation in the present). But it must also include that which is 'already' in a positive sense, even though its appearance is in unlikely form, belonging to children (Mk. 10:14), to the poor (Mk. 10:23–25), and to the servant (Mk. 10:42–45), and even though its presence is not immediately evident, as in the parable of the seed growing mysteriously (Mk. 4:26–29)" (ibid., 236).

47. Ibid., 238.

broader categories for analyzing the modern world. These categories enabled Conyers to identify positive aspects of the present that he felt Moltmann lacked. Third, I turn to the work of the Southern Agrarians and the writings of Richard Weaver, who provided Conyers with a perspective on modernity that he would ultimately use to critique Moltmann and to formulate his own point of view. Conyers braids these three strands to form his particular understanding of conservatism that carries through his mature work.

Johannes Althusius

Johannes Althusius (1557–1638) was born in Diedenshausen, a Calvinist region of Westphalia. He studied law, theology, and philosophy in Cologne, Paris, and Basel, receiving a law degree in 1586. Relocating to Geneva, he completed more studies on law and logic and became acquainted with the ideas of John Calvin. He was then invited to the Protestant Academy of Herborn in October 1594, where he became a member of the law faculty and taught philosophy and theology. In 1603 he published *Politica methodice digesta*, which gained him immediate attention. In 1603, the citizens of Emden chose Althusius to be a municipal trustee. This marked a turning point in his life. His service to Emden allowed him the opportunity to apply some of his theories of autonomy and the freedom of states, especially in Emden's struggle against the Count of Frise. Althusius continued to serve Emden in various capacities from 1603 until his death in 1638.[48]

Althusius provides Conyers a way to order social relations that avoids the hyperindividualism of modernity. At the start of *The Long Truce*, Conyers demonstrates a clear debt to this German Reformed jurist by turning to him as an example of an alternate political path not taken by modernity. Considered by many to be a profound political thinker,[49] Althusius and his work were largely neglected and forgotten until a work on his thought was published in 1880. Since then, scholars have shown more interest and some of his works have been translated, most notably his *Politica methodice digesta*. This work in particular demonstrates Althusius's influence on federalism as a political concept. In fact, as Daniel Elazar states, "Althusius' *Politica* was the first book to present a comprehensive theory of federal republicanism rooted in a covenantal view of human society derived from,

---

48. See Benoist, "First Federalist," 27–28.

49. Ibid., 25.

but not dependent on, a theological system."[50] In order to understand this thinker's influence on Conyers, I will first seek to gain an overview of Althusius and then look more carefully at how he provides Conyers with an alternative political vision as a starting point for navigating the modern world.

Althusius receives attention as "the first federalist" based largely on his work on communities or groups in *Politica*. In that work, he develops a conception of the political that sees the object of politics as "to study all groups, natural and social, from the standpoint of a general physiological community, allowing the possibility to identify the primary properties and essential laws of its association. Its goal is the conservation of social life, which means that it is no longer only a result or a consequence of the state, but also concerns all groups participating in this social life."[51] Politics "is the art of associating men for the purpose of establishing, cultivating, and conserving social life among them. . . . The subject matter of politics is therefore association, in which [those living together] pledge themselves to each other, by explicit or tacit agreement, to mutual communication of whatever is useful and necessary for the harmonious exercise of social life."[52] Althusius rejects the idea of self-sufficient individuals and instead focuses on the fact that being human is a function of belonging to various interdependent groups. He builds on the concept of symbiotic relations, which are established between those who have the same needs and find themselves in various levels and types of proximity to each other. In *Politica*, Althusius deals specifically with the family, the collegium, the city, and the province.[53] Each of these groups is important and has authority based on its nature and function. In addition, the larger groups, such as the province, do not exist on a separate plane from the smaller groups; rather, larger groups are made up of the smaller groups. In other words, the largest-level group is not a group of individuals, in which each individual relates as an individual to the state. Instead, the largest group is a group of groups, relating to individuals on the basis of their existence in other groups. Althusius explains that the largest association consists "partly from private, natural, necessary, and voluntary societies, [and] partly from public societies," and "families, cities, and provinces existed by nature prior to

---

50. Elazar, "Althusius' Grand Design," xxxv.
51. Benoist, "First Federalist," 30–31.
52. Althusius, *Politica*, 17.
53. See ibid., 27, 33, 39, 51.

realms, and gave birth to them."[54] In fact, "the social pact is the progressive organization of organic communities of various sizes, in the formation of which individuals have no part: if they enter into a contract, they do so as members of an already existing community, which does not abandon its rights in favor of the larger community."[55] This organization maintains the integrity of the individual groups while still making cooperation possible.

This relationship between groups influences two other theories that make Althusius significant. First, Althusius promotes the principle of subsidiarity, that the larger groups should only assume functions that cannot be adequately undertaken by the smaller groups. This aims to keep initiatives at the lower level as well as to protect the lower levels from the higher levels. Second, Althusius provides a concept of sovereignty that runs contrary to other influential political thinkers such as Jean Bodin. In brief, Bodin's sovereignty rests upon the idea that the state is central and the source of all authority. Intermediary bodies—such as the family and partial societies—are important, but they cannot infringe upon the powers of the prince. Sovereignty is "unlimited power: having no rival in the political and social order."[56] The law, then, is nothing other than the prince's orders, leading to juridical positivism.

Althusius's view of sovereignty is the opposite of Bodin's. For Althusius, the law emanates from the social dimension and the state is under the law. Sovereignty is not an absolute sovereignty detached from obligations; instead, sovereignty belongs to the symbiotic community and to the sovereign only because he is made administrator on behalf of the community. In Althusius's political thought, all political associations, especially the larger associations, are made up of other, lower-level associations into which humans are born and to which they commit themselves based on various common interests. Authority and sovereignty rise up from the lower levels and are entrusted to the sovereign as an administrator, not as an absolute ruler: "I recognize the prince as the administrator, overseer, and governor of these rights of sovereignty. But the owner and usufructuary of sovereignty is none other than the total people associated in one symbiotic body from many smaller associations."[57]

54. Ibid., 66.

55. Benoist, "First Federalist," 52.

56. Ibid., 43.

57. Althusius, *Politica*, 13. He continues, "These rights of sovereignty are so proper to this association, in my judgment, that even if it wishes to renounce them, to transfer

In the first chapter of *The Long Truce*, Conyers interacts briefly with the thought of Althusius, and "the first federalist" serves throughout the work as a figure representing an alternate path, a different way of conceiving political association in opposition to the large centralized states of the twentieth century. In his brief formal interaction with Althusius, Conyers focuses on two key concepts that form his foundation for approaching and critiquing the development of the modern world. First, he develops Althusius's sense of the nature of politics. For Althusius, "Politics really regards how we live in community with one another; and often the most important group, the group that exerts the most influence on us, is *not* the state. It is likely to be the family, the church, the collegium. . . , the guild, or the regional community."[58] And these groups have coherent projects and goals as well: "These groups each have their own end or goal. In fact, Althusius contended that just as the individual has a vocation . . . so has the group—in its own way and for a given purpose."[59] Any full treatment of politics, then, must respect the reality of these various groups, the significance they provide, and the power they have. Politics "includes the consideration of how and why people live together, a matter prerequisite to any understanding of how they are governed or how power operates in the national life."[60] Political life is about living together, in all the forms it occurs.

Conyers draws another concept from Althusius: the ability to push against thinking of persons in isolation. While certain trends in modern thought make it customary to think in terms of individuals governed by a central administration, Althusius considered it vital to first attend to the function of smaller, nongovernmental associations such as the family and the collegium. For Althusius, political life is more than transactions between individuals and the centralized power, a theme to which Conyers returns in his diagnosis of the "crisis" of modernity. Conyers maintains these ideas of smaller groups and a proper understanding of individuals as he seeks to diagnose problems in the modern world and propose alternate paths. Althusius remains an important example of a path not taken, a path

---

them to another, and to alienate them, it would by no means be able to do so, any more than a man is able to give the life he enjoys to another. For these rights of sovereignty constitute and conserve the universal association."

58. Conyers, *Long Truce*, 14.

59. Ibid.

60. Ibid.

that would not lead to the bipolarity between a sovereign state and autonomous individuals.

Eric Voegelin

The work of Eric Voegelin (1901–85) is the second strand of political influence on Conyers. It provides him with a concept of political order and with an angle for critiquing modernity. Voegelin is regarded as "one of the severest critics of . . . Cartesian subjectivity, its successive philosophical practitioners, and its political and philosophical consequences."[61] Born January 3, 1901, in Cologne, Germany, he studied political science at the University of Vienna and completed his doctorate in 1922.[62] He then learned German constitutional law at Berlin and Heidelberg before becoming an assistant to his mentor, Hans Kelsen, at Vienna.[63] He also studied at Oxford and spent the period 1924 to 1926 in America at Columbia, Harvard, and Wisconsin.[64] After spending some time at the Sorbonne, where he focused on French literature and philosophy, Voegelin returned to Austria in 1927 and became interested in political developments there. He developed a strong concern for examining radical ideologies, and he published two books on the subject of race (both of which the Nazis withdrew from circulation).[65] After Germany occupied and annexed Austria in 1938, Voegelin was fired from his academic position at the University of Vienna. He began to plan his emigration.[66]

Voegelin spent most of the rest of his career in the United States, with a decade-long stint back in Germany. He taught at Harvard, Bennington College, and the University of Alabama before accepting a permanent position at Louisiana State University in 1942.[67] From there, he returned to Germany in 1958 to establish an institute of political science in Munich. The last phase of his career took place at the Hoover Institution at Stanford

---

61. Trepanier and McGuire, "Introduction," 1.

62. Federici, *Eric Voegelin*, 1.

63. Ibid.

64. Ibid., 1–2.

65. Ibid., 4–5.

66. Ibid., 5.

67. Heilke, *Eric Voegelin*, 7.

University, from 1969 to 1974. He continued to work until his death on January 19, 1985.[68]

Before delving into the major features of Voegelin's thought, it is important to note that scholars debate the degree to which they can label him a "conservative." Voegelin himself rejected being categorized so easily. While some vehemently argue that he was a wolf in sheep's clothing, an arrogant conservative pretending not to be,[69] most scholars agree that he does not fit well within any particular category. As one biographer writes, "Whatever one may say of Voegelin's 'conservative' leanings, they consist of neither a neo-classical liberal reaction to the welfare state as in the American conservatism of the 1950s to the 1990s, nor of a wistful longing for the *ancien régimes* of pre-Reformation Europe. . . . Voegelin's political analyses are sufficiently unprogrammatic in political intent that his 'politics' in any prescriptive sense evades ideological categorization."[70] If Voegelin was a conservative at all, it was only as an "adopted son," since conservatives did draw on his thought.[71]

Voegelin's legacy relates to "exploring the nature of modernity and meditating upon the sources of order in human existence."[72] This legacy and his major ideas flow from four primary works. First, Voegelin signed a contract with McGraw-Hill to produce a textbook on the history of political ideas in February 1939, shortly after arriving in the United States.[73] Though the agreement was to produce a two-hundred-page manuscript within a year, two years later Voegelin had written a much longer work (and by 1944 it was three volumes).[74] However, he abandoned the work between 1945 and 1950 due to an important development in his thought.

---

68. Federici, *Eric Voegelin*, 10–11.

69. For instance, see Cole, *Political Philosophy of Eric Voegelin and His Followers*. Cole begins his work by relaying a personal story of feeling humiliated by Voegelin's treatment of a question he once asked in a public lecture. He does little to hide his personal disdain for Voegelin, and that tone carries through his work. He connects Voegelin to two aspects of right-wing politics: business-lobby views and Christian religious conservatism (see ibid., xix). However, others point out that Voegelin's views of Christianity do not mesh well with conservative Christianity. For more on this, see especially Heilke, *Eric Voegelin*, 145–77.

70. Heilke, *Eric Voegelin*, 183.

71. Ibid., 19.

72. Embry, *Philosopher and the Storyteller*, 2.

73. Heilke, *Eric Voegelin*, 5.

74. Ibid., 6.

He came to see that ideas are concrete examples of symbols of order that men and women develop from their immediate experiences. People use these symbols to give meaning to their history and to set up government, which is an attempt at world construction. (Though neither Voegelin nor Conyers uses the terminology, the way that these symbols are explained ties in closely with the idea of the social imaginary.) Ideas can be the subject of inquiry themselves, but describing and understanding political reality requires pushing deeper. Heilke explains this well:

> "Ideas" are the concretized instances of the symbols of order that arise, in turn, out of the immediate experiences of order that men and women have. They use the symbols of order to represent to themselves their experiences and to give meaning to their history. Ideas can be made objects of inquiry in and of themselves, but this is to deform their actual nature as the symbols of lived experiences by means of which human beings express their experience of order, and which they "use" to fashion civilizational order in accordance with those experiences and the symbolizations of them. Consequently, "To set up a government is an essay in world creation," and the "political cosmion" that is created "provides a structure of meaning into which the single human being can fit the results of the biologically and spiritually productive, procreative energies of his personal life, thereby [relieving] his life from the [disordering] aspects of existence that always spring up when the possibility of the utter senselessness of a life ending in annihilation is envisaged." This formulation (written in 1940) was an important breakthrough in the science of politics as Voegelin realized the importance of moving away from the concept of an idea to the concept of a symbol.[75]

Thus Voegelin rejected the ordering premise of the *History of Political Ideas* volumes. Yet, his rejection of the ordering premise did not nullify the fact that he still believed the historical studies in that work to be essentially sound.[76]

Voegelin developed this new angle in two lectures, which evolved into the second and third important works. In 1951, he gave the Walgreen Lectures at the University of Chicago (later published as *The New Science of*

---

75. Ibid., 6–7.

76. Ibid., 83. This belief is important to note because the University of Missouri Press published these volumes in *Collected Works of Eric Voegelin* in the late 1990s. As I will address below, Conyers relied on these volumes for some of his philosophical analysis.

Politics).[77] His inaugural lecture in Munich (1958) was published as *Science, Politics, and Gnosticism*.[78] In these works Voegelin developed his primary angle of critique of modernity: the need for a new science of politics because of gnostic elements in modern ideologies. A new science was needed to overcome distortions caused by applying methods of the natural sciences to politics and history. These distortions include a truncated view of human nature, supposedly value-free social science, and viewing science as a type of saving knowledge.[79] Such moves were developments of earlier positions that Voegelin held. For example, he believed that the problem of National Socialism was indicative of a larger Western crisis. While others were content to critique the Nazis from a moral standpoint, Voegelin probed deeper into the roots of their ideas. As biographer Federici observes, "The identification of these movements and the explanation of their pseudo-spiritual characteristics constituted the beginning of Voegelin's classification of modern political movements as political religions. This insight led to the development of what he would later call 'gnosticism,' a defining characteristic of modernity."[80]

Voegelin saw modern ideologies as variations of the ancient heresy of Gnosticism.[81] By this term he meant the belief that humans can transform the nature of reality through secret knowledge and social action.[82] Gnosticism had three components: "a strong feeling of alienation stemming from a sense that some essential aspect of one's own humanity remains unfulfilled, a revolt against the conditions in the world that purportedly cause this alienation, and the belief that esoteric knowledge and political action will be sufficient to overcome these conditions. *In short, Gnosticism is the belief that human beings have the power to transform both themselves and the order of reality into some sort of magical utopia*."[83] This need for a new science and analysis of modern Gnosticism stemmed from Voegelin's assessment of modern disorder.

77. Heilke, *Eric Voegelin*, 7.

78. Federici, *Eric Voegelin*, 9.

79. McKnight, "Voegelin's New Science of History," 62.

80. Federici, *Eric Voegelin*, 7.

81. McKnight notes that "prominent figures from a wide range of disciplines were exploring equivalences of experience and symbolization between ancient Gnosticism and modern consciousness." He cites both Carl Jung and Hans Jonas as examples. See McKnight, "Voegelin's New Science of History," 60.

82. Cf. Blumenberg, *The Legitimacy of the Modern Age*.

83. Trepanier and McGuire, "Introduction," 4–5. Emphasis added.

The fourth significant work was his five-volume *Order and History*, which explored in depth the concepts of order and disorder as they relate to history and politics. (The first four volumes were published between 1956 and 1974; the final volume was published posthumously in 1987.) Voegelin identified the "quaternarian structure" of order, which consisted of God, humans, world, and society. Proper participation in this structure means order, while alienation leads to disorder.[84] This participation related to religious experience: "Voegelin's analyses of order and disorder in history have among their consistent aims a disclosing of the religious stratum of experience in the creation of the symbols that have structured the human world and guided human energies."[85] Voegelin's relation to Christianity, however, was not straightforward.

Voegelin never belonged to a formal church, though he described himself as a "pre-Nicaean Christian," a "pre-Reformation Christian," and a "Christian humanist."[86] Heilke rightly notes the ambiguous position Voegelin holds among Christian thinkers.[87] On the negative side, Voegelin did lay some of the blame for the Gnostic problems of modernity at the feet of Christianity, or at least Christianity gone awry.[88] Even on the positive side, Voegelin gave Christianity a limited place. The political question at issue in these debates comes down to "the source of moral and even institutional and civilizational authority for political regimes."[89] Voegelin focused on Christianity's civilizational role, not on the Christianity of the local community of faith. Concerned with the quaternarian structure (God-human-world-society dynamic of order), Voegelin saw Christianity as important for a proper orientation of those four elements but did not focus much on particular local expressions.

Voegelin influenced Conyers in three ways. First, the surface of both of Conyers's final books shows an engagement with Voegelin's philosophical thought. Conyers turns positively to Voegelin's *History of Political Ideas* as a source for understanding particular philosophers and philosophical movements. Second, Conyers picks up the emphasis on order at least partly

84. Heilke, *Eric Voegelin*, 67.

85. Hughes, "Introduction," 4.

86. Federici, *Eric Voegelin*, 11.

87. Heilke, *Eric Voegelin*, 145.

88. For instance, he traces the problem to Joachim of Fiore. See McKnight, "Voegelin's New Science of History," 51.

89. Heilke, *Eric Voegelin*, 145.

from Voegelin. Third, he developed a critique of modernity very similar to Voegelin's Gnosticism critique, though he chose to use different terminology. These last two influential elements extend back to the beginning of Conyers's theological work. He includes *Order and History* in the bibliography of his dissertation,[90] and the language of "order" factors into his main critique of Moltmann in that work, as noted above. Conyers also cites both *The New Science of Politics* and *Science, Politics, and Gnosticism* in the published version.[91] Voegelin's influence on Conyers will become more apparent later as I describe Conyers's diagnosis of modernity and his solutions.

Southern Agrarians and Conyers's Conservatism

The Southern Agrarians make up the third strand of political thought that influenced Conyers's "conservatism," and they helped him connect moral order and economic concerns in the modern United States specifically. The work of these "Twelve Southerners" was taken up by a generation of neo-Agrarians, represented most prominently by Richard Weaver, who influenced Conyers significantly via his *Ideas Have Consequences*. Understanding the agrarians provides a clearer picture of the type of conservatism that shaped Conyers and begins to clarify one source of his creative moves in seeking to navigate the modern world.

In 1930, the Twelve Southerners published a book of essays titled *I'll Take My Stand*.[92] The group became known as the Southern Agrarians, due to their focus on the South as a region and on agrarianism as an economic option preferable to industrialism. Nearly all of the contributors were in some way associated with Vanderbilt University. The main organizers of the volume—John Crowe Ransom, Allen Tate, and Donald Davidson, as well as one of the other contributors, Robert Penn Warren—were previously involved in a literary publication called *The Fugitive*, which focused

---

90. See Conyers, "Jürgen Moltmann's Concept of History," 250.

91. See Conyers, *God, Hope, and History*, 163 n. 8.

92. Twelve Southerners, *I'll Take My Stand*. The Twelve Southerners included Donald Davidson, Joseph Gould Fletcher, Henry Blue Kline, Lyle H. Lanier, Andrew Nelson Lytle, Herman Clarence Nixon, Frank Lawrence Owsley, John Crowe Ransom, Allen Tate, John Donald Wade, Robert Penn Warren, and Stark Young. For a helpful treatment of the main scholarship done on this group, see Bingham and Underwood, *The Southern Agrarians and the New Deal*. In their introduction, Bingham and Underwood survey various scholarly treatments of the agrarians in part to argue that many people neglect the essays written after the main book. For a more recent treatment of the influence of the agrarians, and especially Ransom, Davidson, and Tate, see Langdale, *Superfluous Southerners*.

on poetry and was published for a few years in the early 1920s. Later in the 1920s, Tate, Ransom, and Davidson began to experiment with the idea of a symposium on Southern culture and values. Several factors influenced this decision, including feelings that Northerners were imposing their views on the South through events such as the Scopes Trial, as well as the growth of a movement promoting the "New South," which was basically an industrialized and "Northernized" South. (Though these men were not fundamentalists, they disagreed with what they perceived to be a sort of Northern condescension in the handling of the issue of evolution in Tennessee.) In order to defend Southern culture, Ransom, Tate, and Davidson organized the publication of the volume.

In the most basic sense, the Southern Agrarians were concerned with the advance of industrialization and the types of values and ways of life that it imposed upon people, including the concept of progress and the rise of consumerism. They measured a society not by economic progress but by "human product": what sorts of people did societies help produce?[93] While some argued that social values and morals could be dealt with apart from an economic system, the agrarians insisted that they were inextricably tied. Thus, they turned to the South, especially the pre-Civil War South, as an example of a society that was not built around industrialization but instead around agrarianism. For them, the main contribution that the South could make to broader national issues was to remain faithful to this older way of structuring life in order to avoid the evils and aimlessness bound up with industrialism and consumerism. The broader nation was falling prey to the messianic cults of rationalism, scientism, and industrialism.[94] Some of these thinkers were committed more literally to farming than others, but all generally agreed in the distinction between industrial and agrarian.

The individual essays varied in their topics, approaches, and particular views. Writers covered Southern art, education, religion, economy, history, and race, among other subjects. The essays were written with little consultation between the authors, and the variety makes it nearly impossible to find completely coherent positions in the book.[95] While the essays varied, scholars have identified four common themes that characterize the

93. Bradford, *Remembering Who We Are*, 75.

94. Malvasi, *Unregenerate South*, 21.

95. One scholar goes so far as to say that "attempts to group even three essays soon flounder. Sweeping statements about what all the contributors proposed or wanted are simply not worth the paper they are written on." Conkin, *Southern Agrarians*, 78.

essays: family, place, leisure, and religion.[96] Any further unity derived from the volume must come from the initial common statement of principles. For example, "All the articles bear in the same sense upon the book's title-subject: all tend to support a Southern way of life against what may be called the American or prevailing way; and all as much as agree that the best terms in which to represent the distinction are contained in the phrase, Agrarian *versus* Industrial."[97]

"Industrialism," we read in the statement, "is the economic organization of the collective American society. It means the decision of society to invest its economic resources in the applied sciences. But the word science has acquired a certain sanctitude." In fact, "It is out of order to quarrel with science in the abstract, or even with the applied sciences when their applications are made subject to criticism and intelligence. The capitalization of the applied sciences has now become extravagant and uncritical; it has enslaved our human energies to a degree now clearly felt to be burdensome."[98] The statement expands into the issue of "labor saving," which assumes that labor is an evil. The "apologist of industrialism" assumes that evils will disappear once we have bigger and better machines. Consumption is the end that justifies modern labor, "But the tempo of our labors communicates itself to our satisfactions, and these also become brutal and hurried."[99] Religion cannot flourish in industrial society, because "We receive the illusion of having power over nature, and lose the sense of nature as something mysterious and contingent."[100] For the agrarians, a system of values cannot be separated from an economic base, and it cannot be rebuilt without addressing problems at this base. The labor-saving devices and logic of industrialism and capitalism lead to "increasing disadjustment and instability" in society:

> But a fresh labor-saving device introduced into an industry does not emancipate the laborers in that industry so much as it evicts them. . . . Of course no single labor-saving process is fatal; it brings on a period of unemployed labor and unemployed capital, but soon a new industry is devised which will put them both to work again, and a new commodity is thrown upon the market.

96. Ibid., 85–86.
97. Twelve Southerners, *I'll Take My Stand*, xli.
98. Ibid., xliii.
99. Ibid., xlvi.
100. Ibid.

The laborers were sufficiently embarrassed in the meantime, but, according to the theory, they will eventually be taken care of. It is now the public which is embarrassed; it feels obligated to purchase a commodity for which it had expressed no desire, but it is invited to make its budget equal to the strain. All might yet be well, and stability and comfort might again obtain, but for this: partly because of industrial ambitions and partly because the repressed creative impulse must break out somewhere, there will be a stream of further labor-saving devices in all industries, and the cycle will have to be repeated over and over. The result is an increasing disadjustment and instability.[101]

On the other hand, agrarianism stands as a more promising model. It is the idea "that the culture of the soil is the best and most sensitive of vocations, and that therefore it should have the economic preference and enlist the maximum number of workers."[102] Other forms of work should approach the agrarian model. This change is necessary because "if a community, or a section, or a race, or an age, is groaning under industrialism, and well aware that it is an evil dispensation, it must find the way to throw it off. To think that this cannot be done is pusillanimous. And if the whole community, section, race, or age thinks it cannot be done, then it has simply lost its political genius and doomed itself to impotence."[103] The Southern Agrarians put this very question to American society, and in doing so promoted a different way of political organization and being in the world, rooted in a different economy.

While the book *I'll Take My Stand* gained the most attention, both then and in contemporary scholarship, it "was to be only the opening salvo in a much larger crusade."[104] During the early years of the New Deal, the agrarians were very active in making proposals, and they even joined forces with the English Distributists on issues of property reform.[105] Together they edited an Agrarian-Distributist book in 1936, *Who Owns America?*[106] However, this alliance ultimately failed due to jealousies and differences concerning the platform of the alliance. By 1937, Southern Agrarianism

---

101. Ibid., xlix.

102. Ibid., li.

103. Ibid., lii.

104. Conkin, *Southern Agrarians*, 89.

105. Ibid., 101, 111–13. This included famous figures such as Hilaire Belloc.

106. Agar and Tate, *Who Owns America?*

began to fall apart. The various leaders went their separate ways, focusing on their careers and other projects.

It can be tempting to interpret the entire project of the Southern Agrarians negatively because of the racism present in parts. In *I'll Take My Stand*, for instance, only one essay deals explicitly with race, and while it does so in a fairly progressive way for the time,[107] it still affirmed a type of segregation. In addition, Donald Davidson, one of the key figures in agrarianism, was a staunch supporter of segregation throughout his life. However, rather than moving from such facts to the conclusion that the entire agrarian project is simply an attempt to return to a pre-Civil War South including racism, a more nuanced approach is necessary. Political theorist Christopher Duncan makes this point: "Yet focusing only on [racism], while understandable to a point, leaves us in ignorance of the vast majority of what the Agrarians had to say and teach. If what they had to teach us is as important as I and others have thought, then we impoverish ourselves, which seems a shame."[108] In fact, as Duncan argues in his book *Fugitive Theory*, "what is left over once the racism is sufficiently acknowledged and isolated is worthwhile, important, and potentially even politically useful for people interested in sustaining community, morality, and civic virtue in this country."[109] So, while acknowledging the racism present in individual writers, the project overall can be carried on without the racist elements. The vision that the agrarians had for broader society, taken up by later thinkers, does not require racial subordination.[110]

---

107. See Robert Penn Warren's essay, "The Briar Patch," in which Warren argued along similar lines as Booker T. Washington for a separate but equal type of position. Other essays avoided the issue for the most part, though some startlingly racist lines appear at points in some of them.

108. Duncan, *Fugitive Theory*, x–xi.

109. Ibid., 9.

110. For more on the relationship between the race question and the overall project of the agrarians, see ibid., 201–21. Duncan states, "The fact that slavery was a significant part of the antebellum Southern world should certainly be cause for alarm." Various agrarians believed "it was ultimately not an 'essential part of the agrarian civilization of the South'" (207). In fact, "This, in turn, means that for the Southern Agrarians their theoretical contribution, while as susceptible to racism as any other form of government, was neither dependent on it nor essentially enmeshed with it outside of the realm of an important but not controlling historical predisposition found in the region. . . . The structural form of an Agrarian regime was not so severely corrupted that only bad things or predominantly bad things could come of it" (207–8). As Duncan begins to point out, the North's record on the race issue in Northern cities is by no means exemplary (207). Instead of insisting on rejecting agrarian thought because of its connection to racism,

The Southern Agrarians must be understood within a broader political context. The first way to connect the Southern Agrarians to their political context is to look at the tradition in which they are rooted. Scholars have
done this in numerous helpful ways. In *The War Within*, historian Daniel
Singal places the agrarians in a shift from Victorian to modernist thought,
putting them barely in the modernist camp.[111] Eugene Genovese sees an element of southern nationalism present.[112] Richard Gray's *Writing the South*
views the agrarians as embroiled in a sort of "cultural lag," in which there
is "not only disharmony between the material and non-material culture,
but discontinuity and division *within* the non-material culture itself: the
familiar vocabularies, the old codes and customs are seen to be threatened,
there is a perceptible and evidently unbridgeable gap between them and the
material conditions of existence, but they are clung on to—tenaciously, with
increasing difficulty, and with growing self-consciousness."[113] However,
these positions all fail to consider the broader *political* tradition that orients
the agrarians. For this perspective, the work of Duncan proves insightful.
He argues that the agrarian movement is best understood as a Christian
subspecies of classical republicanism, a subspecies that points to the spiritual significance and even sanctity of work and land.[114] Understanding the
agrarians in this light helps explain their enduring significance, for they
challenge the way the relation of means and ends have been changed in
modern society. The agrarians were not simply a reactionary interest group
but one rooted in a particular political trajectory. They creatively applied
that trajectory to their heritage in the South and proposed ways that the

---

we should realize that the race issue is not one that America has simply solved after the
Civil War and the civil rights movement. Instead, as Michelle Alexander argues, "What
has changed since the collapse of Jim Crow has less to do with the basic structure of our
society than with the language we use to justify it. In the era of colorblindness, it is no
longer socially permissible to use race, explicitly, as a justification for discrimination, ex-
clusion, and social contempt. So we don't. Rather than rely on race, we use our criminal
justice system to label people of color 'criminals' and then engage in all the practices we
supposedly left behind. . . . We have not ended racial caste in America; we have merely
redesigned it" (*New Jim Crow*, 2). Just as we have our own blind spots in the "age of
colorblindness" that need to be exposed and corrected, so did the Southern Agrarians.
Rather than throw out their work in its entirety, we should take seriously the fact that
many Southern Agrarians saw race as separable from their project.

111. See Singal, *War Within*, 198–263.

112. Genovese, *Southern Tradition*, 3.

113. Gray, *Writing the South*, 124.

114. Duncan, *Fugitive Theory*, 12.

Old South's conception of moral order and economy might prove helpful in combatting the ills of industrialization and moral disorder.

The second way to connect the Southern Agrarians to their political context is to connect them to later developments in which their thought played a role. For this we turn to Richard Weaver.

Labeled the "Saint Paul" of the Southern Agrarians,[115] Richard Weaver (1910–63) is considered the first systematizer of the Southern Agrarians and one of the most significant figures carrying on their concerns, both in his dissertation on the South (*The Southern Tradition at Bay*, which he wrote at LSU with Cleanth Brooks, who was tied to several of the agrarians) and in later essays and books.[116] Earlier in his life a socialist,[117] Weaver describes his conversion to the "Church of Agrarianism" in religious terms, and "at the core of that conversion was a commitment to restoring 'the kind of poetic-religious vision of life which dominated the Middle Ages,' as well as a conviction that the grounds for such a restoration could be discovered through a more profound appreciation of his cultural heritage."[118] Neo-Agrarian scholarship focused on agrarians' modern poetics and abstract ideas instead of on their political statements.[119] Weaver traced Southern Agrarian ideas back to first principles,[120] and his work in such scholarship cemented him "as the most eloquent spokesman, since the Second World War, for the traditional idea of his region—the notion, that is, that the Old South was an embodiment of Christian, chivalric values, the last outpost of feudal culture in the Western world."[121] In the eyes of M. E. Bradford, another prominent inheritor of the Agrarian tradition, "what was essential to the Agrarian enterprise . . . found its final completion in Weaver's more

115. He was born too late to be one of the original twelve, but he did much to further the agrarian project. The "Saint Paul" comparison is made by Walter Sullivan, quoted by Nash, *Reappraising the Right*, 99 n. 27.

116. Malvasi, *Unregenerate South*, 224. His most influential book was *Ideas Have Consequences*. Its publication marked the high point of his career; see Smith, "Introduction," xxxvii.

117. He joined the American Socialist Party in 1932, the year he graduated from the University of Kentucky. See East, *American Conservative Movement*, 39.

118. Smith, "Introduction," xxxi.

119. Bingham and Underwood, *Southern Agrarians and the New Deal*, 8. Weaver says, "Political claims alter with circumstances. But claims based upon ethical and aesthetic considerations are a different matter; they cannot be ignored at any time, and it was these which furnished the principal means of attack" ("Tennessee Agrarians," 5).

120. Bradford, *Remembering Who We Are*, 76.

121. Gray, *Writing the South*, 275.

general and sustained excursions into social theory, rhetoric, educational philosophy, intellectual history, and related fields."[122]

Weaver's purpose was not only the recovery of ideas but also the recovery of belief.[123] For "in seeking a philosophy sustaining a recommendation of life, Weaver turned to those venerable traditions of Western thought that spoke in terms of meaning, purpose, and truth—in terms of affirmation: He turned to the Platonic-Christian heritage and its manifestation in the American South."[124] On the most basic level, Weaver argued that society's decline was traceable to the rise of nominalism and the rejection of realism, and in the American context the example of the South proved to be a promising way to begin to remedy this problem. His critique of modernity was inseparable from his apology for the South.[125]

In his work on the agrarians, historian Mark Malvasi holds up Weaver as one of two figures carrying on the project (the other being M. E. Bradford). Weaver argued that the Northern interpretation of being American dominated simply because the North won a great war; the defeat forced the living tradition of the South into silence.[126] However, the Southern tradition still "offered a core of resistance to the most powerfully corrupting forces of the modern age: rationalism, positivism, and science. . . . The southern tradition, alternately, enabled men to see that civilization lay not in the accumulation of wealth and power but in the moral and aesthetic conceptions with which men's imaginations informed reality."[127] While modern man had rejected both the past and the transcendent as a source of meaning under the influence of industrialization, Southerners had more reserved demeanors and expectations. Nor was this merely a matter of taste: "Without a vision of order preserved and disseminated by men of virtue, character, and intellect, civilization would collapse into a barbarism and chaos that would inevitably engender despotism and tyranny."[128] Yet Weaver did not give in to a blind materialism or behaviorism. While he pointed out the faults that industrialism encouraged (calling it caustic and seeing it as running rampant over traditions and associations), he insisted

---

122. Bradford, *Remembering Who We Are*, 74.

123. Gray, *Writing the South*, 275.

124. East, *American Conservative Movement*, 67.

125. Malvasi, "*Ideas Have Consequences* and the Crisis of Modernity," 59.

126. Malvasi, *Unregenerate South*, 224–25.

127. Ibid., 225–26.

128. Ibid., 227.

that humans are responsible for the choices they make.[129] Still, systems such as industrial capitalism played a role in shaping people and their choices. For Weaver, modernity was the institutionalization of many of the seven deadly sins and the loss of order.[130]

Order was Weaver's passion: "the inner order of the soul, the outer order of society."[131] In his eyes, modern people "had lost their moral orientation, had become 'moral idiots,' unable to respond to the perversion, brutality, or challenges of their world. Heartless and indifferent, they lived not immorally but amorally, without the capacity even to measure their descent and degradation."[132] If this loss of moral orientation was not remedied, Weaver feared the collapse of Western civilization, which he valued not simply in and of itself, but because it was an imperfect embodiment of important values, such as piety. Piety was necessary to recognize the existence of a Creator and an order outside of the human will.[133]

Weaver did not hold out for a literal return to the Old South and its ways of life. He admits that no one would want that: "The Old South may indeed be a hall hung with splendid tapestries in which no one would care to live; but from them we can learn something of how to live."[134] However, as Malvasi notes, "The achievement and promise of the South, Weaver argued, posed a challenge to the modern world to abandon the demonic forces of science and technology and thereby to save the human spirit."[135] Part of the reason the Southern tradition could serve in this way was that it maintained a religious worldview over against pure science and materialism. According to Weaver, what the agrarians "were saying is that there are some things which do not have their subsistence in time, and that certain virtues should be cultivated regardless of the era in which one finds oneself born."[136] The Old South offered Weaver a pattern for community, a pattern that was the modern world's only resource for reform (or at least the resource closest to the American context).

---

129. Nierman, "Rhetoric of History and Definition," 60, 44.

130. Bradford, *Remembering Who We Are*, 80.

131. Kirk, "Foreword," viii.

132. Malvasi, *Unregenerate South*, 231.

133. One scholar even calls piety the key to Weaver's thought. See Nierman, "Rhetoric of History and Definition," 4.

134. Weaver, *Southern Tradition at Bay*, 380.

135. Malvasi, *Unregenerate South*, 230.

136. Weaver, "Tennessee Agrarians," 8.

Weaver turned to the South as a tradition worth maintaining in order to have true civilization. His most significant contribution to conservative thought, in the eyes of one political scientist, was his delineation of what is necessary for civilization and culture to flourish.[137] In particular, he spoke of "social bond individualism." This idea captured the Southern conservatives' version of Christian individualism, distinguishing it from the bourgeois individualism associated with the Renaissance and the French Enlightenment.[138] In an essay originally published in 1963 in the journal *Modern Age*,[139] Weaver argues that there are two types of American individualism, one worth guarding and the other impossible to build upon. To illustrate, he provides a "prophet" for each. The individualism worth guarding Weaver called "social bond individualism," represented by John Randolph of Roanoke in his defense of state's rights combined with the political prudence to compromise when necessary. For Weaver, social bond individualism "battles unremittingly for individual rights, while recognizing that these have to be secured within the social context."[140] Randolph believed in the limited role of the government, which secured the "individual" side of the equation, while also insisting on the defense of the smaller but "natural" unit over against the state, which pretends a right to rule and to run roughshod over the smaller unit.[141] This defense protects the other side of the equation, the social bond side, recognizing that a proper individualism operates within group bonds.

On the other hand, Weaver called the impossible form of individualism "anarchic individualism," represented by the withdrawal of Henry David Thoreau. This form slips into idealism and seeks to withdraw from every form of association, for "anarchic individualism is revolutionary and subversive from the very start; it shows a complete despite for all that civilization or the social order has painfully created, and this out of self-righteousness or egocentric attachment to an idea."[142] Thoreau's individualism brought him to a studied withdrawal from society, but Randolph's individualism moved him toward political action at the local level.[143] Individual-

---

137. Nierman, "Rhetoric of History and Definition," iii.

138. Genovese, *Southern Tradition*, 3.

139. Weaver, "Two Types of American Individualism," 77–103.

140. Ibid., 82.

141. Ibid., 88.

142. Ibid., 102.

143. Young, *Richard M. Weaver*, 11.

ism, for Weaver, is worth guarding when located within the proper social context. However, modern talk of individualism tends to lean toward the anarchic variety, enthroning the individual apart from and over any other bonds, bonds that in fact secure true individualism. Weaver's criticism of radical individualism separated him from libertarianism and what would become neoconservatism. Weaver thought that the embrace of freedom by men such as Frank Meyer with the *National Review* led to the "anarchic individualism" that Weaver associated with Thoreau.[144]

Conyers demonstrates this same concern with individualism. He deals with it explicitly in two works on theology. In a 1998 article on Baptist theology, he argues that the individualism that is characteristic of modernity is an autonomous individualism.[145] In an article published in 2004, he draws on this theme again in connection with modern theology: "Individualism and rationality are not, strictly speaking, features of modernity, but rather they are features of a Christian view of life that, through the filter of the Enlightenment, were made to conform to what is the heart of modernity and of postmodernism as well."[146] As is shown in these two articles, Conyers operated with a similar distinction between different types of individualism. Not all individualism is nefarious.

Conyers also inherits a concern for religious imagination from Richard Weaver. In *Superfluous Southerners*, John Langdale argues that Weaver ultimately believed that "a revitalization of the religious imagination was essential to resisting ideology's gnostic impulse to debate the spoken and written word."[147] Conyers's work on modernity, which we will explore in full later, turns to just such a revitalization of the religious imagination through the concept of vocation.

When one hears the word *conservative* today, the likes of Richard Weaver and the Southern Agrarians are not what springs most immediately to mind. This is due to political change in the mid-twentieth century, which deserves brief mention here in order to understand the relation of the Southern Agrarians to contemporary conservatism. In the mid-twentieth century, William F. Buckley Jr. fused together various conservatives and

---

144. See Langdale, *Superfluous Southerners*, 95. Russell Kirk also saw "true conservatism" as antithetical to unrestrained capitalism and egoistic individualism. See Nash, *Reappraising the Right*, 78.

145. Conyers, "Changing Face of Baptist Theology," 34.

146. Conyers, "Can Postmodernism Be Used," 303.

147. Langdale, *Superfluous Southerners*, 115–16.

other groups to form what is more commonly thought of as "conservative" in contemporary political thought.[148] Buckley and his *National Review* succeeded because of their "ability to unite antistatist libertarians, who wanted to roll back the New Deal state; socially conservative traditionalists, who opposed the secularism and relativism of liberalism; and anti-Communists, who feared liberal weakness in the face of Communist aggression abroad and subversion within the United States."[149] In proposing a new "conservative" identity, Buckley marginalized older leadership of the Right and newer contenders, transforming right-wing politics.[150] He "paired a politics of liberty (and the pristine market) with a politics of order—an embrace of modernization with a rejection of cultural modernism."[151]

This new conservative identity impacted the agrarians and their reception. Paul Murphy notes, "Radical conservative critiques of progress, such as that of the Southern Agrarians, were marginalized after World War II, not so much by liberals, who tended to be intrigued by conservative anti-modernism, but by the postwar conservative movement, which aimed to co-opt the label 'conservative.'"[152] The degree to which Weaver held together the moral element and the economic element is debated. Murphy charges that New Conservatives like Weaver jettisoned the economic critique of industrial capitalism in order to have their message better received in post-World War II conservatism. In fact, "By the end of the 1950s, Davidson—as well as Tate, Weaver, and others in the Agrarian circle—had planted the seeds of a universalist reinterpretation of Agrarianism, one with only limited criticisms of industrial capitalism and fewer assertions of southern identity."[153] This criticism of Weaver, however, painting him as a compromiser of true agrarian ideals, does not seem to hold. Historian

148. As noted above in relation to Nash's work, some historians consider the movement to have three main focuses: a libertarian economist wing (F. A. Hayek and Ludwig von Mises), a strong anticommunist ideology (Whittaker Chambers and James Burnham), and a traditionalist wing (Russell Kirk and Richard Weaver). See Scotchie, *Barbarians in the Saddle*, 1–2. As mentioned above, however, others place more distance between even Kirk and Weaver. All of this supports the point I am making here: modern "conservatives" are a hybrid of earlier influences, and understanding earlier forms of conservatism such as that of the Southern Agrarians and Weaver (and hence Conyers) requires grappling with these branches.

149. Murphy, *Rebuke of History*, 118.

150. Ibid., 119.

151. Ibid., 120.

152. Ibid.

153. Ibid.

Eugene Genovese argues that Weaver openly attacks capitalism.[154] Other thinkers who did turn away from the economic critique did so to make Southern Agrarianism more palatable and influential in Buckley's new fusionist conservatism. Whether the Southern Agrarians and neo-Agrarians toned down their economic critique as much as Murphy charges or not,[155] Buckley's fusionist conservatism would continue to develop in favor of the free market, defining conservatism from the 1950s onward.

The Southern Agrarians and neo-Agrarians, however, are not truly themselves without the economic critique, and their most faithful followers maintain it. At the root, the Southern Agrarians held that a society's values and morality are inextricably connected to its economic system. One prominent contemporary writer in the agrarian stream of influence is Wendell Berry. Berry's essays on agrarianism in collections such as *The Unsettling of America* and *The Art of the Commonplace*, as well as in fiction centered on the fictional community of Port William, Kentucky, demonstrate a clear connection to the Southern Agrarians and their twin emphasis on the critique of a society's morality and its connection to an economic system. In fact, "The belief that industrial capitalism and Western notions of progress subvert an organic and healthy social order lies at the heart of [Berry's] social criticism."[156] Berry continues the call for rootedness that marked the agrarians.[157]

---

154. Genovese, *Southern Tradition*, 12, 17, 24, 35. Part of the problem seems to emerge in comparing Weaver's *Ideas Have Consequences* to later works. In *Ideas*, Weaver holds to private property as an important element for reclaiming a proper ordering for society because it establishes individuals in communities. In later writings, he would be even more favorable toward capitalism. See Nash, *Conservative Intellectual Movement in America*, 30–42. For reflection on how his later writings inform how capitalist or anticapitalist Weaver was, see Nash, *Reappraising the Right*, 108–11. Nash states, "To the end of his days he remained a critic of industrialism and technological 'progress.' Nevertheless, by the last years of his life Weaver had significantly softened the militantly antimaterialistic, antibourgeois, anticapitalist biases of *Ideas Have Consequences*. Perhaps at the height of the Cold War against an atheistic and collectivist enemy, the United States of America looked better to him than it had in the late 1940s" (111).

155. The degree to which Weaver toned down his economic critique is debated. See above.

156. Murphy, *Rebuke of History*, 264.

157. For more on Berry's inheritance of this tradition, see ibid., 264–72.

Summary of Conservative Influence

The influence of Althusius, Voegelin, and the agrarians worked together to shape Conyers's particular type of conservatism—one source of his creative moves in navigating the modern world. Conyers's conservatism does not contradict his critiques of the modern world or his constructive themes that would seem more at home outside of the conservative movement of today, because Conyers is connected to the Southern Agrarians and what some call a "paleoconservatism."[158] This form of conservatism predates Buckley's fusionist conservatism and its allegiance to the free market. Conyers's connection to this tradition,[159] especially via the work of Richard Weaver, provides the hermeneutic key for understanding his conservatism and the perspective from which he diagnoses and seeks remedies for the modern world. Weaver's influence is most clearly evinced in themes such as place and Conyers's stance of humility and piety. Conyers draws on several significant ideas from these conservative thinkers, including an emphasis on intermediate associations (Althusius), proper individualism (Althusius and Weaver), the importance of order (Voegelin and Weaver), and the connection between economic systems and morals (Southern Agrarians and Weaver). (Each of these ideas will play important roles later, when we explore Conyers's political theology and expand on this admittedly brief mention of these significant concepts.) In a sense, Conyers stands alongside Wendell Berry[160]—two Southern Baptists influenced by the Southern Agrarian tradition and seeking to incorporate its critique into their projects. While Berry's work is more widely known and appreciated, Conyers's

158. For more on this term, as well as the idea of "New Conservatives" and the relevance of Russell Kirk, see ibid., 129–50.

159. Conyers does not explicitly deal with *I'll Take My Stand*, but he does reference Allen Tate and Andrew Lytle in his work, so he was familiar with the work of at least part of this group, and he is clearly influenced by the stream of thought via Weaver. The earliest reference to Allen Tate comes in Conyers, "Revival of Joachite Apocalyptic Speculation," 209. For other references to Tate, see Conyers, *Long Truce*, 218, and "Three Sources," 313 n. 1. Conyers refers to Andrew Lytle, Donald Davidson, and Robert Penn Warren in "Why the Chattahoochee Sings," 100. For another reference to Lytle, see Conyers, *Listening Heart*, 141. Conyers also names the Fugitives specifically as critics of modernity in "Can Postmodernism Be Used," 297. This evidence shows that while Conyers never provided an explicit treatment of these thinkers, he was aware of their work and influenced by it.

160. While Conyers does not interact formally with Berry's work, he was familiar with it. For example, Berry's *Life Is a Miracle* was found among Conyers's books after his death (D. Conyers, phone conversation with author, July 19, 2013).

is more explicitly theological in working out the implications of Southern conservatism. In fact, Berry could be critiqued for not having enough of a place for the church in his work,[161] whereas the church plays a central role for Conyers, as we will see. Now that we understand Conyers's dissertation on Moltmann as well as the three primary sources of his conservatism, we can turn to Conyers's published book on Moltmann (*God, Hope, and History: Jürgen Moltmann and the Christian Concept of History*), which was published nine years after he defended his dissertation. Analyzing this later book on Moltmann demonstrates how Conyers incorporates what he has learned from these forms of conservatism to build a deeper critique of Moltmann and to solidify his own theological foundation.

RETURNING TO MOLTMANN: A NEW CRITICAL ANGLE IN *GOD, HOPE, AND HISTORY*

God, Hope, and History shows Conyers engaged in a more thorough critique of Moltmann, a critique that would help him establish his own foundation for navigating the modern world. Though Conyers drew most of the book straight from the dissertation (70 percent), he added a different framework and critical angle that together show the way he drew from conservative thought. In short, Conyers enters a new topic of engagement with Moltmann (hierarchy and power) that he builds based largely on the work of a new thinker (Richard Weaver), whom Conyers evidently came across between the dissertation and the book, since Weaver is not mentioned at all in the dissertation. Weaver's thought and the topic of hierarchy and power provide Conyers with a critical angle on Moltmann that sets Conyers on a trajectory of theological concern. He fleshed out this trajectory more in his final two books. He retains Moltmann's emphasis on eschatology and the future, and even his "openness" to a degree, but he tempers it by providing it with structure and moral order based on concepts drawn from the conservatives discussed above. Such synthesis helps Conyers overcome the conservative-liberal binary and form creative theological responses.

In the first chapter of *God, Hope, and History*, Conyers introduces one of Moltmann's criticisms related to theology of history. In works such as *The Trinity and the Kingdom*,[162] Moltmann insists that monadic monothe-

---

161. For instance, see Hart, "Wendell Berry's Unlikely Case for Conservative Christianity."

162. Moltmann, *The Trinity and the Kingdom*.

ism has caused problems for the church.[163] He recognizes various evils, such as human domination of nature through science and technology and oppression in the social sphere. These evils, in Moltmann's eyes, are "a consequence of the hierarchical, dominating, power-oriented thinking that inevitably results when philosophical monotheism becomes the ruling principle in theology."[164] For Moltmann, hierarchy favors stability, not freedom, and thus hierarchical views of theology are detrimental to a theology of hope. He sets up a dichotomy between hierarchy and eschatology as two views of reality. Conyers calls this view into question, thus reframing his engagement with Moltmann. While the dissertation focused on expounding Moltmann's theology of history, the book takes on the task of understanding Moltmann's theology of history in order to assess this dichotomy between hierarchy and eschatology, between order and hope.

A different view of hierarchy arises in Conyers's thought. To him, "Both hierarchy and eschatology, order and hope, are ways of speaking about ethical foundations. While hierarchy suggests loyalty to the highest and best, eschatology suggests loyalty to that which is lasting. They are two visions dealing with the same issue of ordering human action and affection. While eschatology raises open questions about the end and goal of things, hierarchy offers a provisional answer."[165] In this new frame for his dissertation work, Conyers asks whether hierarchy might actually be required for a theology of history with an eschatological focus.[166] While Moltmann too easily identifies hierarchy with the abuse of power,[167] this conflation is an unwarranted move in Conyers's mind.

Conyers's fondness for hierarchy and order was encouraged by Richard Weaver, whose *Ideas Have Consequences*[168] is cited sparingly but significantly in Conyers's arguments about hierarchy (Conyers mentions Weaver on page 14 and cites him on page 192). Especially after World War II, Weaver devoted his work to cultural restoration. In a 1945 letter, he stated, "The atomic bomb was a final blow to the code of humanity. I can-

---

163. Conyers, *God, Hope, and History*, 7.

164. Ibid., 9.

165. Ibid., 13.

166. Ibid., 15.

167. Ibid., 185. This also reveals Moltmann's anti-Catholicism.

168. Weaver, *Ideas Have Consequences*. While Weaver did publish other work, including additional books and many shorter writings, *Ideas Have Consequences* is the only source by Weaver that Conyers cites, so it is the only one that we can be sure he knew.

not help thinking that we will suffer retribution for this. For a long time to come I believe my chief interest is going to be the restoration of civilization, of the distinctions that make life intelligible."[169] Much of his work would continue to bear this burden, and the burden is clearly evident in *Ideas Have Consequences*.

Weaver shows that every advanced society explains its values in terms of social and political hierarchy. This hierarchy can reflect different things, whether it be the inescapable state of things (ancient Egypt) or the horizon of hope (early Hebrew society).[170] Conyers connects these problems to the issues surrounding nominalism through the analysis of Weaver. Conyers notes that "while [Weaver] holds in common with Moltmann a critique of dominating power and the will for conquest, he also sees the problem evidenced in the *loss* of hierarchy. It is interesting that Richard Weaver used almost the same language as Moltmann in his critique of the Baconian development in science and technology, but the precise difference is linked to a defense of hierarchy."[171] Conyers's difference from Moltmann moving forward follows along similar lines.

In his concluding chapter, Conyers makes several arguments about hierarchy. He demonstrates how it fits with a proper eschatological understanding of theology and history. Hierarchy causes openness to as-yet-undefined possibilities of existence, an openness toward God. By this he means that "hierarchy in Christian theology is represented not in the concreteness of the cosmological order, where the divine nature of this order is everywhere asserted, but in an openness (from below) toward him who gave measure and value to all things because he is the ultimate value. This hierarchy is 'open,' not because of the power exerted from above, but because of the disposition of reverence from below."[172] Hierarchy also suggests the relative and questionable nature of all earthly powers, because hierarchy is rooted in something that is longed for but not yet fully realized.

Another way of understanding the development of Conyers's concept of order and hierarchy can be seen in a piece he wrote on Henry David Thoreau in 1998. In "Beyond Walden Pond," Conyers deals with the theme of simplicity in Thoreau arguing that there are two types: negative simplicity (the elimination of complexity) and positive simplicity (the ordering of

169. Quoted in Smith, "Introduction," xxxiv.
170. Conyers, *God, Hope, and History*, 14.
171. Ibid., 192.
172. Ibid., 194.

complexity). He argues that while Thoreau is known for the first, he often draws on the second. The ordering of complexity, positive simplicity, comes from a hierarchy of values. For instance, Thoreau would talk about having only the best books, and taking time for good, deep conversation. It is a simplicity of focus. Conyers then connects this to a need for a transcendent order, which provides the hierarchy of values that makes positive simplicity possible.[173]

Finally, Conyers draws on the concept of humility as the way to resolve hierarchy and eschatology. Eschatology's openness to God is expressed in terms of hope in Scripture, but openness to God in terms of hierarchy is humility. This humble hierarchy is different than hierarchy understood as authority exerted downward by some power; instead,

> from the standpoint of a world open to God in humility, hier-archy can mean precisely the opposite of the presumptuous and calculating use of power—in fact it is the restraint of power and becomes so by resisting the temptation of power. Hierarchy as nothing other than the elaborated will to power is hierarchy as a disguise for something else—but precisely the reason it is so use-ful as a disguise is that we all have an intuition that the sense of hierarchy—embodied in the virtues of piety, humility, reverence, and worship—is the very thing that protects the world from un-qualified, self-justifying power that is unbound and set loose upon the world.[174]

Hierarchy properly understood is indispensable for an eschatological un-derstanding of theology.

The new framework for Moltmann's theology of history that Conyers provides in this book focuses on Moltmann's reaction against the abuse of power and his identification of the abuse of power and hierarchy. Cony-ers agrees with the crisis with power, and issues surrounding power in the modern world motivate much of his later work. Thus he begins to lay the building blocks for this later work with respect to critiques of power in the modern world. However, with this new framework and drawing on Rich-ard Weaver's work on order and hierarchy, Conyers distinguishes hierarchy and the abuse of power. He shows that hierarchy can be construed in a way that is properly open to God as the one "who gave measure and value to all

---

173. Conyers, "Beyond Walden Pond," 26–30.
174. Conyers, *God, Hope, and History*, 199–200.

things because he is the ultimate value."[175] Therefore, hierarchy should not be identified with the abuse of power, as in Moltmann. Rightly understood, hierarchy is "an antidote to the predatory tendencies of a society bent on the political, economic, and technological exploitation of the world."[176]

Conclusion

These three steps—from Conyers's early work on Moltmann to the conservative influences back to Moltmann—show the major influences on Conyers's theology and reveal the way he fuses these diverse influences together. This fusion of influences puts Conyers in a place beyond the oversimplification of a conservative-liberal binary that often plagues evangelical discussions because it situates him in a more critical space between the typical labels, from where he can grapple with each in order to develop his own nuanced position. In agreement with Moltmann, he sees eschatology, openness, and hope as important elements of a Christian view of history. However, conservatives such as Weaver lead him to see a place for order and hierarchy that challenges Moltmann's conflation of power with the abuse of power. Against the conservatives, however, he defines both order and hierarchy in a way that does not depend on past structures alone but on the future toward which God is calling his people, again showing the influence of Moltmann's eschatology. By working through these issues in his early work, Conyers lays a firm foundation and trajectory for his theology and for forming a social imaginary and moral vision adequate for navigating the modern world. With this trajectory in mind, we turn to his theological corpus.

175. Ibid., 194.
176. Ibid., 185.

CHAPTER 2

Conyers's Theological Work

INTRODUCTION

This brief chapter extends the thesis of the first: Conyers incorporates various theological and political influences in a constructive manner that points a way beyond the typical "conservative-versus-liberal" rhetoric that colors the evangelical theopolitical imaginary. Here I provide an overview and categorize Conyers's work to demonstrate his primary interests as well as a shift in his writing that occurs later in his career. This chapter shows the influence and trajectory identified in the previous chapter, and it provides the necessary context for us to engage Conyers's mature work beginning in the next chapter. The arguments of this chapter and the previous build on one another to show how Conyers develops his theological foundation. He incorporates "conservative" political influences and his interest in Moltmann's eschatology to forge a unique theological point of view that guided his navigation of the modern world in his mature work.

Tracing Conyers's theological work further demonstrates the impact of the influences we explored in the previous chapter. His work spans from a 1971 article in *Christianity Today* to his final book, *The Listening Heart*, which he finished just prior to his death (published 2006). In what follows, I make a threefold argument. First, Conyers has a primary scholarly theological project—oriented around eschatology and history—that spans his entire theological career and shows the enduring influence of Moltmann. His published works outside the scope of this primary project are church and ministry focused. Second, a shift occurs in 1996, when Conyers's mature work narrows in focus and changes in audience. It is at this point that Conyers expresses his desire for evangelical theology to promote a "truly catholic vision." Third, one of Conyers's final pieces articulated an idea of "vocational theology" that sheds light on what he was working toward in his post-1996 work and provides a clarifying context for understanding his political theology. This threefold argument demonstrates the influence and trajectory identified in the previous chapter, and it provides the necessary context for us to engage Conyers's mature work.

Primary Theological Project

Conyers's early interest in politics, as evidenced by his undergraduate degree (political science), combined with the recommendation of his *Doktorvater* Dale Moody to study the work of Jürgen Moltmann, set him up for a unified theological project spanning from his doctoral dissertation at Southern Seminary (1979) to his final book (2004). At the most basic level, this project was concerned with exploring eschatology and history for different audiences and with different questions in view, including popular-level theology and more academic angles.

In the first chapter of *The End: What Jesus Said about the Last Things*,[1] which I deal with in more detail below, Conyers reflects on the significance of eschatology in his own thinking. He tells a story of walking in Atlanta with his mother as a young boy and seeing an old, frazzled man wearing a sandwich-board sign saying, "The End Is Near." When he innocently asked his mother how the old man knew, she replied simply, "He doesn't." This incident illustrates some "social wisdom" that he learned as a young child: "Those who talk about the end, those who parade with their sandwich signs announcing doom, are not to be taken seriously. And anyone who takes up that subject seriously is at least running the risk of being associated with those old men, those ultimate misfits, announcing doom on the streets of modern cities, where all sensible people ignore them."[2] This social wisdom impacted his eschatology.

1. Conyers, *The End*.
2. Ibid., 13–14.

College and graduate school confirmed for him that eschatology "was a fertile ground for every misspent human expectation."[3] He proceeds in *The End* through a historical roll call of doomsday predictions and adventist movements: Greek chiliasts, Montanists, early Crusaders, Joachim of Fiore, fervor around the Black Death, Konrad Schmid, Thomas Müntzer, and John of Leiden.[4] His reading of Eric Voegelin and Gerhart Niemeyer showed him that the imminent expectation of a final state of being had a deadly influence on Western culture. Modern mass movements, such as Nazism and communism, created social disorder by reducing Christian hope to a this-worldly, imminent expectation.[5] This led to a shift in Conyers's view of eschatology and its relation to navigating the modern world:

> Suddenly I began to see the world of public events in a more vivid and significant way. A light came on—and it illuminated what was happening in my world. From the Nazi movement and its announcement of a Third Reich (like Joachim of Fiore's "Third Age"), which is also called the Thousand-Year Reich (a millennial kingdom), to the communist movement with its expectations of revolution resulting in world peace and prosperity in a secular millennium, I began to see striking similarities with what had gone on before on the fringes of pseudo-Christianity. Modern movements, following in alarming fashion the pattern of Thomas Müntzer and John of Leiden, from dreams to madness, from madness to horrible cruelty, were no longer fringe movements but were setting the fate of whole continents, murdering millions and dragging the world to the edge of an atomic abyss.[6]

It was this view of history—birthed by his reading of Voegelin and Niemeyer—that helped cause a shift from seeing eschatology as a fringe subject to a subject shedding light on the violent world of the twentieth century.

While Voegelin and Niemeyer helped Conyers see the explanatory power of eschatology, the work of Southern Baptist theologian Dale Moody and German theologian Jürgen Moltmann convinced him of the central place of eschatology within Christian thought: eschatology was "a central thrust, a theme that permeated everything, and made the gospel apply to everything, and made sense of everything."[7] This conviction grew stron-

3. Ibid., 14.

4. For Conyers's narration of this historical progression, see ibid., 14–17.

5. Ibid., 18. This concern comes from Voegelin's work.

6. Ibid.

7. Ibid., 20.

ger as world events continued to unfold. Conyers specifically mentions the Jim Jones affair of 1978, when an Indiana minister led his large congregation on a trip that ended in mass suicide in the jungles of Guyana. He came to see that

> the street-walking doomsayers, the flagellants, the Jan Bockelsons and the modern apocalypticists of the secular type—the Stalins and the Hitlers—were only at a very superficial level bringing discredit to New Testament expectations of the last days. In fact, in a much more significant way they were confirming what had been said long ago, when Jesus linked sin to judgment yet promised the ultimate triumph of God, when he taught that the path any man or woman takes leads to an end and can be understood only in light of the end.[8]

In fact, ultimately life's choices come down to a simple and direct religious choice, a yes or a no to God, Christ or antichrist. This growing realization pushed eschatology to the center of Conyers's interests because he was convinced that it was at the center of Christian theology and at the heart of the issues boiling in the world around him.

A brief overview of Conyers's most important works related to eschatology provides a better understanding of the shape of his theological project. In his dissertation, Conyers explored the concept of hope and history in the work of Jürgen Moltmann, as explained earlier. Though it was completed in 1979, the dissertation was not published until 1988 as *God, Hope, and History: Jürgen Moltmann and the Christian Concept of History.* Four of the book's eight chapters were from the dissertation. These four chapters develop the concept of history from Augustine to Moltmann and then work through three of Moltmann's important books: *Theology of Hope, The Crucified God,* and *The Church in the Power of the Holy Spirit.* The final part of *God, Hope, and History* deals with "human perspectives in the history of God," with a chapter on Joachim of Fiore earlier published in *Perspectives in Religious Studies,*[9] a chapter focused on consumer society and ecological concerns, and a chapter on order and hope. The development between the dissertation and the book shows Conyers digging deeper into tradition (especially via the insights of Richard Weaver), and then applying his findings to issues in society around him, as he recounted in his reflections in *The End.* Additionally, his work on consumer society and ecological issues,

8. Ibid., 23.

9. Conyers, "Revival of Joachite Apocalyptic Speculation," 197–211.

focused on the work of Moltmann, begins to show some of the themes that he continues to develop later in his career in his own political theology.

Next, Conyers wrote two books on eschatology at a more popular level. First was *The Eclipse of Heaven: Rediscovering the Hope of a World Beyond*, published in 1992 with InterVarsity Press.[10] In it he developed the basic insight that a loss of transcendence characterizes modern life and evacuates it of moral bearings and meaning. Written at a more popular level than *God, Hope, and History*, *Eclipse of Heaven* sought to popularize his basic eschatological ideas and their relation to the way society is ordered. In 1995, InterVarsity published another Conyers book on eschatology, *The End: What Jesus Said about the Last Things*. Though related to his eschatological interests, this book was again on a popular level. It sought to "recover . . . something of the directness and practicability that was once found in Mark 13 and its parallels . . . [and] a sense of its power to address the real fears and aspirations of the human heart."[11] This book fits within his major project because of its topic, but it is unique in being focused on expositing and reflecting on specific biblical passages, whereas his other works on eschatology take Scripture into account but focus on doctrine and history more fully. Around the time these two books were written, Conyers also published two articles that center on similar themes: "Communism's Collapse: The Receding Shadow of Transcendence" and "After the Hurricane."[12]

Conyers did not publish his next monograph fitting into this project until 2001—*The Long Truce: How Tolerance Made the World Safe for Power and Profit*. While it may seem that this book does not fit with Conyers's eschatological interests, it must be kept in mind that Conyers's interest in eschatology was always connected to progressive theories of history and what was going on in the world around him. His project focused on the centrality of eschatology and its connections to history and culture. *The Long Truce* fits well within this project, for in it Conyers develops the basic thesis that the Christian practice of toleration (which at its roots meant the humility to listen to others) had been warped into the "doctrine" of toleration. This "doctrine" served to relativize religious commitments to private concerns, leading to tolerance being used to minimize any commitments

10. Conyers, *Eclipse of Heaven*.

11. Conyers, *The End*, 8.

12. Conyers, "Communism's Collapse," 466–67; Conyers, "After the Hurricane," 34–36.

or bonds besides the bond between the individual and the modern state. As I will develop more fully in the next two chapters, Conyers connects this basic thesis to issues of morality and theories of history in ways that show how toleration as used in the modern period came to challenge Christian eschatology. Around the time he was writing this monograph, Conyers also published related articles, such as "History as Problem and Hope,"[13] "Simms's Sabbath Lyrics and the Reclaiming of Sacred Time in the Religious Imagination,"[14] and "Rescuing Tolerance."[15]

More than two years after Conyers's death, Spence Publishing released his final book, *The Listening Heart: Vocation and the Crisis of Modern Culture*,[16] which the American Library Association listed among its top ten books on religion for 2007. In this work, Conyers turns again to the themes developed in *The Long Truce* but begins to plot ways that the Christian tradition provides practices that can reorient Christian life around a proper understanding of what it means to live a human life before God. The concept of vocation is one key element of this understanding. Part of responding to God's call is recognizing the eschatological reality that God is drawing his people toward; rather than seeking control, one should assume a posture of faithful response to God and God's work. Related articles include "Why the Chatahoochee Sings: Notes Towards a Theory of 'Place'"[17] and "Vocation and the Liberal Arts."[18]

Conyers's own explanation of his interest in eschatology in *The End*, especially in light of his major works on eschatology, makes clear that he had a consistent, major theological project spanning from his dissertation to his final book. This project can be described simply as "eschatology," but more nuance needs to be added after surveying the various works above. Several elements are essential. First, Conyers was consistently concerned with the doctrine of eschatology because of its centrality for the Christian faith. Second, he found Moltmann's work of particular interest in this connection. Third, he saw eschatology as a main element of the teachings of Jesus. Fourth, he believed that eschatology illumined the major societal issues of his day. His major theological project, represented by both books

13. Conyers, "History as Problem and Hope," 29–39.

14. Conyers, "Simms's Sabbath Lyrics," 15–26.

15. Conyers, "Rescuing Tolerance," 43–46.

16. Conyers, *Listening Heart*.

17. Conyers, "Why the Chattahoochee Sings," 99–106.

18. Conyers, "Vocation and the Liberal Arts," 123–31.

and articles, pursued all of these elements at different times and culminated in his final two books. These books deal with issues of political theology, navigating the modern world, and especially the need for a proper telos, a proper end, to orient human life.

While publishing on his primary theological project regularly throughout his career, Conyers also produced articles and books that can best be understood as arising from opportunities to serve the church. I break these works down into three rough categories: biblical studies, doctrine, and theological imagination.

Conyers published his first book, *How to Read the Bible*, with InterVarsity in 1986.[19] He drew primarily from his own teaching material at Central Missouri State University.[20] In it he deals with the art, the practice, and the importance of Bible reading in the home and in the church. He introduces basic topics such as history, the role of faith, and differences between the Old and New Testaments. A few of Conyers's articles fit into the general category of introductory or popular biblical studies as well. He published in the evangelical magazine *Biblical Illustrator* twice: "James: A Pillar of the Church" (1988) and "A Profile of Levi" (1995). One of Conyers's books relating to eschatology, *The End*, also fits within this category, because the book is structured as an exposition and reflection on Mark 13 and parallel passages. These works demonstrate Conyers's professorial responsibilities and commitment to teaching the Bible for the church.

Broadman and Holman published Conyers's only other book not related to his major theological interests in 1995. It was titled *A Basic Christian Theology*,[21] and as the title suggests, this work serves as an introduction to theology, fit for an undergraduate course or church study. In it he emphasizes that "the whole fabric of theology, if it is in fact Christian, has to do not simply with circumscribing God, or some idea of God, within a system of thought, but it has to do with drawing human beings into the circle of God's redemptive purpose."[22] This statement provides helpful context for Conyers's broader work in theology: he is concerned with drawing people into God's work, not merely describing it. This concern illuminates the connections mentioned above between various aspects of his work on eschatology, seeking not only to describe it but also to see how it connects

---

19. Conyers, *How to Read the Bible*.

20. Conyers and Conyers, "Biography of A. J. Conyers," xxviii–xxix.

21. Conyers, *Basic Christian Theology*.

22. Ibid., 8.

and makes sense of life today. His theological work, as shown in this basic introduction, is rooted in the idea of being called by God into a way of life.

I categorize a mixture of other works under the general idea of "theological imagination." In other words, these works touch on issues of Christian vision and formation, such as ethics and education. This category covers early works such as "Is Patriotism Christian?"[23] and "Teaching the Holocaust: The Role of Theology,"[24] and it extends to later ones such as "Cloning and the Moral Imagination"[25] and "Beyond Walden Pond: Illusion and Reality in Pursuit of the Simple Life."[26] These works again demonstrate that his interests always find their termination in the living of the Christian life today and the formation of Christian communities.

These three rough categories—biblical studies, doctrine, and theological imagination—are admittedly broad and overlapping, because the work of Conyers itself was broad and overlapping. In his work in biblical studies, he sought to bring people into the text that it might be significant for their lives, and in his work on doctrine and theological imagination, he sought to be rooted in the biblical text. Categorizing the works in this way, however, makes clear the breadth of topics on which he published and emphasizes his interest in the lived quality of the Christian life, as well as the necessary rooting of that life in the Bible and right doctrine.

Shift circa 1994–96

In the first half of his scholarly career, Conyers focused fairly evenly between his main theological project and other ministry opportunities in his publications, especially articles. He wrote for *Christianity Today* and produced introductory-level books on biblical studies and theology. However, a shift occurred around 1996, with the publication of "Protestant Principle, Catholic Substance" in *First Things*.[27] From that point on, Conyers published nothing in *Christianity Today*, nothing on biblical studies or introductory doctrine, and no books outside of his main theological project. (My argument here relies on what Conyers actually published during this period. I am aware that he continued to have ideas and even book proposals that

---

23. Conyers, "Is Patriotism Christian?," 11–12.
24. Conyers, "Teaching the Holocaust," 128–42.
25. Conyers, "Cloning and the Moral Imagination."
26. Conyers, "Beyond Walden Pond," 26–30.
27. Conyers, "Protestant Principle, Catholic Substance," 15–17.

veered toward other topics, but the majority of the work he carried through to completion centered on this main project.) Most of his publications after this point were directly or tangentially related to his main project, and his audience shifted from Baptist and evangelical circles more narrowly to evangelical and ecumenical circles more broadly. The mid-1990s represent a sharpening of focus and a broadening of audience in Conyers's work. At this point he developed a focus on promoting a "truly catholic vision" for navigating the modern world.

Conyers endured two major changes in the mid-1990s. First, in the summer of 1994 he moved to Waco, Texas, to help start Truett Seminary at Baylor University. Second, he learned that he was in the early stages of cancer, specifically chronic lymphocytic leukemia (CLL), that same summer.[28] He had no significant publications in 1994, but in 1995 he published two books and one article. All three could be characterized as "popular": *The End: What Jesus Said about the Last Things*; *A Basic Christian Theology*; and an article in *Biblical Illustrator* titled "A Profile of Levi."[29] All three pieces were in process to some extent before his 1994 move and cancer diagnosis. In the two books, he acknowledges Charleston Southern University, his home prior to Truett.[30] His article on Levi, though published in the spring of 1995, describes him as "Chair of the Department of Religion, Charleston Southern University." This description indicates that he wrote the piece prior to transitioning to Baylor.[31] Thus the shift from 1996 and beyond can with some certainty be identified with his move to Waco and his being diagnosed with cancer in 1994, since the 1995 published works predate those events, at least in their genesis.

In November 1996, Conyers published "Protestant Principle, Catholic Substance." This essay marks the shift and in a way serves as a promissory note for the rest of his work. Beginning the article by referring to the dialogue over Mark Noll's "scandal of the evangelical mind," Conyers sets out to answer the question, "Is there something in Protestant thought itself that, doing the work of a computer virus, finally renders impotent even the best of the Protestant intellectual tradition?"[32] He gives an example: the belief in Scripture as a more or less unmediated guide raises objections to academic

---

28. Conyers and Conyers, "Biography of A. J. 'Chip' Conyers," xxxi.

29. Conyers, "A Profile of Levi," 20–22.

30. Conyers, *The End*, 9. See also Conyers, *Basic Christian Theology*, ix.

31. Conyers, "Profile of Levi," 22.

32. Conyers, "Protestant Principle, Catholic Substance," 15.

theology. These same objections can spur anti-elitism among evangelicals. At first blush, the focus on small things and distinctions can seem antithetical to the democratizing spirit of Protestant Christianity. However, Conyers notes that specialists serve others; just as automobiles made by engineers are made for others, theology done in the academy is for others as well.[33]

Pushing deeper on the issue of anti-intellectualism, Conyers ties it to the fact that "in the late middle ages, Western people began to lose confidence in universals."[34] The shift from realism to nominalism, from universals as real to a reality made up of unrelated particulars, led all fields of learning to imitate the natural sciences in the modern era. "Science in the modern sense moves from concrete facts to theoretical principles. The latter are subject to change, and the former exact from modern science the most ardent loyalty."[35] The Protestant movement bought into this imitation in a limited sense, beginning to treat the Bible as a sensible source of facts that could then be shaped into theories, forgetting that "the word of God refers to God—and that God cannot be taken as merely another fact in the universe of facts."[36] Actually, the root meaning of *fact* is a thing done or a deed; so, in scholastic thinking, "facts" were accidental, something participating in truth but subordinate to essential truths. In modern thinking this understanding is turned on its head, for facts are allowed priority and principles, values, and virtues become hardly real at all.[37] So, in trying to give Scripture its proper place, the Reformation also lost fifteen hundred years of Catholic intellectual tradition and the memory that theological thinking arises from pastoral concerns, not merely scholars' speculation.[38] Conyers insists that this loss was never the intention of the Reformers, but once "Scholasticism-gone-mad had been reined in, [Luther's words "faith slaughters reason"] would have a different ring."[39]

This understanding opens up two ways to view the Protestant Reformation. First, we could see the Protestant movement, along with the evangelical continuation of it, as "a rediscovery of a truth that was so valuable to the understanding of the Gospel and the nature of salvation and the

33. Ibid., 16.
34. Ibid.
35. Ibid.
36. Ibid.
37. Ibid.
38. Ibid.
39. Ibid.

Church that it must be defended at all costs against every competing idea." Or, second, "we can see the Reformation as a correction made in the nick of time, at great cost to those who remained with the Western Church and those who left. It was a necessary correction in the course of the Church of Christ. . . . Now considerable time has passed. And the time comes to correct the correction."[40] The idea that councils, creeds, great theologians, apologists, and philosophers could be abandoned was not the intention of the Reformers but a course taken by generations of followers. Conyers's call is clear:

> Perhaps now is the time, now that Protestants are noticing that something is seriously missing, to reach back and affirm a truly "catholic" tradition: one that did not deny philosophy but used it to the glory of God and for the sake of the Church. . . . Now is the time for evangelicals to declare themselves in a very intentional way for the recovery of the intellectual aims that are unapologetically catholic—not as a way of losing their distinctiveness, but as a way of recovering the task that made the separation necessary in the first place: the safeguarding of a truly catholic vision of the world and its redemption.[41]

This call to "correct the correction" and to return to a catholic tradition marks a shift in the focus of Conyers's project and in his audience, as noted above. From this point forward, his publications are tied to this "correct the correction" sentiment, and they are published in venues such as *First Things* and *Touchstone*, known for their evangelical-Catholic engagement. This sentiment also provides a new shape and vigor to his overall theological project. While earlier in his career his works on eschatology were focused on Moltmann (the dissertation) and expositions of Scripture (his two popular-level books), his final two books tie eschatological issues firmly to the quest to understand the shape of Western culture, and to provide a course correction rooted in this "catholic" tradition of which he speaks. Of the articles published from 1996 until his death, only a few are outside of his main theological project, and of those only one or two do not contribute to the shift to "reclaim the catholic tradition."

Two aspects of Conyers's move to Truett Seminary likely played the largest roles in this shift.[42] First, being at a seminary connected to a presti-

---

40. Ibid., 17.

41. Ibid.

42. Discerning the weight of each of these elements, as well as seeking others, merits

gious university such as Baylor afforded him more opportunity to publish and speak in different venues. Second, part of his task as a founding faculty member at Truett was to help craft the curriculum, and he gained a reputation for being passionate about orienting the curriculum around primary texts from the great catholic tradition of the church.[43] This period, marked by the 1996 *First Things* essay, marks a shift in his focus on these issues, and they would characterize his later work. His theological method would be guided by a deep sense of vocation.

VOCATIONAL THEOLOGY

In various works Conyers explains the essence of modernity and why it is problematic. In its essence, modernity is a change in orientation: "This change of orientation experienced in modern times is a profound one: moving the human being from the role of receptive discoverer, listener, and responder to the world, to that of shaper, fashioner, even creator of the world."[44] In fact, "the underlying impulse of modernity was to reject the 'givenness,' the irreducible limits and obligations of human life."[45] Modernity rejected the given nature of the world, preferring to see the human as the shaper of it. Thus, modernity is fundamentally man-centered.[46]

This identification of the essence of modernity influences Conyers's understanding and critique of postmodernity, which he refuses to classify as separate from modernity or free from its problems. Postmodern thinkers often point to individualism and rationality as the key features of modernity, and then critique those features in order to provide something different. Conyers, however, sees these as features that are present prior to modernity and that are simply changed by it: "The impulse of the Enlightenment

---

further treatment but exceeds the scope of my argument here. I am seeking to mark and describe the shift, not provide an exhaustive account of its causes or effects.

43. Robert Sloan, phone conversation with author, August 5, 2013. As founding dean of Truett, Sloan worked with Conyers and others in developing Truett's curriculum, and as president of Baylor University, Sloan also saw Conyers's vision and passion for primary texts challenged by later additions to the Truett faculty. Conyers's passion for the tradition remained even when it was not politically advantageous.

44. Conyers, "Can Postmodernism Be Used," 295.

45. Conyers, "Changing Face of Baptist Theology," 34.

46. Conyers demonstrated concern with the man-centered tendencies of modern movements from the earliest stages of his career. For instance, see his critique of Marxism and theologies that seek to incorporate it: Conyers, "God and Man," 914–16.

cannot be adequately circumscribed with words like 'individualism' and 'rationalism,' but must be seen as the ancient hope to be delivered from necessity and to be free in the sense of one who is autonomous (a law unto oneself) and thus self-created."[47] In his final article, Conyers provides a helpful summary of his understanding of modernity and its relation to postmodernity:

> The heart of my argument is this: it is a mistake to think that postmodernism, as we have come to know it in the writings of Foucault and Derrida, for instance, is in fact a critique of modernity. It is instead an attempt to save the sinking ship of modernity by throwing overboard some of its most inessential features while preserving its essence. Individualism and rationality are not, strictly speaking, features of modernity, but rather they are features of a Christian view of life that, through the filter of the Enlightenment, were made to conform to what is the heart of modernity and of postmodernism as well. The heart of modernity is not individualism per se, but the individual without God—the autonomous individual. And it is not rationalism per se, but a rationalism that is capable of making human beings autonomous. Postmodernity as we have come to know it is perfectly loyal to the project of modernity, while posing as its critic in order to escape what would result in authentic Postmodernity—the return to the idea of a God who creates, sustains, and intercedes in life and Who is therefore the true center and anchor of our existence.[48]

So, for Conyers, "these [postmodern] thinkers are most anxious to preserve that part of the Enlightenment disposition that is most antagonistic to Christianity. . . . For the heart of the matter is the question whether God is acknowledged as God, or whether we wish to be our own gods."[49] Postmodernism does not escape modernism but in fact appropriates its major impetus—human autonomy without God. True postmodernity would not further the underlying essence of modernity but react against it. The issue at this point is not so much whether Conyers's assessment of postmodernism is right or not (such an assessment would take us too far afield) but the fact that he sets up a theological distinction (based on his reading of postmodernity and modernity) that he then utilizes in his political theology as

47. Conyers, "Changing Face of Baptist Theology," 34.
48. Conyers, "Can Postmodernism Be Used," 303.
49. Conyers, "Changing Face of Baptist Theology," 34–35.

it frames the way he understands what it means to be human in the modern world (especially in connection with the idea of the will).

Conyers sets up a theological distinction that he sees as undergirding all of the problems of modernity and postmodernity. A shift occurred from what we will call a vocational theology—in which the world is seen as other, created by God rather than by humans, and in which God initiates and calls humans to obey—to a theology of choice—one in which the meaning of the world is largely created by human willing. Conyers's vocational theology views truth as given by Another, while a theology of choice views truth as made. While postmodernism (rightly) critiques modernity's version of individualism and supposedly neutral rationality, it fails to depart adequately from the modern project because it does not address the underlying theological distinction. This issue of theological method—focusing on God as the one who makes and calls—forms and informs not just theology but ethics as well. It alters our way of being in the world. It is with this overarching concern that Conyers attempts to understand and articulate the crisis of modernity, including the role of toleration in that crisis (toleration being his main avenue for describing it).

Conclusion

In this chapter I have made three main arguments, all extending the thesis of the last chapter. First, Conyers has a primary scholarly theological project, oriented around eschatology and history, that spans his entire theological career. His other published works unrelated to this primary project can be understood as church and ministry focused. This project shows the enduring influence of his early work on Moltmann and eschatology. Second, a distinct shift occurs in the period 1994–96, when Conyers's work sharpens in focus and changes in audience, striving toward a "truly catholic vision." Such language shows how Conyers himself saw his work as beginning to address issues of moral vision and, in our terminology, the social imaginary. Third, the concept of "vocational theology," articulated most clearly in a later article, sheds light on Conyers's conservative theopolitical work on navigating the modern (and postmodern) world. The idea of "vocation" connects the ideas of God's eschatological work and the good hierarchy and order that Conyers sees. This overview of his work further validates the significant influences on Conyers identified and analyzed in the previous chapter.

As demonstrated in the previous chapter, Conyers's unique blend of older forms of conservatism with a deep grappling with Moltmann's eschatology helped him build a foundation for his theological work. This foundation provided Conyers with a perspective that cannot be neatly categorized as "conservative" or "liberal" in today's narrow sense of these terms and thus provides a route away from the rhetoric that so often characterizes evangelical debates on theopolitical issues. Now that we have gained an understanding of Conyers's main influences and the overall trajectory of his work (including the sharpening of focus and broadening of audience in his later work), I turn to analyze his mature work, in which he diagnoses problems in the modern world and begins to plot a way to navigate through these problems. In this work, Conyers serves as a resource for addressing some of the other weaknesses we have found in evangelical theopolitical imagination.

CHAPTER 3

The Myth of "Toleration"

INTRODUCTION

While evangelical theopolitical imagination tends to take the modern institutions of the state and the free market for granted, Conyers exposes the dangers of both. He identifies the problems of modern culture by focusing on the idea of "toleration," how it changed in meaning and use, and how shifting notions of power influenced and benefited from that change. In this chapter I analyze Conyers's diagnosis of modernity by exploring his treatment of the changing notion of toleration and the disorders he identifies alongside this change. Using this process, beginning with Conyers's historical arguments and ending with an analysis of various disorders, I demonstrate that he sees the problems of modernity as rooted in a change in the conception of what it means to be human in the world.

Conyers's significance for theological readings of modernity is more than an explanation focused on some changes in toleration as a concept. Instead, I argue that Conyers's diagnosis of modernity, while most obviously dealing with the issue of toleration, is actually subordinate to a larger concern of articulating a difference between vocational theology and a theology of choice, which we explored in the previous chapter. Failure to see this concern weakens Conyers's arguments and obscures his contribution to questions of theology and modernity and theological method. By using the lenses of toleration and vocational theology, Conyers refuses to take modern institutions for granted or promote them but instead exposes how they form agents counter to Christian discipleship.

Defining the Crisis

Conyers digs deep into the development of the modern world, showing how various changes occurred. To do so, he turns to the idea of "toleration," providing a genealogy that accounts for the shift in orientation that he identifies. Conyers's treatment of toleration can be situated within three different types of studies. First are positive accounts of toleration. Historians have traced the development of toleration as a practice, roughly equivalent to religious freedom.[1] This first group lacks a critical view of toleration, seeing it primarily as an unquestioned good. Second are negative accounts. Theologians have addressed how the idea of tolerance has impacted cultural understandings of truth, leading to a loss of a robust sense of truth in favor of tolerating conflicting views.[2] This group focuses primarily on the cultural consequences for explicitly religious claims and less on how the state or capitalism might find toleration useful. The third view pushes deeper than both of these two, identifying the purpose tolerance serves. Conyers contributes to this perspective by charting out not only how the idea of toleration changed but what power interests the change served and how the change fits within Conyers's larger theological vision. While the first group generally fits under the label "liberal" and the second under "conservative," Conyers's presence in this third group shows another way he defies easy categorization. Having developed his theological vision in the previous chapters, I turn in what follows to understanding Conyers's diagnosis of modernity and the role that toleration played, as well as his particular contribution to understanding the way the idea of toleration has changed.

Conyers provides an overview of his assessment of the crisis of modern culture before articulating his understanding of the provenance of the modern idea of toleration. He does this in four steps. First, he provides a

1. For example, see Zagorin, *How the Idea of Religious Toleration Came to the West*. Also see Grell and Scribner, *Tolerance and Intolerance*. For a work focused on the early American context, see Beneke and Grenda, *First Prejudice*.

2. In 1999, the Eighth Edinburgh Christian Dogmatics Conference dealt with the issue of toleration, and various papers have been published in Morrison, *Tolerance and Truth*. For a recent, popular-level evangelical treatment of the issue, see Carson, *Intolerance of Tolerance*.

brief history of toleration in order to demonstrate that the idea of toleration as an explicit public virtue was born during seventeenth-century trials. Second, he identifies modern toleration as a strategy, not a virtue. Third, he expands on the concept of sovereignty and the question of whether strong central states were inevitable. Fourth, he argues that toleration substitutes for love in the quest for strong, centralized power.

The idea that toleration is a public virtue was born during various trials in the seventeenth century. Conyers highlights three. First, religious wars devastated communities on the continent, and while religious differences were not the only catalyst, they "were also the occasion for the protraction and exacerbation of conflicts."[3] Second, rising nation-states took in large territories and united peoples previously unrelated politically. These new arrangements were not simply the results of the religious wars. In addition, they created the demand and opportunity for concentration of power.[4] In place of the various associations that had previously made up complex human society, Europe saw a growth in larger and more comprehensive governments over the next several centuries. Third (and in line with traditional conservatives such as Richard Weaver), Conyers argues that new social arrangements led to the isolation of the individual. As the nation-states gained power, people viewed themselves less in terms of previously important institutions such as the family, the church, or some other social setting, and more in terms of autonomous free agents. Associations with others began to be considered more and more as accidental and volitional rather than necessary and obligatory. The result of these features set up two distinct features of the modern period: a powerful state and a lonely individual.[5]

Toleration emerged as a public virtue amidst these changes. Toleration, however, is not properly called a virtue but instead relies on other virtues.[6] It eases the tension created by the fact that people are different; it seeks harmony but is not itself harmony. Toleration is better understood as a strategy, and "in the case of a strategy, everything depends upon what

3. Conyers, *Long Truce*, 5. For Conyers's own primer on *Long Truce*, see Conyers, "Rescuing Tolerance."

4. "War was both the emergency that created the demand for and the opportunity to effect the large-scale concentration of power." Conyers, *Long Truce*, 5.

5. Ibid., 6.

6. "[Toleration] calls upon virtues, such as patience, humility, moderation, and prudence; but toleration itself relates to these qualities not as another quality of the same sort but as a policy intended to achieve some other end" (ibid., 7).

purpose that strategy serves."[7] In the context of the increasing power of nation-states, toleration served not simply to help people live in harmony but to neutralize differences (including religious differences) among vast populations in order to provide the central power with an expanding authority over the entire populace.[8] Thus toleration as a modern doctrine is not about helping minority groups survive persecution; rather, it is about centralizing power and destroying other systems of authority in order to do so.[9] Toleration as a strategy serves the increasing power of the nation-state, not in the sense that some group is intentionally using tolerance for this end but in the sense that sovereignty and toleration work together in a mysterious way.[10]

While some scholars view the evolution toward larger states as inevitable,[11] Conyers draws on political resources that provide a path not taken by modernity, inspired in part by the work of Althusius as explained earlier. Conyers likely draws the language of a "path not taken" from Donald Livingston. Livingston argues that the idea of secession, or the right of a smaller federation to withdraw from a larger one, was an important part of the Althusian political scheme. However, Hobbes's notion of consent emphasized the sovereign, central state and left no room for withdrawal for various reasons. Livingston notes a shift in American political imagination from an Althusian orientation to a more Hobbesian orientation after the Civil War. However, "There is no reason why Europe and the United States could not have followed the path marked by Althusius."[12] Conyers urges his readers to "nurture a suspicion" that the seemingly inescapable nature of centralized authority is in fact a modern superstition and that

---

7. Ibid., 8.

8. The state frames reality, insisting that religion is a private matter and that it will take no part in religious disputes, thus neutralizing religious commitments and upholding its power as being of paramount importance. See ibid., 9.

9. As Conyers says, "toleration as a modern doctrine . . . has little to do with the survival of minority groups and everything to do with the centralizing of power," and once we realize that groups have their own system of authority, we realize that "the central power makes peace with groups by detaching them from their spiritual essence and then testifying to its respect for the dispirited remains of what was once both the body and soul of a culture" (ibid., 10).

10. See Conyers's discussion of this in ibid., 10–12.

11. Conyers points specifically to *Sovereignty*, written by F. H. Hinsley, in which Hinsley argues that the evolution toward larger states was inevitable. See Conyers, *Long Truce*, 13.

12. . Livingston, "Very Idea of Secession," 48.

even if centralized powers are going to take care of certain things (such as defense), we do not need to conclude that these same powers must take care of things more naturally belonging to other elements of society. For this option he turns to the work of Althusius. While the state is one kind of community, other human associations exist. Politics is really about how humans live in community, and often the most important group is not the state. In Althusius's thought, "the proper beginning of political thought is the recognition that human beings live in natural communities that occur spontaneously and that nowhere do they live alone—or, if they do, they live in an unnatural state."[13] In the rise of the modern nation-state with its emphasis on a strong centralized power and an autonomous individual, "associations" like the ones drawn on by Althusius (family, collegium, city, province, and church) faded away in influence and power. For Conyers this was not inevitable but a decision to follow a certain path.

Though Conyers acknowledges that elements of Althusius's views are still present, a different view gained preeminence, one focused on all powers being lodged in a sovereign center. Toleration plays an important role on this path: "the issue is partly expressed in the unscientific maxim that groups arise from the power of love and the organization of the state arises from the love of power. However we might want to qualify this 'proverb,' we have the beginnings of a depiction of the modern crisis, which is, in a real sense, the struggle between the love of power and the power of love."[14] Once the search for the good is abandoned in favor of "toleration" and survival becomes the dominant concern, the temptation is to abandon any speculation and instead pursue only practical goals. In one sense, "toleration is the pragmatist's substitute for love."[15] Because the good is neither defined nor sought, toleration takes the place of love in pursuing the goals of power and profit.

Conyers defines the crisis simply: a strong centralized state and autonomous individuals have replaced complex human social arrangements. Toleration serves as a strategy for creating and maintaining this split. In order to establish his view of this moral crisis, Conyers pushes deeper into the historical evolution of the term *toleration* in order to develop the history of this crisis.

13. Conyers, *Long Truce*, 14.

14. Ibid., 12.

15. Ibid., 20.

HISTORY OF THE CRISIS

Conyers spends the bulk of *The Long Truce* advancing his thesis regarding change in the usage of the word *toleration*. However, in drawing this change out he gets into more than just the change in the use of this word. He also provides his views on the development of modernity along the lines of the rise of the nation-state and the rise of autonomous individualism. He deals with two matters that seem to be out of sync: on the one hand, toleration developed in the context of Christian society and the intellectual life of the church, but on the other hand, toleration as a public policy or public virtue did not appear until political life began to be marked by increasing secularity.[16] He deals with these matters in four steps: explaining the ancient practice of toleration, the role of hopes and fears in the change in toleration, the development of a "bipolar vision of society," and the use of tolerance to dissolve social bonds.

The Ancient Practice of Toleration

Conyers distinguishes between the *practice* of toleration as seen in the ancient world and the *doctrine* of toleration developed in modern times. He begins explaining the practice of toleration by turning to the roots of the tradition in the Bible. Developing what he calls a "peculiar paradox" found in Scripture,[17] he notes two key elements. As the product of Hebrew prophetism, the Bible advances the unshakable conviction of "ethical monotheism." In fact, "The trend in biblical traditions, even at its earliest stages, is contrary to tolerance. It is the opposite to openness toward the plurality of religions and the variety of moral communities in the ancient Mediterranean world."[18] However, a paradoxical trend is also present within Hebrew exclusivism (and later Christian exclusivism): "To reject the god of the

---

16. Ibid., 28. Conyers notes that the idea of toleration was rare until the seventeenth century: "In the English language the word 'tolerance' or 'toleration' was rarely used in reference to public policy or public philosophy—even in referring to religious attitudes—until well into the seventeenth century. By the turn of the eighteenth century it had become a prominent idea, a policy in several European states, the cry of religious dissidents, and the doctrine which most obviously marked off modern society from the earlier feudal society with its understanding of the compactness of religion, laws, community, fealty, and piety" (ibid., 26).

17. Ibid., 31.

18. Ibid., 29–30.

foreigner on monotheistic and exclusive grounds is to accept the foreigner himself as a fellow human being, tied in kinship by the fact of their both being created by the same God. In one and the same gesture, one rejects the foreign gods and embraces the foreigner."[19]

In Scripture, tolerance means being willing to hear other traditions and to learn from them, something encouraged by both the Old and New Testaments. This willingness is tied to the virtue of humility,[20] for it is essential in understanding creaturely reality.[21] Toleration in the Bible is rooted in seemingly exclusive monotheism, which believes that all people were created by the same God, and in both the created and fallen state of humanity. Christians both learn from and teach all others.[22]

Conyers next turns to church history to illustrate the ancient practice of toleration rooted in humility. His treatment of the practice of toleration in church history focuses on only three thinkers.[23] First, Justin Martyr serves as an example of a hospitable spirit to pagan philosophies.[24] Second, Clement of Alexandria "cured the church of its fear of pagan intellectual achievements."[25] His synthetic thought engaged the world of pagan philosophy while maintaining the priority of the Christian tradition. Third, Thomas Aquinas aided in rediscovering Aristotle and modeling a way of theology connected deeply to an exchange of various ideas. Thomas was influenced not only by Aristotle but by the tradition of Muslim philosophers as well, such as Averroes.[26] In Conyers's estimation, these examples point to

---

19. Ibid., 30–31. Conyers notes various examples of this paradox, including Jonah's being sent to Nineveh and Ruth the Moabite's place in the line of David and the Messiah.

20. The virtue of humility also plays an important role in Conyers's treatment of Moltmann's view of hierarchy in *God, Hope, and History*, as mentioned above.

21. ". . . even with our best efforts at understanding the things of God, we are prevented from reaching that sublime goal. We are prevented by our creatureliness and by our sinfulness. Therefore, it is a matter of grace that truth comes to us from many directions" (Conyers, *Long Truce*, 33).

22. Ibid.

23. Conyers's paucity of examples in this section may be explained by his attempt to describe the practice of toleration in the ancient world rather than provide exhaustive proof of the prevalence of the doctrine. Still, more than three examples, especially spanning the amount of time that he does, would serve to strengthen his argument about the practice of toleration in church history.

24. Conyers, *Long Truce*, 34–36.

25. Ibid., 36.

26. Ibid., 39.

a humble tradition of openness.[27] This tradition of openness and humility served to root the doctrine of toleration that emerged in modern times.

By "the doctrine of toleration," Conyers means a particular teaching regarding restraint and noninterference. When toleration first began to be used in its new form, "it became a kind of encapsulated speech about the values of a public weary of fighting over doctrinal differences."[28] The term implies that there is something to endure, something to treat with patience. It does not imply neutrality. However, Conyers turns to the Declaration of Principles on Tolerance (signed by member states of UNESCO in 1995) to highlight the main features of the modern doctrine as it now stands. The declaration states, "Tolerance is respect, acceptance and appreciation of the rich diversity of our world's cultures, our forms of expression and ways of being human. . . . Tolerance is not concession, condescension or indulgence. Tolerance is, above all, an active attitude prompted by recognition of the universal human rights and fundamental freedoms of others."[29] Conyers notes that the contemporary meaning of toleration as outlined here is the virtue of restraint or noninterference with the ways of others. And the reference has shifted; toleration is no longer about the classical idea of "the good" but is instead focused on "human rights" or the freedom of individuals.[30] It is meant to be a prescription for community, for noninterference among groups. At its most extreme it is a form of hard individualism. But this shift in referent entirely empties the concept of content; toleration has become merely formal. And because of its focus on individualism, it serves as the community's antibody:[31] "it is a solvent that resists the glue of com-

27. "There was, long before the Enlightenment, a tradition of openness—born of the humility that was counseled by Clement and others in antiquity—that helped to shape the direction of Christian thought and of Western culture. . . . It was a definite practice; and it was a practice and attitude that left the lines of communication open among believing and thinking communities" (ibid.).

28. Conyers, *Long Truce*, 40.

29. Quoted in ibid., 42.

30. Ibid.

31. Cf. Taylor, *Modern Social Imaginaries*. Taylor argues that modern individualism does not mean ceasing to belong—what he calls "the individualism of anomie and breakdown"—but "imagining oneself as belonging to ever wider and more impersonal entities: the state, the movement, the community of humankind" (160). Modernity has meant a shift in social imaginary so that intermediate units of belonging are relegated to the margins. But does such an explanation require an equivocation of the term *belong*? If a person now imagines herself as "belonging" to the state, is that not at the same time ceasing to "belong" in the sense that she would have belonged to more immediate

mon conviction that holds people together," because it evacuates the content of common goals and common values in favor of the formal values of tolerance.[32] A paradox emerges in that it is promoted as a doctrine suitable for living life in community when in fact it weakens communities.[33] Conyers identifies the issue as what sort of community this new virtue serves. The short answer: the rise of toleration fits with the emergence of large nation-states.[34] Conyers further expands on this brief answer.

Hopes, Not Fears: Toleration, Economics, and War

Some scholars define the modern world as a quest for certainty. Certainty is part of the picture, but Conyers sees more nuance in the intellectual climate of the time. For instance, Stephen Toulmin argues that philosophy turned into a modern dead end as a result of the quest for certainty beginning, as the story goes, with Descartes's desire for a secure basis for rational thought.[35] Thus, Conyers concludes, "For Toulmin, the motive for this sudden rigidity in modern thought was that dreadful fear that had come upon Europe in unstable times."[36] Conyers marshals two arguments against this interpretation. First, Toulmin's understanding of modernity as caught up in rigid intolerance with only periodic occasions of relief contradicts most of the evidence. The arguments for religious toleration in the writings of Pierre Bayle, John Locke, and John Stuart Mill, along with the ambiguity and mystery present in the romantic movement of the nineteenth century, defeat this picture of modern rigidity. These examples of toleration emerge from within modernity itself, which Toulmin fails to recognize.[37] Second and more significantly, Conyers argues that modernity is not character-

---

communities? Taylor may claim that she has not ceased to belong, but the features of that belonging change to a large degree, as Conyers's analysis will show.

32. Conyers, *Long Truce*, 43.

33. Ibid., 44.

34. In nation-states, "there is consequently a need for bureaucracy that can deal directly with individuals and not be hindered by the competing loyalties and authorities that create groups within the population" (ibid.).

35. This view hearkens back to the work of John Dewey in *The Quest for Certainty*, in which he argues that society needed the courage and confidence provided by security, but we no longer do.

36. Conyers, *Long Truce*, 48. Toulmin himself was attempting to overcome what he understood as a deficient narrative about modernity. See Toulmin, *Cosmopolis*.

37. Conyers, *Long Truce*, 48–49.

ized primarily by fear and a quest for certainty but by an opportunistic desire for power.[38] Thus opportunism better explains the changes related to toleration.

However, Conyers continues to return to the concept of fear, especially in that it frames his treatment of Hobbes. While he describes the age as one of opportunism rather than fear, the presence of the concept of fear in thinkers such as Hobbes requires him to retain fear in his treatment and description. His argument seems to be that while fear certainly had a place, especially in the description of thinkers such as Hobbes, it was the economic opportunism of the time that drove society toward tolerance. New opportunities created the fear: Hobbes and his contemporaries feared losing what the opportunities presented. So even though fear was present, tolerance became prominent because of opportunism.

Thus, Conyers focuses on the opportunities of the modern period rather than its dangers in order to explain the changes. The collapse of ecclesial power was related to the rise in political power unhindered by church restraints. War resulted from a combination of fragmenting religious loyalties, withering ecclesial restraints, and sudden possibilities for the increase of power for secular authorities. New power had to replace or at least displace traditional forms of social authority. Both sovereignty and tolerance served this purpose. Sovereignty had a twofold relationship with the religious wars, for it was both the means of—and the grounds for—expanding power.[39] Tolerance served as the necessary concomitant feature of this expansion of secular sovereignty, clearing the ground for the broader, more formal power of the nation-state.

Furthermore, toleration stands in a parallel relationship with two other forces that reduce the capacity of a culture to exert traditional authority: economics and war. These three forces neutralize traditional social relationships.[40] We can see this neutralization very simply in economics.

38. "What we find in the seventeenth century is not a rigidity based on fear (at least not as a primary motive) but a new opportunistic spirit motivated by the desire for power. What occurred in that period were surely the terrors of war, just as Dewey and Toulmin had seen. But more than that, there was a new sense of opportunity—unparalleled in any time since the rise of the Roman Empire—for the growth of economic and political influence" (ibid., 49).

39. As Conyers phrases it, "it was both the means by which a sovereign authority expanded its power, and it constituted the emergency that justified such power" (ibid., 50).

40. They "tend to neutralize traditional social arrangements, thus creating a society that no longer operates on the basis of interpersonal relationships, but on the basis of abstraction—that is, on the basis of rationalized categories" (ibid., 52).

Conyers's perspective here is in line with that of the Southern Agrarians, though applied to an earlier time period. For Conyers, "The 'modern' in modern economics is the tendency to free commercial operations from personal relationships."[41] Interests in business enterprises became abstract, represented by money, the universal commodity.

Economics changed in two general ways from the fourteenth century to the end of the seventeenth. First, there was a loss of rootedness or concreteness of the economic system due to the increased use of money.[42] While money had been used in earlier societies, in the modern period it became a way in which vast numbers of people could become literally "invested" in an abstract way.

Second, commerce became increasingly abstract. There was more and more distance in transactions. Though there have long been people dealing in money as investors and lenders, the seventeenth century saw a pair of developments in this regard: vastly increased numbers of people connected to an actual enterprise (whether fishing, building, or domestic commerce) as investors, and the ease with which one person's or company's resources could be employed in vastly unrelated enterprises. Rather than invested as workers, more people were abstractly involved and interested only in money.[43] The radical fluctuations in this new economy, with downturns in 1620, 1640, and 1664, brought great gains and great losses that contributed to a feeling of instability and vertigo.[44] New opportunities drove this abstractness related to the economy, which contributed to growing hopes that in turn gave birth to new fears—fears of losing recently acquired wealth. Conyers's willingness to critique free-market economics demonstrates his affinity with the agrarians and is evidence of another way that he calls into question modern institutions. Also, while his analysis of toleration and the rise of the state might become less important as globalization replaces

41. Ibid., 53.

42. Because of "the introduction of a fluid commodity such as money, that can at once represent grain, beef, gold, oil, the labor of farmers, the skill of craftsmen, the risk of investors, and the wages of workers, we find that the appearance of a localized and concrete *basis* for the economy begins to be lost" (ibid., 54).

43. "People were no longer so inextricably identified with a trade. . . . Their sole interest came to be one thing and one thing only. Their status in society had not to do with a role so much as with the idea of possession. And that possession was expressed abstractly. . . . It was expressed in the precise arithmetic of a monetary sum" (ibid., 55).

44. Ibid., 56.

nationalism as a theopolitical force, his analysis of economics will continue to provide insight.

Related to these new hopes and fears, war also played a role in dismantling natural social arrangements. (While Conyers acknowledges that the wars of religion were more complicated than the name suggests, he maintains that the wars were intense manifestations of religious differences. But at this point in his argument, he is less concerned with the genesis of these wars as with the form that increased militarization lent to society.) Citing William H. McNeill's *The Pursuit of Power: Technology, Armed Force, and Society since A.D. 1000*, Conyers draws on the concept of the "bureaucratization of military administration."[45] There were far-reaching consequences of the development of well-ordered militaries. The military drill, for example, is analogous to what happened to the entire society.[46] As Conyers sees it, the practice of daily drill and rigorous discipline with close attention to details of dress and manner created "a military culture of an entirely modern cast."[47] Under such training, "the huge assembly of compatriots loses those older natural distinctions, and the members of the newly created machine of war are distinguished only by the artifice of military rank and military unit. An army, under the pressure of war . . . becomes a microcosm of society, turning (much more gradually) from its sacred identity—from its blood, its soil, its temples, and its gods—to the secular exigencies of utilitarian purposes."[48] This training results in great

45. Conyers, *Long Truce*, 59. One of McNeill's main insights that Conyers draws on is as follows: "European rulers' remarkable success in bureaucratizing organized violence and encapsulating it within civil society continued to dominate European statecraft throughout the eighteenth and well into the nineteenth century. The victories Europeans regularly achieved in conflicts with other peoples of the earth during this period attested to the unusually efficient character of European military arrangements; and such successes, in turn, facilitated the steady growth of overseas trade which helped to make the costs of maintaining standing armies and navies easier for Europeans to bear. Hence European rulers, especially those located towards the frontiers of European society, were in the happy and unusual position of not having to choose between guns and butter but could instead help themselves to more of both, while their subjects—at least some of them—were also able to enrich themselves." McNeill, *Pursuit of Power*, 144.

46. This is similar to the argument of Michel Foucault in *Discipline and Punish*. See Foucault, *Discipline and Punish*, 167. I do not mean to convey that Conyers draws on Foucault; instead, I merely point out the similarity in this particular analysis. Conyers sees Foucault as exemplifying the trend of an emphasis on human will and power. See Conyers, *Long Truce*, 180.

47. Conyers, *Long Truce*, 60.

48. Ibid.

efficiency in achieving material goals, though simultaneously losing moral and spiritual character. The new military efficiency made possible scalable political economies.

Conyers could push this insight further to trace how the military/war aspects serve to form and disciple people. He stops short of dealing with specific issues of nationalism in addition to war itself. However, especially in the modern West, the military is not the only group habituated into military loyalties and practices. Conyers's treatment would be stronger if he extended his insights beyond the military into the military-entertainment complex.

These forces neutralized the natural social groups favored by thinkers such as Althusius. While natural society is made up of a variety of overlapping groups functioning to pass on obligations, intervene in disputes, enforce rules, and provide culture, a society developing toward a strong central power finds itself in competition with these smaller local authorities. Because nation-states asserted their authority from distant population centers such as Paris or London, they needed to circumvent—either partially or completely—the authority of natural social groups in order to function efficiently.[49] Conyers turns to Hobbes to demonstrate the modern necessity of removing any authority between the sovereign and the individual: "Hobbes's nominalist basis allows him no authority except that of the individual, and through the individual, the state. Other authorities are illusory or seditious. . . . All power and right resides in the individual."[50] This change reduced theology and the concerns of the church to private rather than public matters. However, in the eyes of Conyers this reduction raises an important question: "How can [society maintain itself on this residue of a culture's fundamental commitments] and pretend that the issues once fought out at the theological level no longer matter? How long can it pretend that the character and virtue of a people, that which makes social life commodious and predictable, can simply be taken for granted?"[51] The answer to this question inevitably calls on toleration, either the old form of tolerant practice or the modern form of the doctrine of toleration, which sets aside questions of vocation and purpose.[52] Now that he has set up the

49. Ibid., 61.

50. Ibid., 62–63.

51. Ibid., 64–65.

52. The issue could be explained as a contest of formation: toleration serves to form people for the state project, while the concept of vocation rooted in Christian theology

context for the development of the doctrine of toleration, Conyers moves to treat four thinkers who show this development in their thought: Thomas Hobbes, Pierre Bayle, John Locke, and John Stuart Mill.

Obtaining a Bipolar Vision of Society

Conyers turns to Hobbes and Bayle to establish and critique what he calls the "bipolar vision of society." At its most basic level, this idea refers to modernity's increasing tendency to view all of life as operating between two ends of a spectrum: the strong, central authority on the one hand, and the autonomous individual on the other. Hobbes's thought contributed primarily to the increased tendency to focus on the centralized power, while Bayle's work strengthened the concept of the autonomous individual.

This bipolarity between the state and the individual can be developed further, especially with relation to individual difference and the power of corporations. For example, Sheldon Wolin develops centrifugalism (which fears democracy because it homogenizes, suppressing significant differences, and thus seeks identity more in those differences, e.g., race, class, gender, ethnicity, sexual orientation) and centripetalism (contemptuous of democracy for its weakness yet envious of its appeal; large corporations are an example).[53] Both presuppose that society has had a prior experience of democratization and both exploit that experience. Centrifugal forces rely on the government to protect them, while centripetal forces seek expansion and dominance. Multinational corporations are in a powerful position. The

---

provides another sort of formation. This relates to the social imaginary, or in similar terminology, the interpretive framework. Michael Budde puts the issue well: "Christian formation, when it's done well, is always a lifelong effort to push against interpretive frameworks not rooted in the word become flesh, in the Christ that brings the kingdom of God among us and that calls us to live in the world as if that kingdom has already begun. Putting on the armor of God is as much perceptual as intellectual, as much a matter of changing the operating system of our hearts and minds as it is a matter of accepting new propositions about creation, history and destiny. It means that the process of making disciples is about taking down the scaffolding of some interpretive frames and replacing them with those of the church and the followers of Jesus—dismantling the complexes that make nationalism seem normal, subverting the conventional wisdom that might makes right, and giving people new eyes with which to see and new ears with which to hear all that's been going on around them all the while, but to which they've been oblivious so long as they lacked the right equipment with which to catch, retrieve and act upon this God-soaked reality." Budde, *Borders of Baptism*, 123.

53. Wolin, *Politics and Vision*.

state and the corporation have become partners, and each has begun to mimic functions historically identified with the other. "Corporations are extensively engaged in administering penal institutions and operating health-care systems, and they have assumed important roles at every level of public and private education."[54] The citizen gets blended in this way too, with political behavior becoming assimilated to economic behavior. And corporate money influences elections to such a degree that state actors have become more dependent upon corporate power than on their own citizens. Because of this power of corporations, it could be argued that the bipolar condition of modernity has begun to give way to a bipolarity not of individual-state but individual-multinational corporation. This change is ironic, because just as the nation-state once served to dissolve other associations in favor of its sovereignty (Conyers's bipolar disorder), the nation-state now begins to fall victim to being an "intermediate association" in a greater narrative: globalization.

Hobbes's philosophy was tied to the events of his age. Conyers notes two important influences on Hobbes's life. First, Hobbes served as a tutor and companion to William Cavendish, with whom he traveled extensively. This travel exposed Hobbes to subjects such as Euclidean geometry, which impressed him with its logically and inescapably arranged method. Hobbes hoped other sciences could achieve the same level of certainty.[55] Second, Hobbes's thinking was shaped by viewing reality as a state of motion rather than a state of rest, no doubt partly influenced by his meeting Galileo in Italy: "The world for Hobbes and his successors was a world of no given order, but a world infinitely malleable."[56] The world awaited an order created by human imagination and will. This notion influenced the way that Hobbes conceived of the political.

While Conyers does not work systematically through Hobbes's corpus, he provides his understanding of Hobbes's project as a whole. Hobbes thought it impossible to conceive of philosophy in terms of traditional metaphysics with its appeal to the notion of a moral aim; instead, a new philosophy must replace this moral element with natural science. For Conyers, "This is not only a description of Hobbes's work and his intentions, but it is

---

54. Ibid., 588.
55. Conyers, *Long Truce*, 67–68.
56. Ibid., 68.

the root of the problem which incessantly presents itself in Hobbes."[57] The moral element had to be replaced by human intention.

Conyers identifies two primary intellectual influences on Hobbes. First, Puritanism's analysis of human ills parallels Hobbes's theory of the individual in the social setting. Puritan thought tended toward Gnosticism because of its emphasis on the brokenness of the created order. Puritanism, in this reading, was "a kind of gnostic style of theologizing that finds no good in the created order, in the human nature, or in the institutions arising in such a world. For the gnostic—and, one could almost say, for the Puritan—Christianity is altogether a theology of redemption without the inclusion of a theology of creation."[58] This is admittedly a controversial reading of Puritanism, and one in which Conyers refers to no secondary literature on the topic. Instead, he seeks to draw parallels between what Hobbes thought and how that thought might relate to the Puritanism that was present at Magdalen Hall, Oxford, while Hobbes was there.

This understanding of Puritan thinking fits Hobbes's emphasis on humans in nature as engaged in constant warfare due to a focus solely on one's own interests. Just as the extreme position of some Calvinists led them to believe the worth of the human being relies entirely on God's redemptive purpose, Hobbes saw the salvation of man as entirely dependent upon a different higher power: the state. Conyers identified nominalism as the second intellectual influence. He understands nominalism filtered through the work of Richard Weaver primarily.[59] Hobbes's nominalist stance led again to a focus on voluntarism, moving engagement with the world from the domain of intellect to the domain of the will.[60]

In order to summarize Hobbes's thought, Conyers finds six principles in Hobbes's writing that have nearly an axiomatic status in placing the individual in society and that demonstrate the importance of the two intellectual influences identified. The principles are as follows: (1) "Philosophy

57. Ibid., 70.

58. Ibid., 72.

59. In fact, "it was Hobbes perhaps more than any other who brought nominalistic thought to the surface in modern discourse" because of the dominance of this perspective in *Leviathan* and *Elements of Law* (ibid., 74–75). Conyers provides several quotes from *Leviathan* and *Elements of Law* to illustrate this point.

60. Conyers mentions Richard Weaver in this connection, which is further evidence that Weaver is Conyers's primary source for the nominalist critique and analysis (ibid., 75). In fact, Weaver's *Ideas Have Consequences* is the only source Conyers uses to discuss the decline of logical realism in Conyers, "Three Sources," 313–21.

is the science of reducing things to their causes and determining the consequences of causes."[61] This means that everything boils down to the efficient cause and the material cause, with the formal and final causes not being true causes. Hobbes sets aside the language of the two causes that have most to do with religion and morality. (2) "The individual's motives are governed by fear and (consequently) by the desire for power."[62] Individuals fear others and seek power to achieve their own desires. (3) "The civil order is an artifice; it is not a reflection, as it was for the ancients and medievals, of the metaphysical order of existence."[63] Human progress and technological mastery of nature theoretically know no bounds. Humans work to impose their wills on nature. (4) "Hence, the moral order is an artifice."[64] Only positive law forms the foundation for any moral system. (5) "The commonwealth must be large enough to secure safety or to pursue common advantage among the nations."[65] Justice no longer frames the political order; instead, the *libido dominandi* of the emerging modern state does. (6) "The authority of the sovereign within the social order must be absolute."[66] Hobbes does not deny that government is about coercion.[67] No matter what form authority takes in the modern state (monarchy or democracy), "the authority itself is single; everything is governed from a central point of concentrated power."[68] These principles bring Hobbes to the conclusion that the natural world calls for mastery at the hands of the human will. Knowledge of the world is not for love (as it was for Augustine) but for mastery and possession.[69] For Hobbes, the fears of modern individuals call for the concentration of power in a central authority in order to assuage fears, a central authority created by human will. This is the first pole of Conyers's spectrum creating a bipolar vision of society.

61. Conyers, *Long Truce*, 75.

62. Ibid., 79.

63. Ibid., 80.

64. Ibid., 82.

65. Ibid., 83.

66. Ibid., 84.

67. Here Conyers turns to the example of Althusius again as a positive influence. One of the lacunae in Conyers's treatment of modernity is the lack of positive development of Althusius, toward whom he repeatedly gestures without much explanation, besides what was treated above.

68. Conyers, *Long Truce*, 86.

69. Ibid., 87.

Pierre Bayle's work sets up the other side of the spectrum, developing the concept of the autonomous individual. While it is fairly well known that Bayle played a vital role in changing convictions on the sovereign rights of the individual in matters of conscience, Conyers develops a certain irony in what Bayle championed: "Although the idea of the development of liberal democratic institutions is that they protect the individual from the overweening designs of the state, in fact, Bayle's case against persecution and in favor of protecting the 'erring conscience' was not so much cast against the state as against the traditional social powers of the church and local communities."[70] In short, though Bayle sought to protect the individual from the institutions that were more powerful at the time (like the church), his theory ultimately led to an autonomous individual that had nothing to protect it from the more powerful state, whose power was no longer balanced by the mediating groups.

In Bayle's life, the principle issue was "the friction between the majority Catholic population in France and the minority (Huguenot) population."[71] Bayle came to the conviction that from a human point of view indecisiveness is appropriate: the human conscience is an "erring conscience," requiring toleration as a policy. As Bayle challenged force as a means of conversion, he provided a unique angle by arguing that the conscience has a stronger claim on the soul than group obligations do.[72] Bayle did not occupy a moderate position between warring parties such as Jesuits and Calvinists; instead, he provided a different center, the "individual."[73] An erring conscience had rights in Bayle's eyes, and the idea of the private conscience is important. He moved from this position of rights for an erring conscience to the point that anything done against the lights of conscience is evil. He not only protected the conscience from abuse but enthroned it as "supreme arbiter."[74]

70. Ibid., 89.

71. Ibid., 90.

72. Ibid., 96.

73. As Conyers explains, "he located a new center of gravity for civil and religious responsibility, one that would prove to be the hallmark of modernity. This new center of gravity is no longer any particular public or private authority. It is, instead, the newly emerging notion of the individual—one might say, without exaggeration, the autonomous, the self-ruling, individual" (ibid., 98).

74. "Bayle opened doors that neither Locke nor Hobbes had entered; he opened the way to making the private conscience the supreme arbiter of matters of conscience" (ibid., 107).

Conyers identifies a paradox in Bayle's work on toleration. While Bayle makes strong arguments for toleration in the face of religious persecution, he does not regard the state as a threat.[75] He notes that Bayle's work on Hobbes is remarkably positive; Bayle is clearly more concerned with the church than the state in issues of toleration. But this strong leaning toward political absolutism is striking in the midst of writing on toleration. Bayle's concerns are with nongovernmental authorities, such as the church: "When Bayle spoke of oppression, he had in mind the kinds of oppression from which the individual might be liberated *by the state*. And what if the remedy proved more oppressive than the cure? Such a question apparently did not occur to Bayle in quite that form."[76] In fact, Bayle reminds us that individuals might feel less threatened by a strong centralized power than local ones like neighbors, guilds, and the church. He sacrifices religious authority to the authority of the state for the sake of rescuing the freedom of the individual.

For Conyers, the problem with this change is not only that the nation-state becomes too powerful and thus destroys mediating groups such as the family. It is also that the nation-state differs from natural groups in key ways. The spontaneous loyalties and organization of natural groups resist the heavy level of organization proposed by the state. The two compete: "The organized, rationalized state finds the spontaneous loyalties within families and religions inconvenient to organization."[77] The individual gravitates to bonds of affection, common experience, and common interests, and "the group, or groups, communicate to the person a sense of place and purpose, a complex of ideas through which to view the world, so that one might properly identify both the self and others."[78] However, since the state's need for organization finds such bonds inconvenient, toleration weakens the bonds by implying that the natural groups impose discipline in a restrictive or manipulative way, thereby impeding the individual's

---

75. "Yet what we find in Bayle is not an argument against the powerful exercise of the same sovereignty that had crushed the Huguenot community, sent him and his coreligionists into exile, burned his books, and brought about the imprisonment and death of his brother. Instead, we find that he defends the idea of political sovereignty, even of royal absolutism" (ibid., 115).

76. Conyers, *Long Truce*, 117.

77. Ibid., 119.

78. Ibid., 120. This point again shows Conyers's debt to an older form of conservatism.

freedom and sending the individual into the seemingly protective arms of the sovereign state.[79]

In her published Gifford Lectures, the late political ethicist Jean Bethke Elshtain deals with sovereignty and tells its story through its connection to God, the state, and the self. While she ends up with a similar picture as Conyers does, she takes a slightly different route. For Conyers's bipolar vision, strong state sovereignty and a robust individualism arise together. However, Elsthtain's tale includes an extra step. She argues that changing notions of God's sovereignty led to absolutist state sovereignty. Then, as a second step, individual self-sovereignty emerged from absolutist state sovereignty, not along with it: "As sovereign state is to sovereign God, so sovereign selves are to sovereign states."[80] Elshtain constructs her argument by first turning to the likes of Hobbes and Locke to understand the state, and then turning to Descartes, Kant, and others for the development of the self. What Conyers uncovers is that in the development of a strong centralized power, the autonomous individual was necessary as well. Because a bipolarity was necessary for the state's sovereignty to work and for autonomous individualism to be protected, they arose together, not in separate steps as Elshtain argues.[81]

Together, Hobbes and Bayle demonstrate the creation of a bipolar vision of society. Hobbes exalts the necessity of a strong central power in order to protect humans from one another. Bayle, on the other hand, promotes toleration while at the same time advancing a political absolutism in line with Hobbes. Bayle's work stems from a concern to protect individuals from oppression at the hands of institutions like the church in matters of conscience. For Conyers, these thinkers set up the two poles: a strong central state and an autonomous individual. The natural institutions that once provided connection between people and provided for social norms and other social goods slowly fade from view because of their competition with the nation-state. Conyers's history of this crisis includes one more step, in which he turns to John Locke and John Stuart Mill to demonstrate the full extent to which tolerance dissolves social bonds.

---

79. While pushing this point, Conyers recognizes that such developments were unintended on the part of thinkers such as Bayle.

80. Elshtain, *Sovereignty*, 159.

81. Though they differ on the precise mechanism of these changing notions of sovereignty, I think Conyers would agree with some of the ethical implications Elshtain draws from self-sovereignty, including a changing understanding of personhood.

Tolerance, Dissolver of Mediating Social Bonds

The author of the famous *Letter Concerning Toleration*, John Locke is the philosopher most prominently associated with the doctrine of toleration. While some view Locke as a promoter of toleration when the idea was unpopular, Conyers's description of toleration in Hobbes and Bayle allows him to argue that "we find Locke not the lone champion of an unpopular idea but the respected spokesman for an idea whose time had come, and which by now was being well received in many communities and in some of the most powerful circles in seventeenth-century England."[82] Locke has an important place in advancing this trend of linking state sovereignty and individual rights.

Conyers relies on an alternate interpretation of Locke that challenges Locke's liberalism. Locke's earlier writings serve as an embarrassment to those who view him as a liberal thinker, and neglecting these earlier writings (or explaining them away in light of his later "mature" thought) has strengthened the typical view of Locke.[83] In order to understand the differences between Locke's early (more absolutist) writings and his later (more liberal) writings, Conyers turns to an article by political scholar Robert Kraynak titled "John Locke: From Absolutism to Toleration."[84] Kraynak demonstrates differences between Locke's earlier and later writings,[85] but he argues that a deeper principle unites the two. The background of the Reformation and religious wars situated the problem for Locke. In his mind, "Orthodoxy was employed by the state to bring order, but now orthodoxy was an uncertain touchstone. Locke found that this new circumstance called for rethinking the role of the state in regard to religion."[86] Since one cannot be certain with regard to matters of religion, two options present themselves: "secular absolutism," in which the state establishes one religion without making the claim it is the only true one, or "liberal toleration," in which "religion is no less subordinated to the state: it is relegated to the sphere of the private life and prevented from having meaningful influence."[87] Thus,

---

82. Conyers, *Long Truce*, 122.

83. Ibid., 123–25.

84. Kraynak, "John Locke," 53–69.

85. For instance, many of the early writings (such as *Two Tracts on Government* [1660 and 1662] and *An Essay on Toleration* [1667]) were written to uphold the magistrate's authority over matters of religion.

86. Conyers, *Long Truce*, 127.

87. Ibid.

Locke's writings do not change in purpose or principle, but in strategy. He remains within the general principle of subordinating religion to the state.[88]

Pushing beyond Kraynak's analysis of Locke, Conyers argues that the problem with Locke is not merely some hidden agenda but a mistaken vision of society. Locke describes a nonexistent world, a fatally simplified one formed only around the state and the individual.[89] Conyers observes a narrowing in Locke's view of a federation. While thinkers such as Althusius include families, professional associations, and churches in their theories on federations, for Locke "'federation' occurs only in the contract made among individuals and between the individual and the state, or between sovereign governments."[90] The organized state is Locke's only political body; he fails to see that the role of citizen is not the deepest and most significant relationship in a person's life.[91] His distorted view of reality leads to a reductionist understanding of political association.

Locke's vision of society relies upon a theological point about revelation and reason. Modern "reason" differs in important ways from premodern "reason." Both agree that something is furnished to the mind, to which reason responds. However, premodern reason had a threefold given: revelation, sense experience, and tradition. Experience gives voice to the present, tradition connects to the past, and revelation gives the meaning of things, or the eschatological aim of things. Modern reason, however, has one of two givens: the rationalists began with the distinction between the self and the world, and the empiricists focused on all knowledge entering through the senses. Conyers notes that these not only differ in that modern reason focuses only on experience, but that the type of experience differs as well:

88. Kraynak goes so far as to say "absolutism and toleration are the same in principle despite their great difference in practice." Kraynak, "John Locke," 53.

89. Locke "attempts to describe a world that does not exist, a world that forms itself around two contrary poles, that of the state and that of the individual. It is a bipolar vision of society, fatally simplified because it neglects the social reality that lies about us on every hand: a world of multilayered associations, most of which are not organized and formal" (Conyers, *Long Truce*, 138).

90. Ibid., 140.

91. "One is more likely, for instance, to change citizenship from one country to another than to be dissociated from one's family or one's faith. For the emerging liberal idea of citizenship, however, even the family seems to have no other reason for being except to produce and raise to maturity individuals who then become (by their freely assenting will) citizens of the state" (ibid., 141).

> Earlier philosophies, to one extent or another, depend upon experiences that are *not* available to everyone, which are in fact available to very few. . . . Revelation is nothing other than the idea that truths important enough to determine the ordering of the soul and the culture become known to us through the rare experiences of a very few members of society over a long period of time. It is a tradition, or a custom, of the most refined and rare type. But the implication is clear: because of these few and these rare, the rest of us come closer to understanding the purpose, the nature, and the shape of life.[92]

The premodern envisioned the community benefitting from the experience of the few. The modern, however, envisions everyone in the community having at least the access to the raw stuff by which the community understands itself. Everyone is the same, and all interpretations of the raw material of experience hold equal weight. Locke's toleration gives birth to an undifferentiated, unarticulated society, a mass society. In fact, "Toleration in its modern form is the solvent that dissolves the bonds of interdependency. It therefore makes society fit for the 'new' ordering and regulating powers of the state."[93] Toleration dissolves social bonds, a dissolution creating thoroughly individualized and isolated modern people. While such isolation was not the goal of Locke's emphasis on toleration, our distance has given us the perspective to see such long-term consequences of this type of society.

In the last step of his historical genealogy of toleration, Conyers explores one more shift: the evolution of toleration from Locke into the twentieth century. To do so, he analyzes the use of *toleration* in Locke and then in John Stuart Mill. Mill demonstrates how the term shifts even more. For Conyers, this shift is rooted in the rise and fall of two contrasting beliefs about the human condition: on the one hand, the classical idea of decorum and the Christian idea of grace served to imply limits to human powers, limits that should be observed in order to pursue the good. On the other hand is the contrary sentiment that neither nature nor the supernatural pose any barriers to the human spirit.[94] The former has room for (and calls for) encounters with the divine; the latter divests previous restraints and

92. Ibid., 143.

93. Ibid., 145.

94. Conyers warns against viewing the former as pessimistic and the latter as optimistic. The idea of limits was not to prevent humans from achieving something but as the proper way toward human excellence. See ibid., 150.

seeks limitless progress and power: "[Toleration] as it is used in the era of Locke is found in Mill's time almost freed of its earlier inhibitions and, like Icarus, winging its way to the sun."[95] Conyers illustrates this shift by comparing the toleration of Locke to the toleration of Mill.

While Locke paved the way for thinking in distinctively modern ways, he did not fully forget the earlier sentiment regarding the importance of religious expression.[96] Conyers identifies three arguments in Locke's famous *Letter Concerning Toleration* (1689): the care of souls is not committed to the civil magistrate; the magistrate is ineffective in effecting the inward persuasion of the mind; and salvation would come by an accident of birth if governments imposed religion.[97] Conyers highlights the following principal features of Lockean toleration:

> First, toleration stands as a restraint against the misguided use of force. It admits the ludicrousness of a forced religious faith. . . . Second, it is thereby a defense against persecution—a matter that is decisive in distinguishing Locke's variety of toleration. Third, toleration serves the interest of truth, a truth only apprehended by reason, assisted by revelation, and attained by faith. Fourth, toleration is made necessary by the frailty and inadequacy of human reason, clouded and rendered unreliable by sin. Fifth, toleration is an expression of humility.[98]

Tolerance arises because of the imperfection of human reason and the incompetence of the state to choose for each individual. It does not arise from optimism regarding human society and institutions; rather, it acts fundamentally as a restraint on power, hubris, and the state's imagined moral competence. After Locke, "a very different idea of toleration was projected upon this view." This projection resulted in "the operative language of toleration embrac[ing] a concept that acts not as a restraint against moral presumption but actually becomes the engine for social conformity."[99] Mill's thought evidences this change.

95. Ibid., 152.

96. Conyers uses the language of "sentiment" in a way that corresponds to the idea of "imaginary." For example, see Conyers, *Listening Heart*, 39.

97. Because of the variety of religious opinion, and the fact that governments are divided with regard to it, "salvation would then not answer to the faith of believers but to the chance that one's own government is right—and that, by the same token, other governments are wrong" (Conyers, *Long Truce*, 155).

98. Ibid., 155–56.

99. Ibid., 157.

Mill brings about the utilitarian virtue of toleration. Conyers highlights two important differences between Locke's and Mill's ideas of toleration. First, Mill views toleration as a positive good: "For Locke, the idea of protecting the individual's rights is prophylactic; for Mill, it is generative."[100] Second, Mill appeals to a very particular understanding of truth as the aim of toleration. Here Mill's idea of toleration combines with another aspect of the Enlightenment: the myth of historical progress. Toleration serves the truth of human progress by opening people up to change rather than adherence to custom. Conyers describes the distinction between Locke's and Mill's ideas on toleration by noting the following: 1) Locke's toleration is a negative thing, a check against ambitions, while Mill's is an optimistic unfolding of human possibilities; 2) Locke's toleration restrains human ambition when values transcend utilitarian calculations, but Mill's toleration becomes a strategy for progress; 3) Locke's toleration communicates life as an encounter with the divine, but Mill's toleration communicates the immanent potentiality of the world; and 4) Locke's view restrains sin, while Mill's view restrains restraint.[101] For Mill, progress has become the organizing principle that toleration serves.

Conyers's focus on intellectual history is not the only way to address the issue of toleration in the early modern world. In *Divided by Faith*, Benjamin Kaplan challenges the typical story of the rise of toleration. According to this story, "Tolerance . . . was first imagined by a visionary few, who offered increasingly robust theoretical justifications for it, then it was institutionalized by a small number of forward-thinking rulers, who let themselves be guided by reason. Two genres of historical writing (often combined with one another) have served as the chief bearers of this story: one traces the genealogy of ideas, the other tells a political narrative."[102] Kaplan cites two factors credited for a rise in toleration. On one hand, early modern Europeans supposedly got tired of all of the religious wars and saw toleration as a good alternative. This view does not fit with the evidence that, in the vast majority of the population, the cessation of such conflict did not occur as early as the typical story claims. On the other hand, early modern Europeans supposedly embraced the rationality of the Enlightenment and became more tolerant. This interpretation not only focuses too much on ideas but also oversimplifies the relationship between faith and

---

100. Ibid., 160.

101. Ibid., 165.

102. Kaplan, *Divided by Faith*, 7.

reason. Instead, factors like prosperity, a broad civil society, and individualism encouraged the practice of toleration among the non-elites.[103]

Kaplan argues instead that "contrary to the progressive schema of the Whig interpretation, toleration declined sharply in Europe in the wake of the reformations, and for the next two centuries, from around the middle of the sixteenth century to the middle of the eighteenth, it remained deeply problematic for a majority of Christians."[104] In short, "Religious violence—popular, official, military—continued in many parts of Europe in the late seventeenth and early eighteenth century. The age of religious wars had not yet ended."[105] This fact challenges the rise of toleration not only by questioning whether tolerance was as widespread as it claims, but it also calls into question the source of that toleration. If such problems still occurred so long after the typical story claims ideas changed, then perhaps the importance of those ideas and thinkers is diminished.

Kaplan also identifies other motivations for persons of different faiths to tolerate one another, when they did in fact do so. Like Conyers, Kaplan highlights the economic issues at stake: "Over the late seventeenth and eighteenth centuries, an increasing number came to believe that the wealth and power of their state was their principal responsibility and that toleration could increase these. London's sheriff Slingsby Bethel, for one, condemned 'imposing upon Conscience, in matters of religion' as 'a mischief unto Trade, transcending all others whatsoever.'"[106] The toleration that Kaplan identifies arises out of such decisions to get along on a practical level for practical purposes, not because of some grand progress in the history of ideas.

The story of the rise of toleration needs to be debunked because it is part of a larger construct. According to Kaplan,

103. Here I am summarizing Kaplan, ibid., 336–50.

104. Ibid., 47.

105. Ibid., 343. "Europe's last religious wars were fought in the 1700s and the 1710s, not the 1640s. Ruling elites in Britain, France, and Poland continued to treat certain religious dissenters as potential traitors until the middle of the eighteenth century or later. French and Austrian governments actively persecuted Protestants just as long. Only in the middle decades of the century did Voltaire and others make toleration the rallying cry par excellence of the Enlightenment, and only then did a consensus form within Europe's educated elites that laws and policies needed reform. A hundred years after the writings of Locke and Bayle, the toleration acts of the 1780s improved the position of religious dissenters, but not radically" (ibid., 355).

106. Kaplan, *Divided by Faith*, 351.

> The story of the rise of toleration is an ideological construct that perpetuates our ignorance. It is a myth, not only in being at variance with known facts, but in being a symbolic story, with heroes and villains and a moral—a story told about the past to explain or justify a present state of affairs. According to this myth, toleration triumphed in the eighteenth century because reason triumphed over faith. It triumphed because religion lost its hold on people, and hence its importance as a historical phenomenon.[107]

The Whig theory of history used the rise of toleration to support Protestantism over Catholicism. The secularization thesis then replaced the Whig theory:

> According to [the story of the secularization of the West], around 1650—or even earlier, by some accounts—Europe began to undergo a long-term, evolutionary process. Although it took centuries, by some point in the twentieth century its results were clear: churches lost much of their power and authority; clergy ceased to play major roles in politics, education, and social welfare; religious worship grew less universal; people stopped giving religious explanations for natural phenomena and human events; religious idioms ceased to pervade communications. . . . This story is controversial among scholars, who disagree first as to which aspects of it are empirically true, and second, whether as a story it is not conceptually flawed.[108]

In the case of the Whig theory of history and the secularization thesis, the real story of toleration is neglected in favor of a useful ideological construct.[109]

But did societies become more tolerant? We do not know enough about whether relations between people of different faiths really changed in the eighteenth century. Those who do argue that societies have become more tolerant focus on elite ideas and ignore popular behavior.[110] In fact, Kaplan's work suggests another possibility:

> The history of early modern Europe suggests a different view. It demonstrates that, even in communities that did not know our modern values, people of different faiths could live together peacefully. Even in profoundly religious communities where

107. Ibid., 356.
108. Ibid., 357.
109. Ibid.
110. Ibid., 356.

antagonisms were sharp, religion was not a primitive, untameable force. In the centuries between Reformation and French Revolution, Europeans discovered that, in practice, they could often manage and contain confessional conflict. As limited, tension-ridden, and discriminatory as their accommodations and arrangements were, they can open our eyes to the unique qualities of the toleration we practice today and the possibility of other options.[111]

These examples of people living together peacefully, even before the Enlightenment, line up with Conyers's observations about the "ancient practice of toleration." Kaplan's connection of the "rise of toleration" to Whig and secularization theories likewise lends support to Conyers's observations about the "doctrine of toleration" and its function in an ideology. For Conyers, the myth of toleration funds the state.

Kaplan and Conyers disagree on method but agree when it comes to their conclusions. Conyers uses the sort of "history of ideas" approach that Kaplan critiques in arguing against the typical story of the rise of toleration. But Kaplan's focus on lived practices of ordinary people confirms Conyers's overall thesis about the way toleration changed in the modern period, and the ideological nature of the story.

For Conyers, the rise of tolerance is ideologically tied to the idea of progress. This idea of progress is borrowed from Christian and Jewish eschatological hope, but progress cannot communicate the concept of order that Christian eschatology does. "Progress" means simply the continual development of immanent possibilities. But which possibilities should be pursued? In short, it comes down to a power struggle, a contest of wills, because the concept lacks any notion of order or goal beyond itself.

The New Goal: Power via the Exercise of the Will

In the place of any agreed upon purpose, power becomes the new goal in the modern world. Conyers develops this argument in two steps. First, he explains how power becomes the new goal by looking at a couple of conceptual shifts. Second, he draws on Jürgen Moltmann in order to show how theological concerns inform this new goal. In his own analysis and remarks, Conyers demonstrates how toleration plays into the emergence and maintenance of power.

111. Ibid., 358.

Power Becomes the Goal

From Hobbes to Dewey, the Aristotelian notion of a "final cause" faded away; purpose was rejected. Material and efficient causes explain the world. One way to understand this change is the difference between rest and motion. While the notion of final cause points toward rest, a time when motion is complete, the loss of that notion views the world as being in constant motion. Hobbes gained this idea from an encounter with Galileo and shifted his view of the world to one in which the natural state of things is motion rather than rest. If rest is not the natural state, then the nature of things is not given and discoverable or revealed to humans. Instead, it is always subject to change: "And if subject to change, it is malleable; and if malleable, then the world is essentially unstable. In that case, any order that exists does so either accidentally or because of human action upon things. Order is a product of the human will or it is projected upon things by the imagination."[112] For Conyers, this change in orientation characterizes modern thought.[113] It is another way of seeing the shift from a theology of vocation to a theology of choice.

The shift from viewing the natural state of things as motion instead of rest leads to a shift in posture for engaging the world. If there is a purpose in the world, some goal or rest that the world is moving toward, then humans can become involved in this by seeking to understand what this purpose might be and seek to get in line with it. Acting requires understanding; the intellect is the primary human power needed for this. However, with a changing and malleable world, engagement does not require understanding a purpose but proposing one. Understanding is not essential, but acting is: the will is the primary human power necessary.[114] This shift from intellect to will reflects a change in human engagement from seeking to understand the world to seeking to control the world.

Conyers recognizes that this shift from intellect to will has roots outside of the modern world. For example, nominalism's triumph over realism influenced this shift: "To give up the task of understanding universals (held

112. Conyers, *Long Truce*, 172.

113. In *Long Truce*, Conyers does not always relate the various features of modernity to one another. He speaks of the bipolar vision of society as defining modernity, this change from rest to motion as being characteristic, among others, but he does not explain explicitly how he understands their relationship. In the conclusion to this chapter, I attempt to relate these various shifts to one another.

114. Conyers, *Long Truce*, 173.

to be real by the realists) and to assert that universals or categories are what they are because we *name* them as such is really to say that the intellect is subject to the will."[115] In addition, Conyers briefly treats Kant, Marx, Mill, Nietzsche, Dewey, and Foucault as contributing to this shift in the understanding of purpose and goals, making it a product of human will rather than any created order.[116] The real goal comes out of the power of invention, and we must invent some sort of purpose because humans despair without one. Metaphysics is ruled out of court so as not to distract from the task at hand of exerting power via will.[117] When the will becomes the authority that sets things in order, the void that is left by the loss of meaning is filled by the will to power.

Theology and Power

The rise of power as the new goal emerged from theological debates, and the relation of theology and power in the modern world is an important and complex one. Conyers turns to the work of Moltmann to explore these connections and implications before setting out his own critical engagement and interpretation. Moltmann ties the shift in the understanding of power to the changes of nominalism and the concept of the *potentia absoluta* of God in his *God in Creation*. Nominalism led to a modified picture of God, making *potentia absoluta* his preeminent attribute, and the advance of science and technology increased this tendency to see God's most prominent

---

115. Ibid.

116. For more on these figures, see ibid., 173–80. Conyers also notes that getting rid of a telos was not an option: "While Hobbes, Bayle, Locke, Nietzsche, Dewey, and Foucault all are rather certain about the need to live on the basis of a *telos*—none attempts even to imagine that human life is conceivable otherwise—and they all to varying degrees see some significance to that fact, each nevertheless calculates in various ways how the question of *telos* might be settled in a way less ultimate than the gravity of the choice implies. For Hobbes it is settled vicariously by the magistrate. For Bayle and Locke the matter is relegated more or less to the private sphere. For Nietzsche and Foucault the *telos* is illusory but necessary and must be settled in the realm of myth and the inventive imagination. And for Dewey, the end is a pragmatic concept that responds to the situation at hand (the end-in-view) that only reads and feels as if ultimate" (ibid., 199).

117. "For the sake of intensity and control we have reduced our knowledge of things to a room with objects all of which we can touch, taste, handle, and move. In such a room, windows are a distraction; we cannot after all do anything about the stars. They belong to a speculative order" (ibid., 182).

attribute as absolute power.[118] Conyers notes that this opened the way for power itself to become the goal of human life,[119] because humans sought to be like God in his power alone rather than in connection to other moral attributes such as goodness. This shift in the dominant conception of God also leaned toward the oneness of God, neglecting the Trinity and the way community and harmony of wills impacts our understanding of power.

Conyers considers the modern idolatry of power the touchstone issue for Moltmann.[120] Moltmann identifies a weakness in Western culture, one that can be traced back to Christian theology.[121] Focusing too much on God's oneness leads to an overemphasis on power and neglects other attributes of God. An unselfconscious acceptance of power and all that serves power results from this overemphasis. Moltmann felt strongly about this because of experiences in his own lifetime of the idolization of power and of theologians' affirmation of leaders such as Hitler as the instrument of God's power.[122]

Moltmann turns to two key resources to better diagnose and potentially begin to remedy these problems. First, he draws on the political insights of Johannes Althusius and the federalist tradition. Common life should be organized on various levels, which helps guard against absolutism and the centralizing power of the state. However, the West's emphasis on the oneness of God has actually worked against the insights of federalism, resulting in many federalist political associations giving way to some form of absolutism.[123] Second, he "sees the doctrine of the Trinity being developed among Christians as an effective resistance against the centralization of power."[124] In fact, "Trinitarian thought prepares us for thinking of society in terms of distributed roles, separation of powers, and a federalist view of social associations."[125] These two resources work together in that

---

118. Conyers, "Three Sources," 317.

119. Conyers, *Long Truce*, 202.

120. Ibid., 207.

121. "That subtle weakness is on the side of Christian monotheism. It is the monotheism that early Christianity both cultivated in a certain way and resisted in a certain way, as it encountered and eventually made its place in the Roman Empire" (ibid., 210).

122. Ibid., 208.

123. Ibid., 210.

124. Ibid., 212–13.

125. Ibid., 212.

trinitarian thought protects federalism from the absolutizing tendencies of the Western emphasis on the oneness of God.

After drawing on Moltmann's insights, Conyers provides a critical reading that allows him to construct a slightly different interpretation of the problems existing between theology and power. Pointing back to *God, Hope, and History,* Conyers repeats his basic criticism of Moltmann: "The problem I found in his inclusion of hierarchy in his critique of monarchical monotheism, along with the coercive sorts of power arrangements, is that hierarchy does not always imply power and oppression. We are ruled in different ways. Besides being ruled more or less against our wills by some alien power, we are also ruled by our desires and by our expectations."[126] Love and hope order these desires and expectations: love constructs a hierarchy of values, and hope arranges the world in a type of hierarchy.[127] For Conyers, Moltmann's concern to reveal the problems with the abuse of power neglects the way that hierarchy can serve to orient lives without being abusive. The problem is monotheism alone, not monotheism itself. Monotheism cannot be a replacement for trinitarian doctrine, for the danger lies in the extremes of unity without difference or difference without unity.[128]

The secular emphasis on power, for Conyers, roots itself in an illusion. While secular cultures avoid dealing with the problem of telos, the turn to power as the goal problematically creates an end out of a means. Conyers retrieves Southern Agrarian Allen Tate's definition of secularism: "when the ends are replaced by the means."[129] Stated differently, secular-

126. Conyers, *Long Truce,* 213–14.

127. "If our hopes and loves are directed toward that which is less worthy, then the disorder shows up in our lives. By contrast, the ordered and peaceful life is ruled by properly ordered love and hope" (ibid., 214).

128. "In the Christian understanding of the triunity of God, there is both the unity of God and the differentiation of his three persons. In principle we find theological justification for a view of the world that is Catholic [*sic*] or universal: something that tells us that indeed we are all related to each other and taken up along with the whole of creation into one great destiny. At the same time, the idea of real distinction within the godhead also helps us to know that distinctions are not swallowed up in the unity of things, as some illusion—the *maya* of Hinduism—but they are real and significant. As persons, we are part of the world, and we stand over against the world. Both are true. There is theological justification for our communal existence, even for viewing ourselves as sharing our humanity with all other human beings. And there is also theological justification for thinking of ourselves as individuals. This balance is made real for us in the Incarnation" (ibid., 217).

129. Tate, *Essays of Four Decades,* 6. As noted above, Tate was a prominent member of the Southern Agrarians.

ism occurs when the ultimate goal (which is almost inevitably religious in nature) is replaced with the smaller "goal" of efficient means (which does not necessarily require explicit religious foundations). Put still another way, "It is when much discussion centers around how to do something and not what to do. A secular culture is one in which the ends are largely assumed— and are therefore unexamined."[130] Power becomes the object of pursuit, and when this happens "we are therefore engaging in an illusion. It is rather like the proverbial dog chasing its tail. . . . The illusion of a grand pursuit allows us to imagine that we are in control of life and of our destiny."[131] This pursuit of control is the problem, for "this anxiety for control is a form of despair: having found nothing to 'rest' our hopes in, we grasp for the lesser things of the created order."[132] But the modern world pursues power nonetheless, and it is this pursuit of power that makes toleration so useful. For smaller groups have purposes that compete with the power arrangement built solely on the individual and the state.[133] Toleration serves to dissolve these barriers to the efficient operation of the central administration and centralization of authority and power. Conyers compares it to the old struggle between Baal and Yahweh, "the god of fertility and wealth over against the God of sociability, peace, and righteousness. The modern tale of an ideology of toleration has, as we have seen, increasingly served the priests of Baal."[134] When power is the goal, toleration serves to eliminate all other goals so that they will not curtail the state's power.

This judgment on the shift to power as the primary goal depends on Conyers's acceptance of the criticism of nominalism that he largely received from Richard Weaver.[135] In fact, shifts connected to nominalism undergird the theological concept of vocation versus choice that animates Conyers's entire approach. His acceptance and modification of the nominalist critique is not without controversy within evangelical theology. In his work on Carl F. H. Henry, Baptist theologian Gregory Alan Thornbury mentions Conyers as belonging to a group of evangelicals critical of nominalism

130. Conyers, *Long Truce*, 218.

131. Ibid., 219.

132. Ibid.

133. "The more the group exists on the basis of a *telos* or purpose that transcends in significance the practical purposes of the state (or the ideological vision of the state), it becomes thereby an indigestible, alien, and resistant object that frustrates the simply bipolar power arrangement" (ibid., 223).

134. Ibid., 224.

135. See chapter 1 above.

and voluntarism.[136] For Thornbury, the issues surrounding nominalism and voluntarism boil down to a choice between Catholicism and Protestantism.[137] But is this the case? Is Conyers a Catholic-in-denial, or at least headed toward Rome?

To some degree, the answer to this question depends entirely on the concerns with which one approaches this medieval shift. In his treatment of Henry, Thornbury comes from an epistemological angle. He argues that voluntarism and nominalism were key developments because they led to the idea that the humans can know anything only because of God's initiative.[138] God chose to create, and God chose to make knowledge possible. He set the content and the conditions of knowledge. In Thornbury's mind, voluntarism rightly drew out that the world depends on God's will, "in accordance with his own nature."[139]

On the other hand, Conyers approaches nominalism and voluntarism through the work of Richard Weaver and his concerns with the ethical implications. If Thornbury comes from an epistemological angle to the issue, Conyers acknowledges the epistemological character of the debate but pushes through to an anthropological or ethical angle relating to the ontology developed by nominalism.[140] Conyers sees that the shift in understanding of God toward *potentia absoluta* had an anthropological effect: it led to a greater focus on human willing and autonomy that precipitated anthropological shifts in modernity. Most of the shifts that Conyers identifies can be tied to this nominalist shift. As humans sought to be in God's image, they focused more and more on exercising the will and gaining power. Control became more important. Ultimately, focusing on God's will so strongly, as nominalism and voluntarism did as they were inherited and applied, led to a jettisoning of God from the equation because of the increased

136. Thornbury, *Recovering Classic Evangelicalism*, 47.

137. Ibid., 58.

138. Ibid., 53.

139. Ibid., 45.

140. "The result of this epistemological change is that a sense of cosmic order, which is articulated in a hierarchy of civil and religious authorities, to which an individual gives fealty, is also modified. Social arrangements instead reflect the inviolability of conscience and the moral responsibility of the people. The result is a contractarian theory of political order that was not unlike that of Hobbes, was to be expanded by Rousseau and Kant, and has had a major influence in Western thought and political practice." Conyers, *Long Truce*, 156.

emphasis on human willing and making.[141] Because Conyers focuses on these changes, he sees nominalism and voluntarism as dangerous changes.

Can both Thornbury and Conyers be right? It comes down to how one reads nominalism and voluntarism. If, as Thornbury contends, voluntarism depends on God's will "in accordance with his own nature," then there is room to accept aspects of nominalism and voluntarism while still rejecting the reconception of God as absolute power and the resultant growth of autonomy. Conyers would be comfortable with this approach since he is primarily concerned with the ethical implications. Is God's will positively understood ("in accordance with his nature") or negatively understood (without hindrance; arbitrary)? While this question can be debated at the level of the original writings of Ockham, at the level of reception and the development of modernism, the modern world's emphasis on arbitrary will and autonomy won the day.[142] Whatever Ockham's intentions in connection to God's will, nominalism and voluntarism led to a greater role for human willing and choice instead of responding to a reality created by God and into which God calls people.

So, while nominalism and voluntarism understood in connection to God's nature can provide epistemological aid for those wanting to focus on God's choice to reveal himself, the same concepts approached anthropologically or ethically yield dangerous theological results in the modern period, especially the turn to power as the main goal.

Disorder(s) of Modernity?

Now that we have followed the logic of Conyers's treatment of modernity through the crisis, to his treatment of toleration, to the new goal of power, we can begin to draw together the disorders that he identifies. These disorders of modernity emerge throughout *The Long Truce* and also in the beginning stages of *The Listening Heart*. Understanding his explanation of the development of toleration provides a necessary context for these disorders, since they are all tied to the shifts that he narrates in that treatment. In what follows, I will review important connections that Conyers makes as well as

141. For support of this emphasis on human willing, see Dupre, *Passage to Modernity*.

142. As Elshtain notes in her treatment of nominalism, "It isn't necessary to unpack the entire structure of late medieval argumentation . . . in order to take the measure of a 'climate of opinion' that Ockham either solidified or deepened, if he did not inaugurate" notions of God's radical omnipotence. Elshtain, *Sovereignty*, 36.

the shifts that he identifies in the modern world so that I can set up his basic assessment of the disorders of the modern world related to these problems.

Conyers identifies significant connections between toleration and other aspects of the modern world that are influential in developing modern individuals. First, he calls the modern era a "long crisis," "a crisis testing religion's, especially the Christian religion's, ecumenical claims. Early in the modern period, that ecumenical sentiment was tested by the outbreak of rival visions, each claiming universal validity. Wars in sixteenth and seventeenth century Europe, inflamed by religious conviction, gave rise to fanaticism, fanaticism gave rise to cynicism, and cynicism gave rise to secular expediency."[143] While he does not fully develop each of these connections, he clearly sees them as conceptually and causally related, with the change in tolerance serving as an important element in the shift. Conyers identifies another connection between tolerance and two other elements that play a similar role: war and economics, concerns highlighted by the Southern Agrarians. While tolerance serves to dissolve mediating social bonds by relativizing and privatizing them, economics has the tendency of disconnecting commercial operations from personal relationships, thereby making them more abstract, and war disrupts and dismantles natural social arrangements as well.[144] These two sets of connections are related: the first draws the changes out through different historical events and tendencies, and the second shows how different social elements serve to facilitate the changes that Conyers observes.

In his genealogy of toleration, Conyers points to four significant shifts that characterize the modern world in opposition to what came before it: (1) a shift from love to power; (2) a shift from good to rights; (3) a shift from complex to bipolar vision; and (4) a shift from intellect to will. In the first, Conyers argues that the modern world sees a shift from the "power of love" to the "love of power."[145] Whereas groups at one time arose because of common interests and loves, the rise of the nation-state led to organization occurring on the basis of power. For this change to happen, toleration served as a substitute for love.

143. Conyers, *Long Truce*, 22.
144. Ibid., 49–60.
145. Ibid., 12–20.

The second shift occurred as "human rights" replaced "the good" as the point of reference for restraint or toleration. This shift boils down to noninterference between individuals and groups.[146]

In the third shift, toleration relativized the commitments that once united mediating groups such as the church and family in order to strengthen the bipolar vision of society (in which all of political life is understood as a contract between the individual and the state).[147] Related to the role of economics mentioned briefly above, Conyers argues that the joint-stock company formed the political imagination: the modern failure to take into account the full range of realities that make up any society "is a failure that was especially tempting in a time of the rise of the nation-states and the bourgeois desire to relate to that entity as individual stock holders in a joint-stock company, without the complications brought on by other, and less formal, social groupings. . . . The failure occurs instead at the level of conscious reflection upon the nature and shape of public life."[148] This new economic entity provided a different way of imagining political relationships, simplifying them and focusing primarily on the contract between individuals and the state rather than the other complex associations in life.

The fourth and final shift that Conyers identifies relates to a change in understanding the world: rather than the natural state of things being one of rest, it is one of motion. This view encouraged humans to view themselves as masters and possessors of nature: "The idea of limitless and uniform progress and the inexorable technological mastery of nature was hardly ever questioned. It was until relatively recently, and to a degree remains, our myth."[149] This shift in political and moral imagination impacted the way individuals relate to one another, the state, and the natural world. For example, this view implies the exertion of will over something or someone, and "that thing—so moved by the will—becomes no longer a subject with which one enjoys companionable mutual relationship. It becomes an object. And the more perfectly an object obeys the will, the more it becomes a mere extension of the self."[150] This shift led to engaging with the world

---

146. Ibid., 42.

147. Conyers deals with this bipolar vision and the breakdown of mediating institutions throughout *Long Truce*. For examples, see 44, 89, 117, 120, 194, and 226.

148. Conyers, *Long Truce*, 137–38.

149. Ibid., 80.

150. Conyers, "Three Sources," 317.

through intellect (seeking to understand) rather than through will (seeking to control).[151]

While Conyers focuses on toleration as a lens for understanding modern changes in *The Long Truce*, in *The Listening Heart* he provides other diagnostic concepts that approach modern problems from different angles. He identifies a few specific disorders of modernity that result from the historical and conceptual changes that he maps. These shifts create a world in which isolated individuals seek to exert as much of their own will as they can without overrunning the "rights" of others (no sense of "common good" or "the good") while perceiving their responsibilities as primarily contractarian in nature and between themselves as individuals and the state. Another disorder that Conyers identifies is that the modern world has caused the disorder of social isolation. Isolation stems from the emphasis on the autonomous individual in the bipolar vision of society and from the continuing disappearance of mediating social bonds. While in Bayle's time it seemed as though the individual needed the state's protection from oppressors such as the church, later in the modern age the loss of these mediating institutions left individuals isolated. Conyers goes so far as to say, "It should not be surprising that modernity has been marked by the exaggeration of the freedoms of the individual, the alienation of the person, the dissolution of families, and a culture of pathological loneliness: for these features are in the very design of the organized society which replaces the organic society."[152] The move from organic society to organized society (by which Conyers means the modern nation-state) was facilitated by concepts such as "tolerance" and has produced these modern disorders related to individualism.

Conyers refers to this idea as the development of the "imperialistic self." This self arises out of three modern trends: rejection of absolutes in nominalism, pursuit of power in science, and the loss of distinction in pantheism. Because of these trends, "theology becomes psychology. Talk of ultimate ends becomes meaningless, for the horizon beyond the limited self has disappeared. We can only speak of operations, of practice, of techniques. . . . Under such circumstances, secularism has become complete. The world must discover all over again how to speak about ends. And once again the gospel becomes required reading."[153] The shifts in the modern

151. Conyers, *Long Truce*, 172–73.

152. Conyers, *Listening Heart*, 25.

153. Conyers, "Three Sources," 321.

world have created a new conception of the self, the imperialistic self, an impoverished self.

Pushing further into a diagnosis of modernity, Conyers observes that the modern emphasis on choice and freedom leads to a desire for control and mastery that ultimately yields distraction. "Choice," Conyers observes, "when it is the first in our ethical vocabulary . . . pulls us apart."[154] Freedom, in this view, is understood as the freedom of self-determination, the capacity to use one's intelligence without being guided by another; self-determination has become "a primary virtue."[155] Conyers calls this the "Invictus" principle: "This distinctly modern prejudice might be called the 'Invictus' principle. We think for ourselves; we are the masters of our souls. In ancient texts, such as the Old Testament book of Judges, such a characteristic in society was thought to be the sign of profound disorder rather than a sign of freedom."[156] In the modern world, this sign of disorder has become the hallmark of freedom.

The modern emphasis on choice leads to a desire for control and mastery of both the natural world and fellow human beings. Conyers points to a change in the conception of knowledge to demonstrate this desire for control.[157] The Enlightenment approach to reason "is rather a means of setting out sights on the uses and behavior of specific things so that we might control them. Its earlier aim was knowledge, and its later aim was power."[158] Viewing the human primarily as subject, as possessive of a will that shapes and determines reality, causes a shift from seeking to know in order to *participate* in a reality not of one's own making to desiring to know in order to control, to master. "Reason and the idea of 'humanity as subject,'" Conyers argues, "give us a sense of mastery over nature and reality, but also draw us

154. Conyers, *Listening Heart*, xii.

155. Ibid., 17.

156. Ibid., 19.

157. Here Conyers draws on Moltmann's *God for a Secular Society*. He quotes Moltmann at length, including this: "Scientific reason is instrumentalizing reason, reason whose epistemological drive is utilization and domination. This pushed out the older receptive reason, which was an organ of perception, and the earlier *phronesis*, which clothed reason in the wishes of experience. According to Kant's *Critique of Pure Reason*, modern reason only now sees 'what it itself has brought forth according to its own design,' by 'compelling nature to give an answer to its questions' (Preface to the second edition). This coercion of nature is called 'experiment,' and in the eighteenth century, it was often compared with inquisitions under torture." For more, see Moltmann, *God for a Secular Society*, 7–8.

158. Conyers, *Listening Heart*, 56.

apart from nature and reality, so that we understand ourselves no longer as participants, but as observers and as manipulators."[159] When we emphasize human willing, we closely identify humanity's relation to nature with controlling, manipulating, and mastering.

Finally, the quest for mastery and control leads to distraction because it is based on a misunderstanding of the proper way humans should relate to God's world. Conyers connects knowledge for the sake of mastery with distraction.[160] In describing modern people he states, "We are distracted. To be modern is to exist increasingly in a state of distraction. Our attention is drawn away from those things that have been placed in our care, away from the center of our apparent concern to something abstractly related to that concern, and thus away from God himself who is the center of all things. To be modern is not only to find ourselves thus distracted, but to justify that life of distraction."[161] This problem of modernity is more than intellectual: "it is rather a moral problem and a problem of the affections. We have failed to love properly what we ought to love and we fall away from that love which draws us toward God. Instead we fasten upon that which draws us away from God."[162] While one of the marks of modernity is a spirit of freedom from objects, Conyers views this freedom from objects as a form of distraction from the object of our lives, namely, God.[163] Modernity pulls apart what belongs together. Drawing on Augustine's distinction between use and enjoyment, Conyers argues that modern distraction leads people away from the proper enjoyment of God to the enjoyment of what should merely be used. This results in a lack of an aim in life.[164]

Beyond using this progression to highlight the disorders of modernity, Conyers also paints a picture of modern slavery and an oppressive "submodernity" lurking beneath the surface and derivative of free-market economics. He makes the provocative argument that slavery is the eldest child of modernity, not something finally overcome in modernity. Since

159. Ibid., 59–60.

160. "The 'distraction' that I have described—and which I have claimed to see at the heart of modernity—is opposed by the idea of 'participation.' There is a difference, for instance, in the idea of 'knowledge' that might be stated this way: we can know something in order to have mastery over it—that is what I call 'distraction'; or we can know something in order to participate in the world which we attempt to know" (ibid., 60–61).

161. Ibid., 55.

162. Ibid.

163. Ibid., 56.

164. Ibid., 60–64.

the slavery terminology is highly offensive, modern people tend to reject it when it is visibly evident and instead submerge it in less visible forms. For example, he names trade arrangements with China that employ slave labor, or the public worship of the rich, famous, and powerful. Slavery was more the product of modernity than ancient or medieval Christendom. The modern human being often feels like she "belongs" to the state or the company, finding it difficult to develop this sense of belonging with other associations.[165] Indeed, the sense of belonging to the state or to the company can overwhelm any sense Christians have of belonging to the body of Christ.[166]

Two features of slavery require highlighting because of their clear parallels with views of the human in modern thought: on the one hand, the transformation of the human into an instrument, and on the other hand the decimation of relations within natural groups such as the family or clan in order to isolate the individual. With the former, the

> rich blessings of modern technology inevitably brought with them a new sentiment, [a] new way in which the increasingly urbanized man could begin to think about himself. . . . Man had become increasingly an instrument for production, profit, and warfare. Rather than a participant in a creation that embraced all men equally, and that required a common seeking after the good of a community, this new relationship implied something else. It implied that the naked purpose of existence was production, conquest, and material acquisition—a purpose that indeed sanctified power and possession, rooted somehow in the mystery of pleasure—but a purpose expressive of the human will and its capacity for acquisition and domination.[167]

This view of the human, shifting to an instrumentalization, fits within the concept of slavery, because it emphasizes the *use* of humans for particular ends.

The decimation of natural groups resulted in the instrumentalization and the isolation of the individual. Conyers notes, "With the second feature—the individualizing of human existence—we have made the full

165. Ibid., 38. This idea of the shift in "belonging" also relates to Taylor's argument about individualisms of anomie.

166. For instance, Budde argues that unless ecclesial solidarity becomes something capable of forming people, Christianity will become a parody of what it once was in a world of competing allegiances. See Budde, *Borders of Baptism*.

167. Conyers, *Listening Heart*, 39.

descent. It has been a descent from an idea of vocation that evokes the human person in his full connectedness, as a social being with responsibilities, loves, and a fully social understanding of himself not as mere free agent with an isolated and unhindered will, but as father, mother, brother, daughter, colleague, neighbor, and friend, each with its peculiar role, obligations, and sentiments."[168] The idea was to free the individual from such "petty obligations" so that she might be more useful to the interests of nation-states and international corporations. She becomes an instrument even more so in her isolation.

At root, Conyers wants to redefine slavery so that we can understand that the fate of the modern worker is not all that different from the agrarian slave; in a way, slavery has simply gone underground. (He is not speaking about things like human trafficking and sex slavery, though those forms support the idea that invisible slavery is less troubling to people.) The average worker is like a slave because she has become an instrument, a piece that has been severed from its local community and bonds to such a degree that it can be moved around or interchanged with others with little resistance. Thus it is an issue of the social imaginary: individuals are willing to sever community relationships in order to relocate for the company. Once slavery is seen as not merely bondage to something (a master) but also as opposition to *belonging* to a community in any real way, it becomes clearer how modern economic arrangements have not actually eliminated slavery but simply changed its form. Once slavery is seen in these ways, related to instrumentalization and social isolation, "this might just as well describe the modern middle class worker and bureaucrat as it does the nineteenth century agrarian slave."[169]

We may be skeptical about such an analysis, for the institution of slavery has been formally outlawed, though human trafficking is again gaining attention. But as Conyers counters, "It is true that we no longer have the visible institution of domestic slavery such as existed in the nineteenth century, especially but not exclusively in the American South. But when some populations are living sumptuously at the expense of others who are barely able to feed their young, is that not also slavery, one might ask?" This modern slave system remains out of sight and thus less offensive.[170]

168. Ibid., 42.
169. Ibid., 48.
170. Ibid., 49.

By "submodernity," Conyers refers to the oppressed and suffering who are often ignored, whose suffering is the unintended consequence of modern actions. Drawing on the work of Moltmann again, Conyers argues that all along, an "underside" accompanied the optimistic estimation of human progress in the modern age.[171] This underside includes problems like slavery ("the genuine fruit of modern developments that called for the mastery and organization of the world")[172] and the killing of native peoples: "Thus progress looked very different to the black slave, to the American Indian, and to the Filipino than it might to those who occupied the new nineteenth-century suburbs and road [*sic*] the trains that spanned the North American continent, or to the British and American shipping magnates or industrial barons who were on the 'receiving end' of 'progress.'"[173] This "underside" of modernity is often portrayed as the exception to the progress of modernity or the lingering results of a previous, less enlightened age, but Conyers holds it as a necessary and incriminating part of the modern idea of "progress."

As we have seen, Conyers identifies various disorders of modernity. For him, the disorders are rooted in conceptual shifts such as that mapped with toleration that have led to an individualistic, control-oriented view of human living, which has brought about distraction and violent assertions of power. Those on the "receiving end" of progress are distracted from God, and those on the "underside" have suffered and continue to suffer in myriad ways. However, it is more illuminating to see Conyers as identifying one disorder of modernity that manifests itself in all of these various ways. For Conyers, the root disorder is the shift from vocation to choice. The fallout from nominalism has led to an anthropological shift. The job of humans is no longer to listen to and obey God but rather to choose, to construct, to control. All of the disorders identified by Conyers are genetically related to this one disorder. It has caused the four shifts, and the emphasis on control and mastery that leads to distraction, isolation, and the instrumentalization of the human. These aspects that Conyers labels as "disorders" are more

---

171. For this, Conyers draws primarily on Moltmann's treatment of liberty and autonomy in the Enlightenment era, as well as the total rule of instrumental reason, the loss of liberty and the dissolution of human subjectivity. See Moltmann, *Coming of God*, 220. Conyers then turns to Moltmann's treatment of the issue of covenant versus rationalized modern society in an essay titled "Covenant or Leviathan?" in which Moltmann draws on Althusius. See Moltmann, *God for a Secular Society*, 24–45.

172. Conyers, *Listening Heart*, 109–10.

173. Ibid., 110.

consistently understood as manifestations of the disorder rooted in the shift to individual choice, to the will, as the way to be human in the world.

CONCLUSION

We can summarize Conyers's diagnosis of modernity as follows. Various shifts, facilitated in many ways by a changing notion of "toleration," served to produce a bipolar vision of society focusing on individuals and the state, dissolving mediating social bonds that once served to provide meaning and purpose. In addition, a different view of the natural world led to the belief that meaning and purpose must be imposed by human willing, which leads to power and conflict.[174] This root disorder of individualism and a lack of meaning gives rise to other disorders (or other symptoms of this one disorder) such as violence, in which individuals and states seek to use power to gain more power, since power has become the new goal in the absence of other meaning. Evangelical theopolitical imagination that finds a stake in promoting the democratic nation-state or free-market capitalism is not only blind to such dangers and disorders but can actually serve to promote them and the way they shape social imaginaries.

Conyers's genealogy of toleration and its relation to modernity must be properly situated within his broader theological concerns in relation to the modern world, theological concerns that I first addressed in the previous chapters. He sets up a contrast for Christian theology. There are two modes for approaching theology: "first, 'vocational' in form and content, or, second, one that is formed by the primacy of 'choice' in all human endeavors, even theology."[175] To expand, he explains, "Until the modern period, advances in philosophy and theology borrowed heavily from the sentiment of vocation. Ideas were not true because they captured the imagination, but they captured the imagination because they were true."[176] While previous thinkers sought to discover and conform to a truth independent of themselves (vocation), modern thinkers are pressured to be resourceful and

---

174. This conflict relates not only to decisions between humans but also to decisions made about the natural world: "And if one thing in nature is not inherently more important than another, then the survival of one species or another, and the question of whether bears are not of more service as bear rugs, becomes a question that can only be resolved on the level of power and conflict." Conyers, "Three Sources," 316.

175. Conyers, "Can Postmodernism Be Used," 293.

176. Ibid.

inventive, ultimately responsible for coming up with the truth they espouse (choice).[177] This simple distinction, between vocation and choice, frames the way Conyers views all of modernity, including the relationship between the state and the individual.

Toleration, then, facilitates the shift from an emphasis on the truth of theological concerns to an emphasis on jettisoning such disagreements in favor of a strong state. Once disagreements are demoted to issues to be "tolerated," they slowly lose their power and ultimate significance. Toleration, a sinister doctrine, promises protection from danger, but its price is a notion of truth. Conyers's diagnosis of modernity, then, flows out of this theological distinction between truth as given or truth as made.

While Conyers unpacks this diagnosis in his final two books, he leaves the remedies primarily in the final book, *The Listening Heart*. We now turn to these remedies in order to evaluate whether Conyers has the resources for an evangelical theopolitical imagination—resources that can avoid an oversimplified use of Scripture and inspire consistent and faithful Christian discipleship.

177. Ibid., 294.

CHAPTER 4

The Return of Vocation

INTRODUCTION

Conyers's work confronts modern disorders with a recovery of the theological concept of vocation. Vocation reopens a proper Christian worldview and reestablishes important Christian practices for resisting sin and being the church, thus aiding in the theopolitical imagination. His work on vocation demonstrates how evangelicals can remain committed to the Bible while moving into more nuanced and careful readings of Scripture than can help overcome the oversimplified readings that are often offered.

The Southern Partisan published an essay by Conyers on the topic of religion in the South that illustrates Conyers's careful reading of Scripture. Conyers's overall argument was that religion in the South was becoming more like religion in the North, but that Southern religious communities used to be able to resist certain disorders that plagued their Northern counterparts, such as Puritanism, fundamentalism, and paganism. Of particular interest here is the fact that Conyers's drew approvingly on examples from Southern religious leaders on how to read the Bible: "The Church, however, has traditionally understood its teaching as rooted in the historical and literal, but not confined to it. And the South, as it has been represented in the leaders of her churches, has successfully resisted an extreme preoccupation with the mere 'facts' of the Bible, and instead saw in these facts a more comprehensive truth.["][1] He cited the work of prominent religious leaders, including B. H. Carroll and James Boyce, both of whom founded Southern Baptist seminaries, to show that "there was evidently little dissatisfaction with a less-than-literal reading of the Bible. For Southerners, there was still no problem in believing that truth is conveyed by poetry, parable, and rhetoric, as well as by straight, hard data."[2] In this essay, Conyers discusses the interpretation of Scripture explicitly, especially in opposition to biblicism. His work on modernity, as we will see in this chapter, puts this way of reading Scripture to practice by moving beyond simply translating "hard data" found in Scripture and instead seeking to be formed by the way Scripture informs ideas like vocation and community. He rejects fundamentalism, which "fails to appreciate the subtlety of the intellect, thinking that truth presents itself in univocal and transparent ways to a mind innocent of paradox or metaphor."[3]

In his later writings, Conyers not only paints a picture of the crisis of modern culture but also proposes a theocentric, constructive project for navigating the modern world. He connects various other constructive themes to vocation in order to begin to build a response, one cut short by his death. To understand his response fully, and to extend it where it is undeveloped, we must turn to its roots. I argue that there are three primary roots. I have already explored the first root: Conyers's concern for highlighting the theological binary between vocation and choice guides his response. The second root is William Gilmore Simms, a nineteenth-century literary figure who provides some of the content for the practice-centered constructive themes that Conyers begins to develop. The third root of Conyers's response is a group of constructive themes—both practice-centered and more explicitly theological—that he turns to in developing his remedies to modernity. I argue that while some of these resources are no longer usable, others show promise. Since we dealt with the first root in previous chapters, we will turn to the second and third roots.

Conyers and William Gilmore Simms

Conyers's diagnosis and remedy of modern ills depends on his encounter with the work of William Gilmore Simms (1806–70), though this fact is not

1. Conyers, "Real Old Time Religion," 17.

2. Ibid., 18.

3. Ibid., 19.

immediately apparent. A prestigious man of letters in the mid-nineteenth century, Simms lived in Charleston, South Carolina. [4] His literary output was astounding: "one poem and one review a week, on average, over forty-plus years,"[5] and scholars argue that the roots of great Southern writers such as William Faulkner and Robert Penn Warren are to be found in Simms.[6] He left behind a large amount of correspondence, and he excelled in fiction, nonfiction, and poetry. He was not only important because of his literary contributions, but also "as an editor of periodicals; as a molder of political strategy; as an articulate spokesman for causes; as an early exponent of environmental protection and agricultural reform; as an antiquarian enamored of history, books, and art."[7] There is now an active scholarly journal, *Simms Review*, devoted to his life and work. Simms's basic social theories "center upon the importance of home, the need for stability, the value of work, the requirements of leadership, the protection of the environment, and reverence for the past—all consistent with the philosophy of the Southern planter class: noblesse oblige."[8] Identified with the Old South and himself a slaveholder,[9] Simms's reputation and significance did not survive the Civil War, and it was not until the 1970s and 1980s that he again began to receive scholarly attention.

In 2000, Conyers published an essay in the *Simms Review* approaching some of Simms's poetry and social criticism from a theological perspective. The article's main task was to interpret Simms's *Sabbath Lyrics*, and Conyers draws on poetry and social criticism in his treatment. He argues that Simms's thesis in the *Sabbath Lyrics* is that "a restless society is a more or less barbarous society, and a more or less violent society."[10] Simms sees (even his mid-nineteenth-century version of) the modern world as a restless society that has lost any sense of purpose and therefore resorts to barbarism and violence. His poetry and social criticism expose this aspect of society and hold out Christian notions such as purpose and rest as

---

4. For biographical information on Simms, see Guilds, "Introduction," 1–35. Edgar Allen Poe once called Simms "the best novelist which this country has, upon the whole, produced" (ibid., 26).

5. Ibid., 15.

6. Ibid., 18.

7. Ibid., 13.

8. Ibid., 24.

9. Ibid., 29.

10. Conyers, "Simms's *Sabbath Lyrics*," 15.

important remedies. In this poetry, Conyers finds both incisive diagnosis and hope for society because of the scriptural imagination that saturates Simms's work.

Tucked in a short chapter in *The Listening Heart*, one central passage of Conyers's final book shows him drawing on Simms again. (And it should be noted that this chapter is a reworking of part of the 2000 *Simms Review* piece.[11]) While we will deal with the specific content of this particular chapter below when explaining how "rest" plays into Conyers's treatment, the chapter merits brief mention here because Conyers provides some insight into the influence of Simms on his entire project. Conyers begins the chapter by noting the way that Hobbes helped facilitate a shift from seeing human life as pursuing purpose and rest to seeing human life as motion dependent upon will. He then states,

> My own awakening to the importance of these matters in the lives of families and communities, however, did not come from the philosophy of Aristotle or the theology of Thomas Aquinas. And it did not come from the numbers of thinkers in this century, capable as they are, who are showing clearly the dangerous fissures in the modern edifice. Nor did it come from even those who, like Dietrich Bonhoeffer, have helped to point the way to a better life in community. My awakening came instead with the almost accidental acquaintance that I made with the writings of [Simms].[12]

He goes on to note that Simms's social criticism is "a kind of theology, for he understands society always in the light of its being called into being by God, the creator and redeemer."[13] One of Simms's themes is that "while life is effectively wounded by the powerful ravages of change, it is continually *shaped* by the promise of that which is its constant goal. The wounding and the healing take place simultaneously and in the same present world." But a difference is found "between those who believe that the wounding is always mortal, and those who trust that the healing of persons and communities will always prevail in the end."[14]

---

11. The book chapter focuses less on *Sabbath Lyrics* but employs the work Conyers did on Simms's social criticism. In the article, the primary focus is *Sabbath Lyrics*, while in the book Conyers shifts his attention to the rootlessness of modernity, the emphasis on motion, and the need for rest that Simms identifies.

12. Conyers, *Listening Heart*, 156.

13. Ibid.

14. Ibid., 160.

Simms advances these themes through a deep, Scripture-formed imagination, especially in *Sabbath Lyrics*, which was the first piece Conyers wrote about. Each of the poems contains a Scripture reference under the title, and the theme of the individual poem is informed by that passage. Simms's Scripture-saturated imagination is not one of simple proof-texting, but of deep meditation on passages. Simms's work was not simply *informed* but *formed* by the text of Scripture.

Conyers's short portions dealing with Simms reveal that Simms is one source for the major theme that orients Conyers: the concept that he would later articulate as "vocational theology," an insistence on the calling of God being primary over the choice of humans. At the same time, Conyers links this theme to his eschatological orientation: part of the purpose that Christians cling to is rooted in hope that God prevails in the end.

Constructive Themes in Conyers's Work

Now that we understand the guiding role of Simms, I turn to explaining Conyers's constructive themes for resisting problems in modernity. Conyers provides a helpful foundation by pointing to both the role tolerance plays in modernity and the change that occurred in the application of tolerance itself in society. The most value in his work, however, comes from his constructive themes, from what he has to say when he turns to the question of what Christian communities can do to resist modernity's problems. In what follows, I explore these constructive themes in two stages. First, I analyze "practice-centered themes," focusing on what Conyers proposes to do in light of modern problems. Second, I analyze "traditional doctrinal themes," seeking to understand the role that theology plays in Conyers's constructive moves. These two stages of exploration assume one another and are intertwined, though it is helpful to separate them to understand each better.

Practice-Centered Themes

Vocation

Conyers builds his response to modernity on the Christian idea of vocation. Vocation is

> a view in which human life is drawn toward some purpose that is greater than the individual, one that stands above national interests, that invests life with nobility and beauty, and that creates "room" for the common life. More than "work" and more than a "religious identity" or membership in a religious community, it is the notion that being human means one is drawn toward a destiny—and not simply as a worker or as a religionist, but as a soul that properly belongs to that which is yet dimly seen, but which already lays claim to one's very existence.[15]

This concept has four distinguishing features that are nonmodern. First, the concept of the call implies an external agent outside of the one being called. Second, this summons is often *against* the will of the one being called.[16] Third, the calling almost always involves hardships that must be overcome to answer the call. Finally, the greatest danger lies in the possibility of being diverted or distracted from the call.[17] Christians must recover the idea of vocation in order to counter modern problems.

Vocation points to the fact that we respond to a reality greater than ourselves, a reality constructed by Another. It includes an attractional component,[18] and the greater reality to which we respond is personal in nature.[19] For Conyers, "The generating influence of this sentiment that lies so deeply within us, and which we call 'vocation' out of a certain loss for knowing quite what to call it, is a constant reminder that something besides human choice defines the true nature of those ties that bind a people together and to their world."[20] Vocation is more than just an individual call to do something; it is an entire context in which people exist.

That there has been a loss of community in the modern world is a common observation, but Conyers goes beyond this observation and ties the loss of community to a loss of vocation.[21] In the Enlightenment, the human will became the substitute for listening for a call.[22] Vocation was

---

15. Ibid., 7.

16. In fact, one of the changes Conyers notes is that in the Enlightenment, reason became a replacement for vocation. One could just make reasoned choices. See ibid., 14.

17. Ibid., 13–15.

18. Ibid., 32.

19. Ibid., 101.

20. Ibid., 33.

21. Ibid., 9.

22. Conyers ties the decline of vocation to six consequences of the development of the modern world: (1) the myth of progress; (2) the growth of cities; (3) the machine model

replaced by choice.[23] In this reading, modern secular society has been a long experiment in elevating choice to the level of a basic social principle.[24] Conyers draws out this contrast by setting up two views of society. In the natural view, "the main task of human life together is to cultivate those habits and practices that allow us to 'connect' with a purpose already inherent in the world." However, in the Enlightenment view, "the point is to liberate individuals and voluntary associations for the pursuit of 'happiness' defined largely in market terms of private comfort, safety, and material or physical satisfaction."[25] Focusing on vocation shifts the way one conceives of one's life. The life-forming question is not "What shall I make of myself?" but "How shall I enter wisely and profitably into the life in which I find myself?"[26]

Conyers also ties this loss of vocation to the increasing presence of violence in the modern world. He charts three theories on violence: Hannah Arendt suggests that where power in the sense of effective action is missing in a community, violence takes its place; René Girard claims that violence provides focus and strengthens the community by helping it turn against a scapegoat or enemy; and Eric Voegelin teaches that once society is closed to transcendent meaning and instead focuses on worldly goods, only violence and revolution satisfy the competing demands.[27] While these theories differ, Conyers sees them overlap at a critical point: "human beings naturally reach for meaningful action, and not finding it, resort to irrational and destructive action."[28] When vocation is lost, the only calculus left is an

---

replacing the agrarian model, both in reality and metaphor; (4) governments formed for efficient organization of large territories and opposition to barriers that hampered economic growth; (5) social organization mimicked the logic of the machine world; and (6) social consciousness shifted from local, place-oriented communities to urban centers of manufacture, trade, and government. These changes resulted in a shift in sentiment regarding how people viewed themselves: they lost a sense of anything permanent undergirding their existence, and their only sense of belonging came from the state (ibid., 34–39).

23. Ibid., 18.
24. Ibid., 4.
25. Ibid., 106.
26. Ibid., 105.
27. Ibid., 5.
28. Ibid., 5–6.

instrumental calculus, seeking what works or what is useful for advancing the ends chosen by the individual will.[29]

Vocation illuminates a conflict between power and love in the modern world. Love and power compete as ways for motivating community and relationship. Societies—and human relationships and actions in general— are dominated either by the strength of love (attraction to one another, to beauty, to justice, etc.) or by the will, power, and choice invested in another and represented in law. Actions are determined by love or force.[30] Love draws people toward one another; power forces people apart. In fact, "It is the rivalry between power in the sense of force as the means of social organization, and affection as the tie that binds people together, that binds them to their proper tasks, that binds them in creative and loving ways to their places and their things."[31] Both ways are necessary, says Conyers, but it is the Christian hope that love will win out and bind everything together in a web of divine calling.[32] Conyers argues that power became an end in itself because nominalist thought led theology to identify God with absolute power. This identification changes the imitation of God from participating in his goodness or love to emulating his power.[33] And power itself imitates love in a tempting way: "Since power (in terms of obligation, law, coercion, rule, organization) imitates the works of love, and indeed has a role in giving them a 'place' in which to work, we are tempted to think it is a worthy substitute for love. . . . It short-circuits the cultivation of the human spirit, and compels instead the cooperation of people through the agency (at one level or another) of fear."[34] Power offers relief from the suffering that love requires; "it tempts us to believe that it can accomplish quickly what love does only through patience and only fully accomplishes at the End of All

---

29. Conyers develops the importance of vocation for a true understanding of the place of the liberal arts. An instrumental view of education does not have room for the liberal arts, because "the classic understanding of liberal studies centers upon the work to be done *in* the learner, not *by* the learner." See Conyers, "Vocation and the Liberal Arts," 123.

30. Conyers, *Listening Heart*, 12.

31. Ibid., 32.

32. "Power as coercion has its place because the world is fallen. The power of affection or love has its place because the world longs for redemption" (ibid).

33. Ibid., 93–94.

34. Ibid., 71.

Things."[35] Where the modern world has chosen power over love, it has lost something valuable for community.

In contrast to power, love draws people together and provides a better foundation for community.[36] Love surpasses the obligation that power forces: "Through love the person is not driven but drives, for love has no need of rules; it has outstripped obligation already."[37] Vocation connects to the power of love, because "vocation appeals but does not intrude; it points the way but does not compel; its power consists in that it *attracts*, not that it drives. It is attractive rather than coercive. It moves us as does a beautiful poem or painting, not as a threat or an obligation can move us. It is love, not law. In philosophical language, it has to do with the final cause of things, not with the efficient cause."[38] True community requires vocation and its concept of the binding power of love rather than arbitrary force.

Vocation stands for an entire way of viewing the world. It acknowledges that the world precedes humans and is dependent on Another, a personal being who calls humans into community and into fellowship. This concept coincides with the theme of piety developed by Richard Weaver. Vocation aligns with the power of love, for vocation works by its attractive properties, not by coercive properties. When the modern world turned away from vocation, it turned toward a conception of the world dependent upon power and force, which are detrimental to true community. In a sense, Conyers diagnoses modernity's problems as in part fostering an antipathy toward vocation. Thus, the remedy for this antipathy is to reverse it through specific practices centered on themes. He identifies five such themes: attention, tolerance, place, rest, and imitation. These five themes show what it means to nurture practices that strengthen individuals' and communities' sense of vocation. Conyers begins with attention in general before directing that attention toward others (tolerance), toward that from whence we come (place), and toward that which calls us to our destiny (rest).[39] This series leads to the concept of imitation, which Conyers employs to describe the way the Christian community functions.

---

35. Ibid., 33.

36. Community is "uncoerced association and a certain communing of persons based upon common interests, a common vision of life, common experience, kinship, and place" (ibid., 97).

37. Ibid., 71.

38. Ibid., 103.

39. Conyers, *Listening Heart*, 113.

Attention

By attention, Conyers means something fairly simple: "to contemplate [an object] along with its purpose, its highest good, its *telos*."[40] Its opposite is the distraction that plagues the modern world. Conyers argues that modern people are distracted because we do not attend to the objects with which we deal. In the modern world "a thing becomes of value in a way that is rationally divorced from the thing itself, while in the traditional society the value is worked *into* the object and becomes identified with the object itself."[41] We are distracted because we shift from thinking of objects in their full sense (including teleology) and instead think of them via an abstract category such as money. This abstraction moves us away from God as the center because it denies the broader, God-constructed and God-sustained reality of which all objects are a part.[42]

Attention is the appropriate response to vocation.[43] To develop this concept, Conyers turns to the thought of Simone Weil, specifically an essay titled "Reflections on the Right Use of School Studies with a View to the Love of God."[44] In it, she argues that studies develop the practice of attention and that attention always ultimately turns us toward God. As Conyers observes, "No matter what the attention first turns us toward, it is in its highest and purest form always a reaching toward God, or more to the point, a waiting for God."[45] Attention means overthrowing "vain imaginations" and disposing of a self-centered view of existence.[46]

Conyers finds the concept of attention in the eschatological teaching of Jesus, especially in Matt 24 and 25. Here he identifies seven parables that prescribe alertness and watchfulness, an awareness extending beyond the present time to when the master returns: "it is the kind of awareness that sees *even in the present* the coming of the Lord."[47] Conyers relates attention to vision, noting that oftentimes in the Gospels the sign that the Messiah has come is that the blind recover their sight: "It announces the end of the

40. Ibid., 65.
41. Ibid., 54.
42. Ibid., 55.
43. Ibid., 114.
44. Ibid., 119.
45. Ibid.
46. Ibid., 121.
47. Ibid., 122.

inattentiveness that Isaiah described as the fundamental disorder of Israel, an inattentiveness occasioned by the unwillingness to listen or look."[48] These concepts do not center on the self but on something external and greater.

Attention focuses on the truth of reality rather than the anesthetizing power of wishes. It acknowledges that we are called into a journey with and toward God, a journey that requires pain because any true, deep, and lasting change or growth requires pain. The danger is not pain but distraction from the true way that things are. We become conformed to the things to which we attend, and the things to which we attend also influence the types of communities we form together.[49] Rather than seek the supposedly inevitable progress that the modern world advertises, we must truly attend to the world as God created it and seek to be conformed to what God calls us to be. Only then will we understand properly how to relate to others in community. Attending involves us in "that which it means to live in the promised and anticipated image of God, and that which is the concrete reality of the moment."[50] Attending focuses on concrete reality illuminated by the high purpose toward which God is calling people.

Tolerance

Next Conyers applies the concept of attention to interaction between people, especially with regard to differing ideas. He returns to the concept of tolerance, covering the ground from his book *The Long Truce*: "For more than three hundred years now, the term 'toleration' or 'tolerance' has served the purpose of disguising the agenda of powerful states and centralized bureaucracies—the great engines that help to produce a mass society."[51] After briefly reviewing the thesis of the previous book, he connects it to vocation

48. Ibid., 123.

49. "The biblical writers—the prophets and the Apostles—knew that ultimately we become conformed to that to which we most faithfully 'attend.' And to say that we are made in the *imago Dei*, means that that is the image for which we are made to conform. Attentiveness, faithfully engaging the truth, is the beginning and the true mark of progress of a genuinely human life. It is also the process out of which a human community comes into being. For the ends toward which we each are drawn, proves finally, to be the ends toward which we all are drawn in our several ways. Thus the openness of life toward the truth is also the openness of life toward one another" (ibid., 127).

50. Ibid., 66.

51. Ibid., 128.

and argues, "the lure of power and wealth in early modernity served as a highly potent distraction," because it theoretically justified setting aside the central vocation of humanity for the sake of power and wealth.[52]

In opposition to this false toleration, Conyers suggests the practice of toleration as a key aspect of recovering good habits necessary for vocation and life together. He explains that toleration "has more akin to silence than to discourse. It is the habit of not cutting off your interlocutor before listening to what he or she has to say."[53] Rooted in the "idea of truth that can be common to everyone because it is *real* for everyone,"[54] tolerance opens to the truth and recognizes that the truth is true for all people. Recovering a true sense of vocation requires the habit of carefully listening to others for the sake of discerning real truth rather than smoothing over differences using various modern strategies. Truly attending to people requires the genuine practice of toleration.[55]

Place

Next Conyers turns to the notion of place,[56] for "the concreteness of vocation depends upon the fact that it is addressed to real people who reside in real places; and apart from real places, there are no real people."[57] He first shows this concern for "place" and its importance for theology in a 1983 article on liberation theology. There he argues that speaking on the concrete level of real individuals in real places connects to people of any age and place: "No matter how concrete and particular we get, there is something

52. Ibid., 134. Conyers also started to develop the theme of distraction in "Rescuing Tolerance," 44.

53. Conyers, *Listening Heart*, 135.

54. Ibid., 136.

55. This "return" to the practice of toleration is the weakest of Conyers's practice-centered themes. Since he has gone to such great lengths to problematize toleration in connection with the modern world, it would be wiser to turn to other Christian virtues than to try to rehabilitate a lost practice that can be confusing in connection with modern abuses. Instead of proposing right toleration, Conyers would be better served by focusing on virtues such as humility, hospitality, forgiveness, and love. He sees these as undergirding the practice of toleration, but by turning again to that language he produces more confusion rather than clarity and a path forward.

56. An excellent article on Conyers's understanding of place is Conyers, "Why the Chattahoochee Sings," 99–106. This article, written in 2001, serves as the basis for the treatment of place in *Listening Heart*.

57. Conyers, *Listening Heart*, 141.

so common, so inalienable, in humanity that we can each view that bit of experience with sympathy and profit."[58] This view provided him with a critique of liberation theology, which, though claiming to deal in the concrete, actually dealt more in the "middle" at the level of categories of people, not with real, actual people. The idea of "place" and concreteness continued to play a role in his thought on modernity, and it ties in clearly with the thought of the Southern Agrarians and Richard Weaver.

Conyers notes that in modern times, the tendency to abstraction weakens the importance of place, and the modern spirit of conquest changes the way people relate to real places.[59] However, people are not called to be *conquerors* of places but *stewards* of places. The modern world "is about the dream of always transcending limits. 'Place' always ties us to earth, to the land, to the dust from which we came, and to the good creation that is not our own creation but is made by Another. 'Place' humbles us, but it also causes us to think (as Gerhart Niemeyer used to say) about real possibilities instead of possible realities."[60] In an earlier work Conyers's expressed the sentiment well: "The realm that moves beyond actually existing people and things necessarily moves beyond love."[61] Place provides the real context for human living.

Place is significant not only in being particular but also in the way that it connects individuals to universal reality. "A place is significant, and we speak and sing of it, because it offers to us a door by which we know what is true for all people, everywhere. It doesn't just speak of itself—though it never ceases to speak of itself—but it speaks of that which is truly catholic, truly universal—not bound by, but prior to, time and space."[62] Conyers relates this way in which place ties us to the universal to the incarnation. The way that the incarnation as a doctrine functions in Conyers's argument will be dealt with in more detail later. He turns to Eudora Welty to argue that place is important because it is where people put down roots, roots that reach a deep and running vein that is eternal and consistent.[63]

58. Conyers, "Liberation Theology," 306.

59. Conyers showed the intuition that the concrete serves to root the universal and provide access to it. In dealing with patriotism, Conyers argued that many will talk about love in the abstract but are unable to love their real neighbor. See Conyers, "Is Patriotism Christian?," 11–12.

60. Conyers, *Listening Heart*, 147.

61. Conyers, "Revival of Joachite Apocalyptic Speculation," 211.

62. Conyers, *Listening Heart*, 151.

63. Ibid., 152.

Rest

In turning to the practice of rest, Conyers draws on the idea of purpose that orients life. He briefly covers ground from his diagnosis of modernity, pointing out the fact that the modern world shifted from viewing reality as pursuing rest or purpose to viewing it as being in constant motion. This diagnosis critiques the loss of final causation and the exaltation of the material and efficient causes as the only causes worth considering.[64] In this conception of the world, human willing imposes any meaning or purpose. Meaning is not something already put there by Another.

To draw out the concept of rest, Conyers turns specifically to the work of Simms.[65] Reflecting on some of Simms's poetry, Conyers notes that the theme "underscored the remarkable difference between a society whose aim is a settled and harmonious life, and one whose aim is pressing toward the limits of industry and dynamism."[66] Conyers views Simms's social criticism as a kind of theology, "for he understands society always in the light of its being called into being by God, the creator and redeemer."[67] Three themes emerge in Simms's social criticism: "domesticity and civilization, the sirens of money and commerce, and the idea of vocation or purpose in life."[68] The concept of "domesticity" refers to the intention to be in a place long-term. Mobility and transitoriness decrease people's power to develop civilizing institutions because they do not think about long-term needs. Money and commerce tempt people to reductionism, because they subordinate social goals to money and social life to commerce. This reduction has the same effect that rootlessness has, working against the cultivation of life-sustaining institutions that cultivate a broader perspective, vocation, and purpose. Simms's primary concern is to cultivate permanence in order to better achieve a sense of vocation and purpose.[69] He "uses terms

64. Ibid., 167.

65. Conyers focuses on the following Simms works: *Sabbath Lyrics: Or, Songs from Scripture* (1849); *The Social Principle: The True Source of National Permanence* (1843); and *Self-Development* (1847). One of these pieces, *Social Principle*, is considered the key to Simms's social philosophy. See Guilds, "Introduction," 28.

66. Conyers, "Simms's *Sabbath Lyrics*," 15. This attitude toward industry also demonstrates how Simms serves as one of Conyers's connections to the concerns and themes of the Southern Agrarians.

67. Conyers, *Listening Heart*, 156.

68. Ibid., 161.

69. Conyers explains Simms's overarching concern: "The life of a community, if it is to afford those forms of experience for which the human being is made, must with some

such as permanence, purpose, 'rest,' stability, eternity, and 'place' as the fundamentals of civilization. This contradicts the modern preference for movement, change, dynamism, progress, and revolution as indicators of health and prosperity."[70] Rest is an ancient idea: "In the ancient and medieval mind, the contrary of this inexorable ruin to which all things run in time is the notion of 'rest,' which means that time runs toward a goal or purpose—an eschatological goal, a telos—that is secure against the ravages of Chronos."[71] Simms's work develops the importance of both place and rest, but especially the overarching importance of purpose and vocation in giving order to human life and human communities.

Morality itself is at stake in the theme of rest. For "if motion is simply motion and there is no purpose in any motion, then the world itself is without any possible moral structure and our lives have no moral existence in which to participate."[72] In order to shape communities that have humane and generous expectations, we must see life itself as bearing moral purpose and the world "as a place in which the hardships, the suffering, and the uncertainties are but stations on the way to that for which each of us is cast into the world."[73] Without this sense, communities become places for individual wills to be brought into conflict, and power and violence serve as the only arbiters. While Conyers draws on Simms explicitly in connection with rest, Simms's shadow lurks in much of Conyers's response, especially in connection with vocation as an overarching theme.

Imitation

Conyers turns to the concept of imitation to draw vocation-centered practices together to propose a return to community. Ultimately, the vocation of the Christian is imitation of God facilitated by the body of Christ, the

---

degree of success discover and cultivate permanence in the midst of the inevitable flux, restlessness, and change in human existence" (ibid., 164).

70. Ibid., 165–66.

71. Conyers, "Simms's *Sabbath Lyrics*," 17.

72. Conyers, *Listening Heart*, 169.

73. Ibid., 170.

church.[74] Imitation is participation, a holistic following of a way.[75] Conyers situates this theme in the mimetic theory of René Girard. Girard explains violence by arguing that human desires are mimetic (drawn from others), and they thus lead to violent rivalry. Violence taken out on a scapegoat brings temporary peace. Conyers argues that the gospel, in contrast, disarms the scapegoat mechanism by taking the point of view of the victim and promoting self-giving. The power of imitation then is transferred to imitating Jesus, to the following of a way. Imitation works on the power of attraction, not the power of coercion.[76]

Though Conyers is obviously not the only theologian to deal with Girard, extensively comparing him to others falls beyond our scope because Conyers does not develop a Girardian theory. Instead, he uses a basic understanding of mimetic theory as a basis for imitation of God. Two works prove useful in providing more theological context to this discussion: Michael Kirwan's *Discovering Girard*[77] and *Girard and Theology*.[78] Put simply, mimetic theory "is a theory which seeks to elucidate the relationships—one might say the complicity—between religion, culture and violence." The theory has three parts: "the mimetic nature of desire; the scapegoat mechanism as the way in which societies regulate the violence generated by mimetic competition; and the importance of the Gospel revelation as the way in which the scapegoat mechanism is exposed and rendered ineffective."[79] Kirwan divides Girard's work into three groups: (1) three classic texts in which mimetic theory takes shape (*Deceit, Desire, and the Novel*; *Violence and the Sacred*; *Things Hidden since the Foundation of the World*); (2) other books in which mimetic theory is applied; and (3) important but less accessible sources such as interviews, journals, or books not translated into English.[80] In Conyers's treatment of Girard in *The Listening Heart*, he cites *The Scapegoat*.[81] While it is judged to be a good introduction to Girard, it

---

74. Conyers calls the church the "imitative community" (ibid., 185). Though he does not develop ecclesiology strongly in *Listening Heart*, his focus on vocation and imitation, and the idea of the church as imitative community, implies the centrality of the church and a strong role for ecclesiology.

75. Ibid., 178–79.

76. Ibid., 95.

77. Kirwan, *Discovering Girard*.

78. Kirwan, *Girard and Theology*.

79. Kirwan, *Discovering Girard*, 5.

80. Ibid., 7.

81. Girard, *The Scapegoat*. Conyers cites this same book in *Long Truce* when he makes brief mention of Girard. See *Long Truce*, 200, or 259n4.

would fall in Kirwan's second group of texts, "other books in which mimetic theory is applied." It was written in 1982, almost five years after the last of Kirwan's "classic texts." While Conyers's use of Girard alludes to an acquaintance with other texts as well, *The Scapegoat* is what he uses.

While Kirwan's *Discovering Girard* provides a basic outline of mimetic theory, his *Girard and Theology* provides helpful connections between Girard's work and its reception among theologians: "What cannot be denied . . . is the extraordinary generative power of Girard's mimetic theory: its capacity to generate or provoke additional theoretical work of enormous range and calibre, which is relatively independent of Girard's own intellectual commitments."[82] Kirwan explores the influence of Girard on Dramatic Theology, associated with the University of Innsbruck and Raymund Schwager, and the convergence of Girard's thought with Karl Rahner's "theological anthropology." Finally, he explores the impact of Girard on theories of sacrifice and atonement, biblical criticism, and political and liberation theologies. Kirwan shows that theological uses of Girard are diverse.

This brief foray into Kirwan's work leads to a guarded assessment of Conyers's use of Girard. Conyers is quite brief and basic: he takes Girard at face value and then draws conclusions from what Girard says. He does not develop it but uses it as a basis for arguing for the imitation of God. He focuses not on the mechanism as related to explaining violence, but as related to imitation, which he traces back into early Christianity.

The early church encouraged imitation through the teaching of Jesus and the apostles and through the use of imitation in cultivating Christian lives. On one hand, Conyers makes room for violent power, acknowledging that it will stand alongside the new order of the gospel as long as the fallen world exists. Violent power is meant to restrain evil while the gospel works positive good in the world.[83] However, Christians build community around a calling to imitate Christ's generosity, what Conyers calls "the mimetic rivalry of giving" built around a pattern of serving, giving to, and loving others.[84] This notion leads to the concept that all members of the community are one—not equal—in that they receive *different* gifts that contribute to the overall unity.[85] In this way, "the church itself is an imitative community,

---

82. Kirwan, *Girard and Theology*, 32.

83. Conyers, *Listening Heart*, 180–81.

84. Ibid., 182.

85. Elsewhere Conyers develops this concept of gift in connection with the way we

one devoted to learning the pattern of life found in Christ and practiced by those in the church."[86] This mimetic pattern flows from God and continues into the life of every believer.

The recovery of vocation via these practices has at least three important features that Conyers identifies. First, the sense of divine vocation is communal: the call of God embraces the world and all who are in it, drawing people not into a mimetic rivalry of violence but a mimetic rivalry of generosity. Second, the virtues of generosity, kindness, mercy, and forgiveness fit better in this view of life. Third, this concept of vocation has more room for true difference, for

> races, genders, language groupings, and the like, are classically points of misunderstanding and conflict. But they also represent ways in which we grasp the world differently, through different cultures and sentiments, through various metaphors and syntax. As such, each of these human differences can be the basis for understanding existence in a valid, albeit partial, way. Thus with our insights, shaded toward different emphases, enjoying and using the world in our slightly different ways, we are enabled to enrich the greater community.[87]

In fact, "While giving expression to what is temporally divided, we begin together to give witness to what is finally united. For the end of all things is the God who calls us, in whom we find rest, by whose one light we find our separate ways toward that city 'not made with hands, eternal, in heaven.'"[88] For Conyers, it all boils down to an essential argument: "Only when members of a community understand life as a response to a large and generous world, created by a great and merciful Providence, will the possibilities of life together become more fully realized."[89]

Conyers's "practice-centered themes" serve as footholds for developing healthy communities, the bonds of which help counteract the modern tendency to isolate existence between the twin poles of the sovereign centralized power and the autonomous individual. They focus on recovering

---

conceive of life itself, arguing that "our experience of the world moves us toward one or the other of opposing attitudes. Either life is a gift or it is a product of my will. The more we move toward that latter expression of life, the more the absolute necessity of grace eludes us." Conyers, "Living Under Vacant Skies," 16.

86. Conyers, *Listening Heart*, 185.

87. Ibid., 192.

88. Ibid.

89. Ibid., 193.

and sustaining the Christian idea of vocation. In order to better understand what undergirds this turn to vocation and the associated themes, we turn to the role that traditional doctrinal themes play in Conyers's work.

Traditional Doctrinal Themes

While most of Conyers's constructive work on navigating modernity focuses on the idea of vocation, traditional doctrinal themes play two roles: he often brings doctrines explicitly into the discussion, and doctrines also implicitly support other themes. Two in particular are important: the Trinity and the incarnation. For Conyers, a proper understanding of the Trinity impacts our understanding of what the *imago Dei* is and what it means to imitate God. The incarnation provides the logic for the importance of the particular, especially with regard to place, as hinted at earlier.

Trinity

The doctrine of the Trinity corrects inappropriate conceptions of power in the modern world. After the shift to nominalism, God became more identified with absolute power, and thus imitating God meant exercising power over the world.[90] This change fed into the modern desire for control and the emphasis on the human will as the creator of meaning and significance: "God, therefore, whose reality ultimately expresses the end of all existence, is identified with power."[91] However, Conyers, drawing partly on the work of Moltmann, points to the Trinity as a helpful corrective to this tendency.

Focusing on the Trinity redefines the way we understand God, moving away from identifying God with power through the assertion of the divine will and toward a concept of love. God's unity in diversity opens up better possibilities: "For, by virtue of the Trinitarian nature of God, the significance of God's unity is shared with his diversity. In answer to the question, 'What is real, the unity of things or the diversity of things?' the Trinity answers *both*."[92] This idea helps Conyers accept the critique of power of someone like Moltmann without entirely rejecting hierarchy. Monotheism taken as a replacement for trinitarian doctrine is dangerous because it irons

90. Conyers, *Long Truce*, 202.

91. Ibid., 204.

92. Ibid., 212.

out difference and emphasizes power, but a proper trinitarian view of God opens up space for difference while still being oriented to a hierarchy of love and goodness.[93] For "love itself constructs a hierarchy of values: we love, or should love, those things most valuable more than those things that are of less value. We make judgments on the basis of that hierarchy of values. We anticipate or hope for things that are of proximate and immediate importance, or of ultimate importance."[94]

The function of the Trinity in Conyers's thought becomes clearer when brought into conversation with contemporary work on the Trinity, specifically social trinitarianism (ST). ST of various sorts uses the Trinity as a model for social relations, and this approach has fallen victim to a significant amount of criticism.[95] ST emerges from a trend in contemporary systematic theology to reclaim the doctrine of the Trinity, which by many accounts was neglected in the theological writings of the preceding several centuries. In an essay promoting the ST viewpoint, John Franke ties various thinkers to ST: John Zizioulas, Jürgen Moltmann, Wolfhart Pannenberg, Leonardo Boff, Colin Gunton, Alan Torrance, Millard Erickson, and Stanley Grenz.[96] In essence, ST argues that there was a divide between the way the Eastern and Western churches understood the Trinity. The Western emphasis on oneness, channeled particularly through Augustine, came to negatively impact the modern world. On the other hand, the Eastern emphasis on relationality among the persons provides a corrective to these Western problems.

This use of the Trinity has come under significant criticism recently. In an essay analyzing the problems of ST, Mark Husbands notes two primary issues. First, he argues that ST fails to preserve an ontological distinction between God and humanity, a distinction needed to maintain an order consistent with their distinct natures. For Husbands, "The inherent danger in failing to maintain this ontological distinction is the possibility that one's doctrine of God will be eclipsed by any number of contemporary social, cultural or political concerns."[97] Second, he argues that while social trinitarians claim to hearken back to an Eastern understanding of the Trin-

---

93. Ibid., 217.

94. Ibid., 214.

95. See, for example, Leftow, "Anti-Social Trinitarianism," 203–50. See also Holmes, "Three Versus One?," 77–89.

96. Franke, "God Is Love," 113.

97. Husbands, "Trinity Is Not Our Social Program," 121.

ity, especially in the work of the Cappadocian fathers, they in fact fail to read these sources correctly. Husbands provides a helpful overview of contemporary historical work on these issues, done primarily by Lewis Ayres and Michel René Barnes,[98] and he also gives his own reading of Gregory of Nyssa that shows the problems with ST.

Beyond the question of whether ST uses the doctrine of the Trinity correctly—especially as received from the early church—is the question of whether Christians are to *use* the doctrine of the Trinity at all. Kathryn Tanner broaches this idea in an article on the Trinity in particular connection to political theology. She argues that we should not focus on the Trinity simply to apply what we learn to ourselves; instead, we should learn from the Trinity what God is doing for humans, which then has implications for how humans relate to one another.[99] As Daniel Treier and David Lauber explain it, "We learn about the Father, Son and Holy Spirit not to reproduce trinitarian relations, but to participate in appropriate human relations with the triune God and accordingly with each other."[100] The trend in contemporary theology is away from ST and its use of the Trinity.

The issue of ST brings up two questions related to Conyers's treatment of the Trinity. First, where does Conyers fit with regard to ST? Second, how exactly does the turn to the Trinity function in Conyers's work, and if he uses the Trinity inappropriately, is his project marred beyond repair?

Conyers draws on the diversity within the Trinity to counter the emphasis on absolute power seen in modern politics, following the work of Moltmann, whom some consider the leading figure in ST. A close examination of what Conyers does with the Trinity and the social implications he draws distinguishes him from a "hard" ST: he does not argue that the various roles within the Trinity correspond to various roles within society, and he does not explicitly argue that individual Christians are called into the trinitarian relations. Instead, Conyers proposes what I call a "soft" ST: he argues that the existence of threeness in God short-circuits any attempt to identify God with absolute power and instead tends Christians toward forms of order that recognize difference. This in turn weakens the tendency to seek power and control in the world, but it does not equate certain

98. For instance, see Barnes, "*De Regnon* Reconsidered," 51–79; Barnes, "Augustine in Contemporary Trinitarian Theology," 237–50; Barnes, "Rereading Augustine's Theology of the Trinity," 145–76; Ayres, *Nicaea and Its Legacy*; Ayres, *Augustine and the Trinity*.

99. Tanner, "Trinity," 319–32. Treier and Lauber draw on Tanner positively in their treatment of these questions. See Treier and Lauber, "Introduction," 16.

100. Treier and Lauber, "Introduction," 16.

aspects with certain Persons of the Trinity. Conyers turns to the Trinity to counteract the *potentia absoluta* of nominalism more than he seeks to make the Trinity a social program.

Approaching the question of Conyers's relation to ST from another angle, we turn to his teaching on the Trinity in his *Basic Christian Theology*. In trying to explain the concept of "person" in a way that avoids modern notions of individualism, Conyers turns to the idea of relationality. He says, "This brings us to the heart of what is meant by the persons of the Godhead. It is seen in this, in fact, that God—and, by extension, reality itself—is profoundly and even essentially relational."[101] In this work he does not make the typical ST moves from the Trinity to social programs, but his reliance on relationality clearly connects him to the dominant thought of ST.

Next we turn to the second question, regarding the viability of Conyers's project in light of what, in the eyes of some, would be termed trinitarian missteps. Assessing this requires understanding the role that the Trinity plays, what "work" it does. While Conyers's use of Moltmann and his emphasis on the diversity in the Trinity certainly connect him to ST in some way, the Trinity functions merely to counter absolute power in his argument, not as the major foundation for any particular social ordering. The connection to the influence of ST cannot be denied due to the connection to Moltmann and the language Conyers often employs, but his project is not tied to the fate of ST because Conyers's "use" of the Trinity plays a minor role in the entire project.

For Conyers, the doctrine of the Trinity does not provide a specific pattern for social relationships so much as it shifts our emphasis from power to love and prepares us for different conceptions of power.[102] Conyers demonstrates a similar move from trinitarian doctrine in an earlier work on cloning. He says, "The questions raised, coincidentally, correspond to three values inherent in the Christian view of life: the distinction within life, the unity of life, and the givenness of life. As the Trinity combines distinction, unity, and self-giving, mutually receiving love, so the natural experience of birth seems to give daily witness to those same three qualities. The ethical must come to grips with those three."[103] Here he is not proposing the

101. Conyers, *Basic Christian Theology*, 44.

102. "In a word, Trinitarian thought prepares us for thinking of society in terms of distributed roles, separation of powers, and a federalist view of social associations." Conyers, *Long Truce*, 212.

103. Conyers, "Cloning and the Moral Imagination," n.p.

Trinity as a pattern for social relationships but shows how qualities related to the Trinity connect to modern concerns. He does not so much *use* the doctrine of the Trinity for certain social ends as he shows how the logic of the Trinity promotes certain values and counters abuses in modern life. Just as Conyers saw the Trinity serving to form the moral imagination in relation to cloning, here he draws on it to form the theopolitical imagination. The Trinity protects against the modern quest for power and control by preventing monotheism from being used to legitimate forms of power.

In the end, Conyers's use of the Trinity does fall victim in some ways to the critiques of ST. However, this problem does not devastate the entire project. For the most part, Conyers uses the Trinity to reject the conception of God as pure power that occurred after the rise of nominalism; such resistance could be made from other theological quarters as well. ST explanations of the Trinity are not vital to this move, because Conyers could just have simply rejected the nominalist turn that exacerbated this problem with power. This argument would work the same way in his overall project. Thus, while Conyers's connections to ST are rightly questioned and criticized, it does not negate his contribution. In fact, as Stephen Holmes notes, "*social trinitarianism uses the doctrine of the Trinity to answer questions the fathers answered by Christology*,"[104] for while Christians are not told to imitate the Trinity, we are told to imitate Christ. Conyers makes this move as well. His positive work is more dependent upon other doctrines, such as the incarnation, which connects more clearly to the practice of imitation that he highlights in his work.

Incarnation

Conyers rightly holds the incarnation to be central to Christian theology.[105] This focus starts with his treatment of toleration. The doctrinal basis for this practice of toleration is the incarnation.[106] Conyers founds toleration not with speculation or abstract principles, but by calling attention to the

104. Holmes, "Three Versus One?," 88. Holmes's italics.

105. In *Basic Christian Theology*, Conyers, referring to various aspects of orthodox Christology, says, "These points of reference about the person of Christ proved to be the essential cornerstone of Christian theology" (103). However, he did not develop the connections to the doctrine of place as he did later in his work, which is understandable since *Basic Christian Theology* is meant to be an introductory-level textbook.

106. Conyers, *Long Truce*, 232.

historical fact "that here is a pervasive belief that has had enormous impact upon the traditions of the West, is at the same time not confined to the West, and offers a basis for practice. And the practice it engenders is, by the force of its own internal logic, one of tolerance and openness toward other human beings."[107] The incarnation inspires a certain level of humility that allows for listening to others: "To do so—to listen in expectation of hearing truth from others whose doctrine differs from our own—is the highest form of loyalty to the insight that we all rely upon a common reality, created by the One God who makes himself known in human flesh."[108] The incarnation provides a path forward in three ways. First, it asserts that there is meaning in existence without reducing meaning to a set of given propositions. Instead, the meaning of existence is seeking the telos that can only be found in God.[109] Second, the incarnation reveals the paradoxical relationship of authority and humility. The humiliation of God's becoming human in the incarnation is at the same time the exaltation of humans in God: "Power is truly exercised as it is given up. Humiliation and exaltation go together."[110] And third, the incarnation opens the way toward trust rather than fear as the key to relationships between individual humans and between humans and the world. The incarnation "asserts that though the world is full of suffering, and often warrants fear and mistrust, it is nevertheless not destined to remain that way, and it is therefore not essentially a reality to be feared and distrusted."[111] The incarnation turns from fear and points to trust.

The theme of "place" and its importance for vocation also rests to a degree on the doctrine of the incarnation. The incarnation ties together the particular and the universal.[112] Conyers states, "The 'incarnational' truth of place is that particular places, with their own regional characteristics, and their own kind of community, nevertheless speak of that which is true for all people everywhere, and for all time."[113] In fact, the importance of place reflects "the Mystery of the Incarnation. That is, God himself, made himself known, in a particular man, of a particular people, in a particular

107. Ibid.

108. Ibid., 233.

109. Ibid., 237.

110. Ibid., 239.

111. Ibid., 240–41.

112. "The truth of the Incarnation is that the eternal and the particular are forever tied together." Conyers, *Listening Heart*, 150.

113. Ibid.

place. And he did so not in order to lead men to *that* place (as thousands of pilgrims thought), but in order to lead them to their own place—and through that place to the God who made them and *placed them there*."[114] In this case, the particular nature of the incarnation combats the abstracting tendencies of the modern world in order to strengthen the importance of particular people in their particular places. This is not because there is no universal, but because access to the universal comes through rootedness in the particular. Conyers uses the incarnation to combat the universalizing tendencies of modernity, as well as the tendencies of nominalism, which holds that only individual things truly exist. The incarnation helps us understand that place is particular but it connects to the universal.[115]

Conyers's reflections on modernity are theologically guided and determined, although the various doctrines in play tend to exist below the surface of other themes that he draws on. This treatment of Trinity and incarnation demonstrates how these two particular doctrines undergird and provide substance for his project.

CONCLUSION

We can summarize Conyers's response to modern problems with the concept of vocation. It forms his critique of modernity and postmodernity (vocational theology versus theology of choice), and it informs his vision for navigating the modern world. For him this idea includes choices of theological method and visions of the world generated by figures such as William Gilmore Simms, but it is also firmly rooted in a biblically formed imagination. It yields important related themes that can serve as resources for resisting modern ills. His work also resists easy conservative-liberal categorization, exposes problems in modern institutions, and uses the Bible as a nuanced and powerful resource, employing it to shape vision, imagination, and themes and avoiding oversimplification and proof-texting. But there is one more way that Conyers work addresses the weaknesses earlier identified in evangelical theopolitical imagination: he also serves as a bridge to dialogue with the wider world of Christian political theology.

114. Ibid., 153.

115. In another article, Conyers writes, "The incarnation does not mean that God became nature, in which case nature becomes our master. Nor does it mean that God conquered nature, in which case nature is seen as our foe. Instead, He made Himself at home in nature. As John the Evangelist said, 'He "made his dwelling among us".'" Conyers, "Simms's Incarnational Theology," 84–92.

CHAPTER 5

A Vocational Political Theology

INTRODUCTION

The works of Baptist theologian A. J. Conyers and the works of Roman Catholic theologian William Cavanaugh provide an opportunity for drawing together evangelical and Catholic thought on questions of political theology. Their writing is analogous in many ways, and they can strengthen one another while also leading to a common social imagination for navigating the modern world, especially with regard to the state,[1] consumerism, and globalization.

Over the last twenty years, Cavanaugh has become a leading voice in Christian political theology, seeking to influence Christian moral imagination. Cavanaugh describes his project:

> I am a Christian theologian, and I write in the first instance for other Christians. My principal concern is to help Christians to be realistic about what they can expect from the powers and principalities of the present day, especially the nation-state and the market, and to urge Christians not to invest the entirety of their social and political presence in these institutions. My goal as a Christian

---

1. In this chapter, I use "state" and "nation-state" synonymously, since I find the same in Cavanaugh. However, one critique of Cavanaugh, which I will address below, is that he pays insufficient attention to the role of nationalism outside of the state's purview. See Anderson, *Chosen Nation*.

theologian is to help the church be more faithful to God in Jesus Christ. In the present day, I think that faithfulness means taking a hard look at political and economic structures many Christians take for granted.[2]

Cavanaugh provides a compelling description of the faithful church with reference to the nation-state, consumerism, and globalization and develops important ways to re-conceptualize the Christian understanding of space and time. He deconstructs how the modern world determines and shapes Christian imagination in directions that are counter to Christian theology—Christian soteriology, in particular—and he draws on theology as a source for resisting these conceptions.

I group Cavanaugh's work into four clusters: three related to his diagnosis (the nation-state, capitalism and consumerism, and globalization) and one related to his remedy (the Eucharist). For Cavanaugh, the Eucharist serves as the remedy because it provides an explicitly Christian formation that corrects the problematic formation of modernity. We will consider how the Eucharist informs his view of the nation-state, consumerism, and globalization and forms his solutions while also informing his very diagnosis of modernity's problems. The Eucharist "brackets" Cavanaugh's treatment of modernity; it serves as his standard for evaluating modernity and as his basis for remedying the problems he identifies.[3]

Conyers's "vocational theology" serves a similar function, bracketing the diagnosis and remedy. As I progress through these clusters of Cavanaugh's work, I bring Conyers and Cavanaugh into dialogue to show how each strengthens and challenges the other.[4] Conyers's work contributes depth in diagnosing what modernity is and provides an ecclesially broad response that Cavanaugh lacks, a response motivated by Conyers's desire for evangelical theology to develop a "truly catholic vision." Making such a comparison demonstrates the constructive potential that Conyers's work

2. Cavanaugh, "If You Render Unto God," 607.

3. I must thank Nathan Willowby for pointing this "bracketing" out to me in one of our many conversations on the development of this book.

4. While no reference to Cavanaugh exists in Conyers's corpus to my knowledge, Cavanaugh does demonstrate at least some exposure to Conyers. In his "Killing for the Telephone Company," Cavanaugh cites Conyers's *Long Truce*. However, he does not interact with Conyers's overarching thesis in the book; instead, he merely employs a minor portion, Conyers's treatment of Locke and the common good. See Cavanaugh, "Killing for the Telephone Company," 253–54. Alternatively, see the reprinted version of this essay, in *Theopolitical Imagination*, 21–22.

provides for a new wave of evangelical political theology, a wave that takes the nation-state more critically and seeks more nuanced approaches to forming Christian moral imagination in relation to navigating the modern world.

CAVANAUGH'S DIAGNOSIS OF MODERNITY

Cavanaugh's diagnosis of the modern world clusters into three frames. First, his work on the emergence and dominance of the nation-state shows that the nation-state employs various types of liturgies that discipline Christians to see the world and serve the state in a certain way. Christians then often fail to consider the full implications of the state's project or its origin. Second, his work on consumerism shows how the logic of the market has come to influence Christians' lives. Third, his analysis of globalization and its connection to both consumerism and the nation-state challenges the optimism with which many Christians view the world. We explore each of these in turn to better understand Cavanaugh's vision of modernity's problems.[5]

Nation-State

Cavanaugh's attention to the nation-state's power has spanned his theological career, from his dissertation on torture (Duke University, 1996)[6] to his book *The Myth of Religious Violence* (2009) and beyond.[7] It has also garnered him attention in the field of political theology. At the root of his various arguments about the nation-state, Cavanaugh shows that the nation-state operates soteriologically: it has become a simulacrum, offering the definitive solutions to humanity's problems. As he states, "public devotion formerly associated with Christianity in the West never did go

---

5. In this analysis, I rely primarily on Cavanaugh's published books because in most cases they serve as the most developed version of his ideas expressed in earlier essays. For instance, three of the books are collections of previous essays, which demonstrates Cavanaugh's own perception of those essays as important enough to his project to merit republication in book form. In the case of his *Myth of Religious Violence*, he worked on the themes from the publication of his 1995 "A Fire Strong Enough to Consume the House" to the publication of the book in 2009. While I will turn to other essays at times, the books will be the central component for these reasons.

6. Published as Cavanaugh, *Torture and Eucharist*.

7. For instance, see Cavanaugh, "Invention of Fanaticism," 226–37.

away, but largely migrated to a new realm defined by the nation-state."[8] The nation-state shapes the way Christians perceive reality, both what is real and what is possible. In what follows I expound Cavanaugh's work on the nation-state by first explaining his exposure of the nation-state's creation myth, and second exploring the way the nation-state frames reality and posits an alternative soteriology.[9] Setting up this foundation allows us to move on to Cavanaugh's treatment of consumerism and globalization, which are connected to his work on the nation-state.

The nation-state maintains its relatively unquestioned power by telling a tale of its origins that sets up a problem for which the state is the only solution. In *The Myth of Religious Violence*, Cavanaugh dismantles the idea that religion is a feature of human life that transcends historical or cultural considerations—one that is essentially distinct from "secular" features such as politics and economics and that has a particularly dangerous inclination to violence.[10] He calls this idea the "myth of religious violence," and it is a "myth" not (only) because it is untrue but because it wields power in forming a particular view of reality. Once the myth is accepted, something must tame religion by restricting its access to public power. The nation-state then appears as natural, because it corresponds to the universal category of "religion" and protects citizens from religions' excesses.

Cavanaugh dismantles this myth in four stages. First, he challenges the definition of the term *religion* in its contemporary use. Academic arguments that view religion as absolutist, divisive, and nonrational fail because they cannot find a coherent way to separate religious violence from secular violence.[11] This confusion is due to the way we understand religion

8. Cavanaugh, *Migrations of the Holy*, 1. The "migration" terminology comes from the work of Sheldon Wolin, whose 1960 *Politics and Vision* has recently been rereleased in an expanded edition. For an analysis of Wolin's use of migration and its relation to the work of de Lubac, see Pecknold, "Migrations of the Host," 77–101.

9. Cavanaugh's development of these ideas does not follow this order, since he began with his dissertation work on Pinochet in Chile. In that work, Cavanaugh argued that torture serves as the nation-state's anti-liturgy, disciplining and forming a social body, and that the church's main resource for counterformation is the Eucharist. See Cavanaugh, *Torture and Eucharist*.

10. Cavanaugh, *Myth of Religious Violence*, 3.

11. "The arguments I examine attempt to separate a category called religion, which is prone to violence because it is absolutist (Hick), divisive (Marty), and nonrational (Appleby), from a secular, or nonreligious, reality that is less prone to violence, presumably because it is less absolutist, more unitive, and more rational. As we shall see, such arguments do not stand up to scrutiny, because they cannot find any coherent way to separate religious from secular violence" (ibid., 16).

as a result of the modern nation-state and its constitution of power. The older term *religio* was used to refer to clergy in orders rather than diocesan clergy, or to a virtue, not to a category as the modern term *religion* does.[12] In modern times, *religion* is used to describe a much broader concept: a universal genus of which the various religions are species. Each religion is demarcated by a system of propositions, and religion is identified with interior impulse. It is thus distinct from secular pursuits like politics and economics. The functionalist definition of religion (focusing on how people behave and what provides meaning to that behavior) is better than the substantivist one (focusing on religions as certain types of belief systems), but really the functionalist approach just ends up being tautological: people do violence on behalf of those things they take seriously enough to do violence for. It also clings to essentialism, thinking there really is something called religion out there. By drawing out these problems with the term *religion*, Cavanaugh shows that it is not as stable as it first appears.

Second, Cavanaugh shows that what counts as religion depends on who is in power and what it is advantageous for those in power to do:[13]

> Within the West, religion was invented as a transhistorical and transcultural impulse embedded in the human heart, essentially distinct from the public business of government and economic life. . . . Outside the West, the creation of religion and its secular twin accompanied the attempts of colonial powers and indigenous modernizing elites to marginalize certain aspects of non-Western cultures and create public space for the smooth functioning of state and market interests.[14]

In order for the state to exercise power and for the market to run smoothly, differences such as religion had to be neutralized. For the state and the market to gain power, religion had to be defined in a way that would eliminate or privatize differences problematic to the state's and market's functioning.

Third, Cavanaugh recasts the common narrative about the wars of religion as the "creation myth" for the modern nation-state because it describes why the nation-state came to be and secures its continued necessity. Cavanaugh identifies four features of this creation myth: (1) combatants opposed each other based on religious difference;[15] (2) the primary cause

12. Ibid., 60–69.
13. Ibid., 59.
14. Ibid., 120–21.
15. Ibid., 142.

of the wars was religion, as opposed to merely political, economic, or social causes;[16] (3) religious causes must be at least analytically separable from political, economic, and social causes at the time of the wars;[17] and (4) the rise of the modern state was not a cause of the wars, but rather provided a solution to the wars.[18] These features describe the "wars of religion" as they are customarily understood in history and social science.

Cavanaugh questions these accepted features. In the wars of religion, a significant portion of the violence occurred between members of the same church, and members of different churches often collaborated. It is impossible to separate religious motives from political, economic, and social causes. And the idea that the advent of the state solved the violence ignores abundant evidence that state-building was perhaps the most significant cause of violence.[19] So, while the traditional version of the wars of religion makes the nation-state seem necessary to curb violence, Cavanaugh exposes this interpretation as problematic at best and shows that it masks the nation-state's own complicity in and instigation of violence.

Fourth, Cavanaugh analyzes the way this myth functions in contemporary society, focusing on separation between church and state, international relations, and the justification of violence against non-Western Others, especially Muslims. His point is not to deny that violence sometimes occurs because of religious motives but to broaden the scrutiny of violence: "We must restore the full and complete picture of violence in our world, to level the playing field so that violence of all kinds is subject to the same scrutiny."[20] Cavanaugh argues that the myth of religious violence allows critics to label state violence as "rational," as opposed to the "irrational" violence of religion. The myth, then, legitimates some forms of violence and delegitimizes others, resulting in a phenomenon in which American Christians would never kill for their God but would take killing and dying for their country for granted, without questioning the challenges this might make to the supremacy of the Christian God.

This myth advanced by the nation-state establishes the state itself as the necessary savior in the face of "violent" religions. In fact, Cavanaugh argues that the modern state is best understood as an alternative soteriology

16. Ibid., 151.
17. Ibid., 156.
18. Ibid., 160.
19. Ibid., 177.
20. Ibid., 230.

to that of the church.[21] The state serves as a simulacrum, a false copy, of the body of Christ.[22] In the state's conception of reality, all individuals are related to the sovereign head, the state. Individuals are in danger of having their rights interfered with by other individuals and institutions, so the state serves to safeguard individuals and their rights.[23] This relationship of the state and the individual replaces an earlier understanding of social relations as rooted in participation with an understanding of social relations as rooted in individualism:

> The state *mythos* is based on a "theological" anthropology that precludes any truly social process. The recognition of our participation in one another through our creation in the image of God is replaced by the recognition of the other as the bearer of individual rights, which may or may not be given by God, but which serve only to separate what is mine from what is thine. Participation in God and in one another is a threat to the formal mechanism of contract, which assumes that we are *essentially* individuals who enter into relationship with one another only when it is to one's individual advantage to do so.[24]

And when each individual relies directly on the state, older forms of social solidarity are weakened and replaced.[25] In fact, "The main conflict of modern politics is not state versus individual, but state versus intermediate social group. The main actors today are the state and the individual. To protect the individual from interference, the state has had to overcome the power of other social groups."[26] The individual and the state are the supreme realities, and all other groups are evaluated by how they function in connecting these two.

Cavanaugh argues that Christians unwittingly accept the way that the state frames reality and thus view religion as a private matter. He likens the nation-state to a liturgy, which "can come to rival the church's liturgy for our bodies and our minds."[27] The state claims to be the keeper of the

21. Cavanaugh, *Theopolitical Imagination*, 9. Chapter 1, "The Myth of the State as Saviour," is a revision of "'A Fire Strong Enough to Consume the House,'" 397–420.

22. Cavanaugh, *Theopolitical Imagination*, 10.

23. Ibid., 44.

24. Ibid.

25. Cavanaugh, "Separation and Wholeness," 27–28.

26. Cavanaugh, "Body of Christ," 173.

27. Cavanaugh, *Migrations of the Holy*, 115. This chapter was originally published as "The Liturgies of Church and State," 25–30.

common good,[28] and the state and civil society "have become increasingly fused, such that little significant social action takes place wholly outside the funding, direct implementation, or regulation of the state."[29] So the state has become all-encompassing by fusing with civil society and absorbing "mediating institutions" to further its own project. In many ways, Christianity then becomes a servant of the state, meant to shape good citizens but not to challenge the state as the broader, orienting reality. The church and its operations take place on the stage set by the state.[30]

Cavanaugh's work can strengthen Conyers's by providing additional explanatory power that Conyers's position needs in two different areas. First, Cavanaugh's myth of religious violence provides an understanding of the development of the nation-state that harmonizes with Conyers's treatment of tolerance and can serve as an example of how the logic of toleration extended into other terminologies and concepts. Employing the insights from Cavanaugh's myth deepens Conyers's diagnosis of modernity while maintaining a similar trajectory. In addition to extending Conyers's diagnosis, taking into account Cavanaugh's myth helps Conyers deal with the rise of the nation-state in a more nuanced fashion. While Conyers acknowledges that the wars of religion had complicated issues as their cause, he still repeatedly accepts the basic version of the wars of religion, seeing them as an important step in the shift of the use of the term *toleration*, one of the central explorations of his political theology. The problem is that if one accepts the traditional understanding of the wars of religion, it could be argued that the idea of toleration needed to shift in order to promote the protection that the state provided against religious passions. So while Conyers's work does demonstrate how the term shifted and was used, taking into account the strengths of Cavanaugh's position would lead to a fuller concept of the development of the nation-state and other features of modernity.

Second and more significantly, Cavanaugh's work on intermediate associations identifies and remedies a limitation in Conyers's treatment of the same topic. In Conyers's diagnosis of modernity and proposals for

28. For more on this, see Cavanaugh, "Killing for the Telephone Company."

29. Cavanaugh, "If You Render Unto God," 614.

30. Instead, Cavanaugh thinks that Augustine's concept of two cities is relevant here. The state and the church are like two different plays being enacted on the same stage with the same props. The state is not the larger reality that situates the church. For more, see Cavanaugh, "From One City to Two," 299–321. This essay was republished as the second chapter of Cavanaugh, *Migrations of the Holy*.

remedies, he focuses on the idea of vocation. As he develops this concept, he emphasizes that God calls particular people to particular places and that a sense of place and community are significant. The strengthening of intermediate associations flows from this conviction, corresponding to his critique of the increasing bipolarity of life between isolated individuals and the strong, centralized state, which he develops in his diagnosis. For Conyers, one can begin with a commitment to calling and local situatedness and work from there to challenge the problematic bipolarity that he identifies in modern politics.

Cavanaugh's work, on the other hand, problematizes this approach. Like Conyers, Cavanaugh recognizes that the development of the nation-state in modernity demolished the sense of intermediate groups and associations that once provided security and guided people in their understanding and experience of life. Conyers uses language such as "dissolving" of intermediate associations and of their loss. However, Cavanaugh observes that these associations did not simply diminish; instead, they took up a different role, one subservient to the state. So, intermediate associations—where they do still exist and provide meaning and structure to individuals—usually take up their place on the stage as set by the nation-state. In other words, they promote the nation-state's picture of reality and serve to better assimilate individuals into it. The answer then cannot merely be to strengthen these intermediate associations, for this would be to strengthen the role of the state. Without Cavanaugh's more thorough critique of intermediate associations and the way that they serve the state's conception of reality, Conyers's focus on vocation can also be co-opted into the state's project.

The problem with intermediate associations can be clarified by drawing a recent critic of Cavanaugh into the conversation. In *Chosen Nation*, Brad Anderson articulates how nationalism emanates from within church communities when Scripture is co-opted and altered to shape American identity. In setting up his project, he argues that theopolitical scholars, in particular Cavanaugh, fail to see how nationalism can sprout up in places that are not controlled by the state. Thus, because Cavanaugh focuses so much on the state, Anderson charges that he fails to account for other sources of nationalism, such as the church. Cavanaugh's work "falters at crucial points in accurately discerning the church's own direct and even primary agency in the problem of nationalism. This is not to say that Cavanaugh ignores or rejects church complicity, but rather that he provides an incomplete account of the nature of the relationship between theology and nationalism, and hence of the church's role."[31] Cavanaugh fails to address the church's role because of his supposed inability to see church complicity.

For Anderson, the church is an example of a "non-state actor" that fuels nationalism via syncretism of particular theological and national narratives.[32] According to this perspective, Cavanaugh cannot account for the fact that "many nationalist movements are born and catalyzed apart from the state, led by a different set of elites quite apart from state operations, and driven by independently derived goals that are sometimes even a threat to the state establishment."[33] These movements rely on "prior elements of identity," demonstrating that the state is not the only driver of nationalism.[34] In fact, "it is key to an understanding of Christian nationalism as a process, not of *departicularizing* faith communities into an amorphous religious impulse, but rather of *reparticularizing* specific narratives of salvation history in new contexts for nationalist purposes."[35] In Anderson's assessment, Cavanaugh's argument cannot adequately account for this type of discourse, because Cavanaugh focuses on how the nation-state universalizes "religion" in order to marginalize it.

Anderson identifies a problem in Cavanaugh's thought, but the problem is actually solved by another aspect of Cavanaugh's work. On one hand, Anderson is correct that Cavanaugh's analysis does not account for the very particular way that Christian nationalism reparticularizes salvation narratives. On the other hand, Anderson does not see clearly how another element of Cavanaugh's work does in fact account for the phenomena Anderson observes in Christian nationalism. Cavanaugh argues that intermediate associations (which the church has unwittingly become in many ways) are not the same today as they were in the medieval period. While they once were able to challenge the state's power, they have become mediators of the nation-state's project. They facilitate the relationship between the autonomous individual and the strong, centralized power. Thus, everything that Anderson observes about church complicity in Christian nationalism fits with this observation: the church in these cases has taken up a role as a complicit intermediate association, serving the state project.

31. Anderson, *Chosen Nation*, 13.
32. Ibid., 19.
33. Ibid., 23.
34. Ibid., 26.
35. Ibid., 28.

Anderson perpetuates the same misunderstanding that Conyers does, but in different ways. Both see intermediate associations as too independent of the state. Anderson sees them as too strong and pushing in the wrong direction; Conyers sees them as too weak and as a potential for change if strengthened. For Anderson, these "non-state actors" promote nationalism apart from the state and thus must be accounted for separately in understanding the power of the state. For Conyers, these intermediate associations, if strengthened, can provide hope in resisting what he identifies as the "bipolar disorder" of modernity—the binary of the autonomous individual on the one hand and the powerful state on the other. Both Anderson and Conyers fail to take the disciplinary power of the nation-state as seriously as Cavanaugh does. Cavanaugh recognizes that while intermediate associations do indeed predate the modern state and appear to have powerful prior elements of identity, they have become complicit in promoting the state project. The theological shifts that Anderson sees in the church (on American exceptionalism and providence, for example) do not in fact challenge Cavanaugh's notion of the state but instead serve as further evidence that he is correct: the state has risen to such a level of disciplinary power over the very imagination of these other associations that they have reformed themselves to serve the state. The theological shifts Anderson identifies, though they occur in an association that predates the state, are evidence of the state's power.

The example of a local church that promotes Americanism can illustrate these differences. For Anderson, the local church that promotes Americanism is at fault for promoting national identity, and studies of nationalism must grapple with such churches as non-state promoters of nationalism. For Conyers, the local church is too weak due to an emphasis on a strong state and an independent individual, but if it were strengthened it could help solve some of the problems. For Cavanaugh, the local church promotes Americanism because of the state's forming power and reorientation of intermediate associations. The church is not an unfaithful or weak intermediate association but a complicit intermediate association, one ordered to the nation-state, subject to its taxonomy. If simply strengthened, it could strengthen the state's conception of reality rather than challenge it. So Anderson's solution is to stop the Americanism in the church, and Conyers's solution is to strengthen the notion of intermediate associations and the idea of vocation. Cavanaugh's solution takes into account the disciplinary power of the nation-state and sees that power as the primary problem, not nationalist churches or the weakness of some churches in forming people. Cavanaugh and Conyers are mostly on the same page with the importance of intermediate associations, but Cavanaugh is more explicit about the disciplinary power of the state and the need for more than strengthening what used to be referred to as intermediate associations. The entire power dynamic must be addressed. Many churches will continue to promote the state's view of reality, even if vocation is recovered, if the larger disciplinary power is not challenged.

Thus, Anderson's critique of Cavanaugh provides a clearer understanding of the importance of properly situating intermediate associations in the broader spectrum. Conyers takes the first step in situating these associations—he identifies the "bipolar disorder" but then fails to adequately take it into account in formulating his resistance to it. Appropriating this observation into Conyers's work requires taking more seriously the forming reality of the nation-state and the extension of that logic into globalization, another insight from Cavanaugh that can strengthen Conyers's work. While Conyers's starting point for diagnosing and resisting modernity can still work by focusing on vocation, the degree to which the nation-state has reshaped the logic by which people view and imagine the world forces a more basic reevaluation of intermediate associations. Conyers's emphasis on vocation, in other words, must consistently challenge the nation-state and not simply take its place within the nation-state's view of itself. Cavanaugh demonstrates that strengthening intermediate associations cannot be a first step, or even an early step, because these associations are all too often ordered to the nation-state already. Thus, Cavanaugh's more fundamental exposure of the way that the state serves as a religious simulacrum strengthens Conyers's position. Cavanaugh's perspective not only emphasizes the importance of intermediate associations but also the need for those associations not merely to serve as a way to assimilate individuals into the state's reality.

Conyers's work can strengthen Cavanaugh's treatment as well. Cavanaugh's treatment of the nation-state points out the disciplinary power of the way the state frames reality. This treatment, though relying on other explanations as well, focuses primarily on the relationship between the nation-state and violence. He explains that once the nation-state claimed to be the keeper of the common good and the protector of individuals from the violence of mediating groups such as the church, it gained the power it needed to attain prominence.

Conyers's genealogy of toleration strengthens Cavanaugh's analysis of the state by providing additional explanatory power. The heart of Conyers's insight is that the idea of toleration shifted in modernity from a practice rooted in humility to a doctrine meant to erase social differences that were problematic to the rising power of the nation-state. In fact, toleration, a practice that was rightly considered a positive idea, subtly shifted and became an idea used to undermine the importance of the very differences it was once used to protect. The relationship between the strong central power and the individual grew stronger, and toleration was invoked in relation to almost everything else in order to protect the primacy of the relationship of the individual to the state. We must tolerate differences that "do not matter," and what does and does not matter is defined by the rising power of the state.

Conyers's genealogy fits coherently with Cavanaugh's analysis, and it extends the issues of toleration more clearly into contemporary debates by calling into question how toleration comes into play. For example, in *A Brutal Unity*, Ephraim Radner critiques Cavanaugh's understanding of the wars of religion.[36] While Cavanaugh blames the rise of the liberal state for violence, Radner takes the opposite track and argues that the church is better for being embedded in liberal democratic societies, which serve to check the sinful power ambitions of religions. He sees Cavanaugh's work on religious violence as "a kind of political ploy to shift the liberal state's responsibility for bloodshed onto a falsely construed religious zealotry."[37] Instead, "Religion . . . does in fact *need* the liberal state, not so much to protect it from itself (although this could be said in some cases) as to provide a framework for self-accountability; and the civil state needs the churches in order to wrest from her [*sic*] any illusion of holding moral monopoly, or indeed any moral standing of its own apart from the values it is able to receive from her citizens, many of whom will inevitably be religious."[38] Radner makes three arguments. First, he argues that Cavanaugh does not properly grasp the significance of "religion" with respect to violence. Second, Cavanaugh cannot properly engage examples of religious violence today because his explanation of religious violence is deficient. Third, Cavanaugh obscures the relationship between religion and the liberal state today.[39]

36. See Radner, *Brutal Unity*, 19–56.
37. Ibid., 22.
38. Ibid.
39. Ibid., 23–24.

Conyers's work on toleration helps Cavanaugh counter some of these criticisms. According to Radner, "One major difficulty with [Cavanaugh's] argument is that it fails to take seriously the actual attitudes of participants in what is called 'religious violence.'"[40] In other words, focusing on a history-of-ideas approach to religion misleads Cavanaugh.[41] Radner thinks that if most of the people involved in the violence would have used religious categories to explain it—even if they did not have that exact category—then *ipso facto* those are important categories. While there is some merit to this argument, failing to recognize the ways in which terms change or are enlisted in a particular power shift can lead to a misreading of the history.

For example, Radner repeatedly uses the idea of toleration to promote the gains of liberalism and to criticize the myth of religious violence. He states,

> What Cavanaugh and contemporary antiliberal revisionists do not address, then, is the fact that the notion of religious tolerance over and against religious violence was later overthrown by the ongoing and spectacular failures of *Christians* especially in the midst of and in the face of violence in which they participated: it is this that has inflated a narrative into a "myth," but one for which the greatest blame—a term I use deliberately—lies with the churches themselves.[42]

So, in Radner's judgment, the concept of religious tolerance is a key notion, one that was exacerbated by Christian failures that caused religious violence to inflate into a myth. In this telling, the liberal state is actually a product of Christians, "by and large trying to figure out a way to deal with their own internal weaknesses, temptations, and sins."[43] What Radner fails to see, and what Conyers's treatment would help Cavanaugh to develop, is the fact that the term *toleration* itself is loaded with the nation-state's preferred view of reality. "The notion of religious tolerance" is not something that Radner can so easily bring into the discussion over against the myth of religious violence. He must define *toleration* more clearly before he can assume it to be a good: if it is a toleration employed in the logic of the nation-state to destroy difference and "intermediate groups" for the sake of power, it is much different than if it is the practice of toleration rooted in early Chris-

40. Ibid., 25.
41. Ibid., 46.
42. Ibid., 55.
43. Ibid., 49.

tianity and other religions as well.[44] Being attentive to this change, charted by Conyers, strengthens our understanding of religious violence and also the terms of the debate in today's world because it shows how even when people give certain reasons for their behavior, those reasons still must be understood in a broader context. Conyers shows just how problematic the context of "toleration" is in this case.

Conyers's treatment of toleration and the way that it dissolved social bonds works well with Cavanaugh's more thorough work on intermediate associations to address another of Radner's concerns. Radner thinks that the church is to blame for much of the violence because Christians killed and because Christian reasons supported it. At this juncture, the concept of intermediate associations again comes into the picture to situate properly the church in relation to civil society and the nation-state. If Cavanaugh is right (and Conyers's work suggests that he is), then intermediate associations are fundamentally different after the rise of the nation-state, because they are enlisted in the nation-state's project. While Christians have committed and do commit violence, and even give "Christian reasons," we cannot discount the fact that even intermediate associations have been influenced by the state's view of reality. They have been disciplined to a certain degree. Thus Cavanaugh can incorporate Radner's evidence on Christians and violence as evidence for the way that the church has been unfaithful by taking its place alongside other intermediate associations in so-called civil society, supporting the nation-state project.

This collaboration addresses Radner's argument that the church actually needs the liberal state because of the church's sins. While Radner rightly points out that what participants said about their violent motives does matter, his own failure to take into account the way a term like *toleration* changes and was co-opted into the rise of the nation-state weakens his attempt to show the church's failures and need for liberal democratic frameworks. Radner cannot simply point to the rise of religious tolerance within Christian circles as evidence for Christians creating the liberal state to help restrain their own sins. The case is more complicated than that, and both Conyers and Cavanaugh are more nuanced in their arguments, especially with regard to intermediate associations, than Radner's criticism of Cavanaugh allows.

---

44. Not that Conyers's focus on toleration as a practice is without limitations, especially considering the degree to which the meaning of the term has changed, perhaps beyond the point that it is worth trying to reclaim.

Furthermore, Conyers's reading of Hobbes helps adjudicate another difference in Cavanaugh and Radner, since Hobbes is a bone of contention between these two. Cavanaugh and Conyers are both critical of Hobbes, while Radner is appreciative. However, as we will see, Conyers's focus on toleration helps adjudicate the debate and situate Radner's appreciation. Radner criticizes Cavanaugh's reading of Hobbes, noting that for Cavanaugh, Hobbes and Locke are key "myth makers" promoting false consciousness by claiming that certain arguments about Christian faith promote violence.[45] Cavanaugh charges that Hobbes ignored the economic and legal factors that led to religious conflict and instead laid the blame at the feet of Christian preaching; for Hobbes, "the problem begins in the pulpit, where simple people are led astray by seditious preaching."[46] According to Hobbes, violence results from an improper distinction of temporal and spiritual power. Cavanaugh sees Hobbes as mistaken, while Radner sees Hobbes as identifying a key danger illustrated in the religious wars. For Radner, "we must still ask what kind of religion or Christianity would permit such killing. What kind would provide the motivating conceptual structures of meaning to legitimize it?"[47] Hobbes's role, then, is not a negative one of marginalizing religion, but in fact falls in line with a medieval notion of the valorization of the peacemaking sovereign, "who acts according [to] the imposition of law, and who stands over the Church's claims to some alternative and generally divisive route to social order."[48] For Cavanaugh and Conyers, Hobbes is a key figure leading to modern problems; for Radner, Hobbes is a helpful figure providing important distinctions.

Radner's positive use of Hobbes focuses on Hobbes's development of "conscience." Radner turns to Hobbes for navigating the public/private continuum of conscience and the reality of multiple consciences. Hobbes is interested in "peacekeeping" and therefore shows that "the difference between private and public lies not in procedures as in the purposes that guide and hold accountable the otherwise fluid character of human knowing, feeling, and decision making."[49] The very act of living together creates the need for multiple consciences, so that an individual's private conscience can hold one thing, while the public conscience does not insist upon that

45. Radner, *Brutal Unity*, 41.
46. Cavanaugh, *Myth of Religious Violence*, 125.
47. Radner, *Brutal Unity*, 41.
48. Ibid., 54n75.
49. Ibid., 361.

particular truth for the sake of peace and unity. For these purposes Radner calls upon the concept of toleration, which rightly rings problematic to us at this stage in understanding Conyers's work. For the sake of toleration, the individual is willing to sacrifice conscience itself (Radner uses this language of sacrifice).[50] For Radner, Hobbes is a hero precisely because he helps facilitate this toleration that allows for the operation of multiple consciences; for Conyers, Hobbes is a problem for this very reason, because Conyers sees the public conscience and its allegiance to the state as problematic for other associations.

Conyers strengthens and advances Cavanaugh's work on the nation-state. Conyers does not simply save Cavanaugh from the criticisms of scholars such as Anderson and Radner, but his work illuminates a way to take the dialogue forward that strengthens Cavanaugh's overall approach in light of the criticism. The work that Conyers has done on the changing nature of toleration serves as a key explanation of the way that the nation-state has altered conceptions of reality, and how it has ordered other intermediate associations to its project through such terminology. "Toleration" diminishes the importance of intermediate associations and disciplines them to find their place within the dynamic of a strong, centralized state and an autonomous individual. Cavanaugh's criticism of the modern world, however, does not end with the state.

Consumerism

The free market and consumerism stand alongside the state's conception of reality in Cavanaugh's analysis. In his 2008 collection of essays, *Being Consumed: Economics and Christian Desire*,[51] Cavanaugh explains how the free market and consumerism mask reality in the name of economic freedom. In the face of this unreality, Cavanaugh focuses on how Christian concepts and practices create true freedom.[52] He is clear that he is not focused on blessing or damning the free market but instead on creating really free markets, "economic spaces in which truly and fully free transactions—as judged by the true *telos* of human life—can take place."[53] Toward this end,

---

50. Ibid., 396.

51. Cavanaugh, *Being Consumed*.

52. Ibid., viii.

53. Ibid., x.

he develops three primary angles for engaging capitalism, the free market, and consumerism.

First, Cavanaugh reframes the discussion of freedom in relation to economics. The standard narrative of the "free market" is that it provides the opportunity for "free" transactions, defined as transactions that are both voluntary and informed.[54] But Cavanaugh points out that there is a difference between "negative freedom" (freedom *from*) and "positive freedom" (freedom *for*, "a capacity to achieve certain worthwhile goals").[55] While the free market may be free in the negative sense—because there are limited hindrances—it is not free in the positive sense because it lacks treatment of the purpose of human existence, of a true telos. Cavanaugh turns to Augustine for this understanding of desire and freedom: "What is required is a substantive account of the end of earthly life and creation so that we may enter into particular judgments of what kinds of exchange are free and what kinds are not."[56] Desire properly conceived rests not on individual choice but is instead a social product, "a complex and multidimensional network of movement that does not simply originate within the individual self but pulls and pushes the self in different directions from both inside and outside the person."[57] Many Christians take for granted the "freedom" of capitalism; Cavanaugh problematizes that conception by drawing on a fuller sense of freedom that the market clearly lacks and in fact competes against.

Second, Cavanaugh focuses on the idea of "attachment" to material things and argues that consumerism actually reflects detachment, not attachment. The usual Christian picture of greed does not capture what goes on in the consumer economy, for it focuses on an inordinate attachment to things. Consumerism, instead, encourages detachment: "People do not hoard money; they spend it. People do not cling to things; they discard them and buy other things."[58] The spiritual tone of consumerism is set not

---

54. Cavanaugh turns to Milton Friedman for this definition. See ibid., 2. This chapter, "Freedom and Unfreedom," was originally published as "Unfreedom of the Free Market," 103–28.

55. Cavanaugh, *Being Consumed*, 7–8.

56. Ibid., 2. Cavanaugh also turns to Augustine's treatment of desire in "Coercion in Augustine and Disney," 283–90.

57. Cavanaugh, *Being Consumed*, 9.

58. Ibid., 34. The chapter "Detachment and Attachment" was originally published as "Consumer Culture," 241–59.

by having, but by having *something else*.[59] Consumers are detached from production, producers, and products.[60] And this detachment influences the way people understand and interact with the world: "In the Christian tradition, detachment from material goods means using them as a means to a greater end, and the greater end is greater attachment to God and to our fellow human beings. In consumerism, detachment means standing back from all people, times, and places, and appropriating our choices for private use. Consumerism supports an essentially individualistic view of the human person, in which each consumer is a sovereign chooser."[61] Thus the problem of consumerism is not precisely the traditional problem of greed, but a problem of detachment that hides itself under material acquisition.

Third, Cavanaugh explores the logic of scarcity and abundance, arguing that consumerism is based on the former (because it assumes scarcity) while the Christian narrative centers on the latter. As he puts it, "We live our lives at the intersection of two stories about the world: the Eucharist and the market. Both tell stories of hunger and consumption, of exchanges and gifts; the stories overlap and compete."[62] Economics is a science of scarcity because individuals continue to want. Augustine identified the constant renewing desires that humans experience, but he moved from this to the conclusion that material things cannot satisfy; humans must turn to God. This turn to God contrasts with consumer culture: "Marketing constantly seeks to meet, create, and stoke new desires, often by highlighting a sense of dissatisfaction with what one presently has and is. . . . Rather than turning away from material things and toward God, in consumer culture we plunge ever more deeply into the world of things."[63] Even the material problems in the world are solved by this plunge: "Through the mechanism of demand and supply, the competition of self-interested individuals will result in the production of the goods society wants, at the right prices, with sufficient employment for all at the right wages for the foreseeable future. The result is an eschatology in which abundance for all is just around the corner. In the contemporary consumer-driven economy, consumption is

---

59. Cavanaugh, *Being Consumed*, 35.

60. Ibid., 37–47.

61. Ibid., 52–53.

62. Ibid., 89. The chapter "Scarcity and Abundance" was originally published as "Consumption, the Market, and the Eucharist," 88–95.

63. Cavanaugh, *Being Consumed*, 90–91.

often urged as the solution to the suffering of others."[64] The eschatological hope provided by this logic, however, often "fades into resignation to a tragic world of scarcity."[65] Scarcity, not abundance, is the dominant reality in a society whose imagination is shaped by the free market. Because the free market is based on the assumption of scarcity as a simple fact, it promotes a view of the world that centers on scarcity. Cavanaugh is not so interested in whether scarcity is a fact in a fallen world as in the way that the free market's focus on scarcity pushes scarcity to form more than just the economic reality. Such terminology shapes Christian moral vision and moral imagination as well.

This idea of viewing and imagining the world brings us to another way that Cavanaugh's work can strengthen Conyers's. Cavanaugh takes seriously the ideas of moral vision and moral imagination—the way that concepts shape how people see the world as it is and consider what it might be like. Conyers does not use this exact terminology (though he does speak of a vision of the world), and doing so would clarify the way he wants his insights to influence Christians. The concepts of moral vision and imagination would aid Conyers in proposing how his diagnosis and remedies for the modern world might inform and guide ethical praxis in the church. Though this change is not a large one, utilizing this terminology better connects history and theory to the practice of the church. It does so by more clearly exposing the idea that the nation-state imposes a vision and encourages a type of imagination on all who are part of its project. Bringing people's attention to this fact by utilizing the terminology would expose the state's power more clearly and help Christians see better how the moral vision and imagination of the state in fact disciple or discipline individuals into certain ways of life. And these ways of life may run counter to the moral vision and imagination of the gospel.

Conyers's work contributes to Cavanaugh's analysis of consumerism in three ways. First, Conyers provides more conceptual background on how the growing use of money and the increasing abstraction of the economy in previous centuries altered the way that individuals viewed and interacted within the economy. Second, Conyers makes strong arguments about economic instrumentalization—going so far as to call aspects of the free-market system "modern slavery"—that add more weight to a critique of consumerism. Third, Conyers connects consumerism to issues

64. Ibid., 93.
65. Ibid., 94.

of technology and the notions of power that shifted in the modern world in a way that provides a broader context for understanding and interacting with consumerism.[66] Such critiques demonstrate Conyers's sympathy with the type of work Cavanaugh has done in exposing consumerism.

Globalization

The third way that Cavanaugh analyzes the ills of modernity is through his treatment of globalization, which he relates to the project of the nation-state and the logic of free-market capitalism.[67] On the one hand, globalization results from the spread of global capitalism, but on the other, Cavanaugh argues that it is in fact "a hyperextension of the nation-state's project of subsuming the local under the universal."[68] Globalization is an aesthetic that promotes a consumer subject and a homogenizing culture.[69]

The rise of the modern state was marked by the universal's triumph over the local in the form of the sovereign state's "usurpation of power from the Church, the nobility, guilds, clans, and towns."[70] The medieval conception of complex space, with multiple, overlapping associations, was replaced and flattened. Associations were recast as "intermediate associations," not just because they were smaller than the state and larger than individuals, but also because their job was to mediate the state project to the individual. The local mediates the universal, and the institutions of civil society are educative and disciplinary.[71] And while the nation-state benefited from the destruction of localizations that challenged its power, the nation-state is now the victim of the same logic: "Just as the nation-state freed the market from the 'interventions' of local custom, and freed the individual to relate to other individuals on the basis of standardized legal and monetary systems, so globalization frees commerce from the nation-state, which, as it

66. For instance, see his "Hope and Crisis in a Consumer Society," in *God, Hope, and History*, 177–86.

67. While Cavanaugh often treats this in connection with economics and consumerism, I am treating it separately in order to make clear how it is connected to his reading of both the nation-state and the free market, not simply the free market.

68. Cavanaugh, *Theopolitical Imagination*, 99. The chapter "Myth of Globalization as Catholicity" was originally published as " World in a Wafer," 181–96.

69. Cavanaugh, "Balthasar, Globalization," 324–25.

70. Cavanaugh, *Theopolitical Imagination*, 99.

71. "The universal is mediated by the local; the institutions of civil society, as Hegel saw, are educative, or as Foucault would later say, disciplinary" (ibid., 101).

turns out, is now seen as one more localization impeding the universal flow of capital."[72] Globalization extends the logic of the nation-state, a logic that casts aside the nation-state itself as too local and particularized; the logic of the nation-state has sawn off its own branch.

This subsumption of the local under the universal diverts attention from the fact that globalization produces new forms of division. Competition leads diverse places to tailor their uniqueness to attract capital development; they model themselves after other, "successful" places.[73] And "global mapping produces the illusion of diversity by the juxtaposition of all the varied products of the world's traditions and cultures in one space and time in the marketplace. . . . For the consumer with money, the illusion is created that all the world's people are contemporaries occupying the same space-time."[74] Yet local traditions are slowly lost to the mass, universal culture of successful corporations such as Coca-Cola: "Local attachments are loosed by the centrifuge of ephemeral desire, which is fueled by global capitalism's ever accelerating need for growth."[75] The divisions between rich and poor are reinforced, and local cultures fall victim to a false sense of the universal.

Conyers also develops the dynamic between the local and the universal, but Cavanaugh's work helps Conyers connect these concepts more explicitly to globalization, which is becoming a more important reality for theological engagement. In his focus on place, Conyers deals with both the particular and the universal. The modern tendency to abstraction and the modern spirit of conquest weaken the importance of particular places, but Conyers notes that the local is the context for human living and flourishing. In addition to this, Conyers argues that universal reality comes to us through the particular: "A place is significant, and we speak and sing of it, because it offers to us a door by which we know what is true for all people, everywhere. It doesn't just speak of itself—though it never ceases to speak of itself—but it speaks of that which is truly catholic, truly universal—not bound by, but prior to, time and space."[76] So we cannot abandon the local in favor of the universal, for then we lose both the particular and the universal.

This opinion is similar to Cavanaugh's argument regarding globalization and false senses of the universal. In this case, Cavanaugh does not so

72. Ibid., 104–5.
73. Ibid., 108.
74. Ibid., 109.
75. Ibid., 110.
76. Conyers, *Listening Heart*, 151.

much strengthen Conyers's work as he demonstrates an area where it can be extended. While Conyers deals tangentially with globalization, he does not extend his critique into the economic realities in play as thoroughly as Cavanaugh does. Extending Conyers's work in this way would help bring his theological sensibilities to bear on not only the importance of being rooted in particular places but of being aware of the way in which the culture of globalization pushes against this notion.

These three elements of modernity—the nation-state, consumerism, and globalization—serve as the primary loci for Cavanaugh's diagnosis of modernity's ills. The nation-state privatizes religion and sets itself up as a substitute savior, forming Christians according to its logic. Consumerism removes a true understanding of human ends, encourages detachment, and operates on a scarcity that runs counter to a Christian understanding of reality. Globalization, finally, extends the logic of both of these problems to a great degree and provides a false sense of catholicity. For each of these problems, Cavanaugh finds the Eucharist to be the primary remedy and location for resistance.

CAVANAUGH'S REMEDY

In simplest terms, Cavanaugh answers the problems of the modern world with "Eucharist," which is "one privileged site" for Christian reimagination of space and time.[77] It provides and enacts a conception of space and time that counters the detrimental aspects of the nation-state, consumerism, and globalization. Analyzing the way the Eucharist counters each of these aspects deepens our understanding of Cavanaugh's constructive project centered on the Eucharist, because the Eucharist not only forms the substance of his solutions but also serves as the reality by which he evaluates the modern world and identifies its problems as outlined in the previous section.

But first, what does Cavanaugh mean by "Eucharist"? The Eucharist is the sacrament of unity, in which people find communion with God and with one another. It both symbolizes and works to bring about unity in Christ.[78] The Eucharist is the proper response to the ways in which the world violently disciplines or shapes people because through the Eucharist the church is reminded of Jesus's own torture at the hands of the powers

---

77. Cavanaugh, *Theopolitical Imagination*, 4.

78. Cavanaugh, *Torture and Eucharist*, 76–77.

of the world.[79] At the same time, the Eucharist is not something that we apply; instead, "the eucharist makes the church itself a political body. The church practices the politics of Jesus when it becomes an alternative way of life that offers healing for the wounds that divide us."[80] The Eucharist, then, not only unites Christians and calls to memory the sacrifice of Christ but also helps expose and remedy the various ways that the world—modern or otherwise—wounds and divides people. With this basic understanding in mind, we can move to how the Eucharist particularly informs the three ways the modern world shapes people.

The Eucharist counters the forming power of the nation-state by challenging its conception of reality and exposing it as a soteriological simulacrum. Cavanaugh develops this angle with respect to the nation-state generally and the state use of torture specifically. The nation-state promises unity and peace, but the cost is the loss of the local and the particular: "The state thus succeeds in separating people from each other yet creating a direct and powerful link between the state and the individual. The state does not merely wish to make its citizens feel as independent as possible from each other, but also seeks to make them as dependent as possible on the authority of the state."[81] In the face of this "promise," the Eucharist disrupts the logic of contract and exchange in modern social relations.[82] While the state depends on the subsumption of the local and particular under the universal, the Eucharist gathers the many into one but without subordinating the local to the universal.[83] Instead, the Eucharist's unity is "an anticipation of the eschatological unity of all in Christ."[84] But this anticipation is dependent on each local expression; it does not replace the local in favor of the universal. Our true hope should not be in the peace and unity that

79. Ibid., 2.

80. Cavanaugh, "Body of Christ," 177.

81. Cavanaugh, *Torture and Eucharist*, 47.

82. Cavanaugh, *Theopolitical Imagination*, 47.

83. The conservative influence on Conyers can be extended here to the relation of the local and the universal. According to scholars like Donald Livingston, it is the strong centralizing emphasis of the Hobbesian path that leads to problems because of strong centralization and the destruction not only of other authorities but also of the relationship between overlapping authorities. Problems such as those Cavanaugh identifies with the subsumption of the local under the universal emerge because of this path. The Althusian path offers more promise in relating the two without the total subordination of local to universal that occurs in the modern state. See Livingston, "Very Idea of Secession," 38–48.

84. Cavanaugh, *Theopolitical Imagination*, 49.

the state promises, because "the Eucharist is not simply a promise of future bliss outside of historical time. In the biblical and patristic witness we find the Eucharist as an earthly practice of peace and reconciliation."[85]

In *Torture and Eucharist*, Cavanaugh develops how the Eucharist counters torture, which forms the social body of the state primarily through isolation: "The Eucharist, as the gift which effects the visibility of the true body of Christ, is therefore the church's counter-imagination to that of the state."[86] He explains that "isolation is overcome in the Eucharist by the building of a communal body which resists the state's attempts to disappear it."[87]

Cavanaugh expands the importance of the Eucharist by exploring an inversion in Catholic thinking on the Eucharist. Patristic and early medieval tradition spoke of a threefold distinction of the body of Christ: "(1) the historical body, meaning the physical body of Jesus of Nazareth, (2) the sacramental body, or Christ as present in the Eucharistic elements, and (3) the ecclesial body, that is, the church."[88] However, Henri de Lubac's *Corpus Mysticum* shows that in the twelfth century there was an inversion of meaning: the altar became the site of Christ's *corpus verum*, and the church was seen as his *corpus mysticum*. In the older meaning, both the Eucharist and the church are together the contemporary performance of the true body: "Christians are the *real* body of Christ, and the Eucharist is where the church *mystically* comes to be."[89] The inversion led to changed relationships: "Now the historical and sacramental bodies form a pair, and the gap is between them and the ecclesial body. . . . The visibility of the church in the communal performance of the sacrament is replaced by the visibility of the Eucharistic object. Signified and signifier have exchanged places, such that the sacramental body is the visible signifier of the hidden signified, which is the social body of Christ."[90] De Lubac was concerned with a tendency that emerged from this inversion: the Eucharist was reduced to a mere spectacle for the laity,[91] and "the increased localization of the sacred

85. Ibid., 51.
86. Cavanaugh, *Torture and Eucharist*, 251.
87. Ibid., 206.
88. Ibid., 212.
89. Ibid.
90. Ibid., 212–13.
91. Ibid., 213.

in the Eucharistic host in effect secularized all that lay beyond it."[92] Thus "the adjective 'mystical,' when applied to the church . . . signals a retreat in varying degrees from any interruption of historical time by the Kingdom of God. We look for the Kingdom outside of time. The eschatological significance of the body of Christ, and the sacramental action which produces it, is effectively denied."[93] When the church is seen as the "mystical" rather than "true" body of Christ, it encourages a view of the church as disincarnate, hovering over the temporal world, uniting Christians in soul alone.[94]

After tracing the inversion of true body and mystical body in Catholic theology, Cavanaugh examines the Eucharist with reference to the future, past, and present. He draws on the eschatological nature of the Eucharist: "In contrast with secular historical imagination, the Christian story is intrinsically eschatological. . . . The Eucharist is the true heart of this dimension of the church's life, because it is in the Eucharist that Christ Himself, the eternal consummation of history, becomes present in time."[95] The Eucharist also changes the way we understand time, focusing on the disruptive character of God's gracious giving rather than the monotonous succession of events: "The Eucharistic present is not just one moment in the regular sequence of secular historical time—one damn thing after another. Eucharistic time is marked by charity, the gratuitous and disruptive presence of the Kingdom of God."[96] Then he points to the past element of the Eucharist, which is an *anamnesis* of the past. He defines anamnesis not merely as remembrance but as a performance that is the imagination of the church.[97] Third, he treats the present nature of the Eucharist, which he explains as "that performance which makes the body of Christ visible in the present."[98] In this context he deals with excommunication, which he deems necessary for types of sin, like torture, that impugn the identity of the body of Christ.[99] In fact, excommunication done well is an act of hospitality because it tells someone he is outside fellowship and how he might return.[100]

92. Ibid., 214.
93. Ibid., 220.
94. Ibid., 207.
95. Ibid., 223.
96. Ibid., 228.
97. Ibid., 229–30.
98. Ibid., 234.
99. Ibid., 247.
100. Ibid., 243.

These imaginations of space and time, torture and Eucharist, are strikingly different: "A crucial difference in these imaginations is that the imagination of the church is essentially eschatological; the church is not a rival *polis* but points to an alternative time and space, a mingling of heaven and earth."[101]

The Eucharist also provides a new logic of consumption that challenges the way consumerism shapes being in the world. First, the Eucharist "is a particularly important locus for the Christian practice of consumption,"[102] for in it "the insatiability of human desire is absorbed by the abundance of God's grace in the consumption of Jesus' body and blood."[103] The Eucharist is not just another commodity to be consumed; instead, the Eucharist is God's gift, and consuming the Eucharist challenges individual consumption because in consuming the Eucharist the consumer is taken up into the body of Christ. Thus "the act of consumption is thereby turned inside out: instead of simply consuming the body of Christ, we are consumed by it."[104] We do not consume the gift, but the gift consumes and remakes us. Second, the Eucharist tells a different story of hunger and consumption, for "it does not begin with scarcity, but with the one who came that we might have life, and have it abundantly."[105] And this abundance is not one to be consumed individualistically and privately; through consuming the Eucharist one becomes part of the body of Christ. And this abundance presented by God's grace is *now*, in the present. God breaks in. It is not the gradual progress promised by the market but the kingdom received as gift.

Finally, the Eucharist exposes the ruse of globalization's supposed catholicity and produces an alternate, localized center. Cavanaugh argues that "the Eucharist overcomes the dichotomy of universal and local" by collapsing spatial divisions not by mobility (as in globalization) but by gathering in local assembly.[106] The Eucharist is then a decentered center, for it is celebrated in multiple local churches scattered around the world but gathered up into one. In addition, "the Eucharist not only tells but *performs* a narrative of cosmic proportions, from the death and resurrection of Christ, to the new covenant formed in his blood, to the future destiny of all creation. The consumer of the Eucharist is no longer the schizophrenic

---

101. Ibid., 65.

102. Cavanaugh, *Being Consumed*, 53.

103. Ibid., 54.

104. Ibid.

105. Ibid., 94.

106. Cavanaugh, *Theopolitical Imagination*, 113.

subject of global capitalism, awash in a sea of unrelated persons, but walks into a story with a past, present, and future."[107] Participation in the Eucharist changes the way space is experienced, for the consumer walks "in the strange landscape of the body of Christ, while still inhabiting a particular earthly place. Now the worldly landscape is transformed by the intrusions of the universal body of Christ" in particular, local spaces.[108] The Eucharist draws the consumer into the universal body of Christ through the local reality of the church and the practice of the liturgy. And the local practice of the Eucharist is local in a way that the local franchise of McDonald's is not. McDonald's erases difference in favor of universalism, while the Eucharist points to Christ, the one concrete universal.

In the end, Cavanaugh's remedy is the Eucharist alone, but not only the Eucharist. On the one hand, I simply mean that Cavanaugh acknowledges that the Eucharist is *one* Christian doctrine that yields fruit, not the only one. But on the other hand, I mean something more: in his work so far, Cavanaugh has repeatedly returned to the Eucharist as a remedy. He has not developed other potential remedies, or at least not nearly as fully and explicitly. So for Cavanaugh the remedy is the Eucharist alone. However, as Cavanaugh turns to the Eucharist, it is never a "bare" concept; it is not alone. Instead, it overflows into other concepts and practices as implications of its own plenitude of significance. The Eucharist serves as a central practice of abundance, a gift that overflows into other remedies. For instance, it effects the communicability of pain from one person to another as all are united in one body, thus underlying the obligation to feed the hungry.[109] The Eucharist also anticipates future reconciliation,[110] because part of taking the Eucharist includes the command to "discern the body," a Pauline command that Cavanaugh connects to being aware of divisions and seeking to remedy them.[111] Thus Cavanaugh's one remedy leads to other identifiable concepts and practices.

One potential limitation of Cavanaugh's focus on the Eucharist is developed by David Fitch in connection with the work of Nathan Kerr. In *The End of Evangelicalism?*, Fitch identifies three beliefs that evangelicals have reified and turned into Master-Signifiers that shape the evangelical

---

107. Ibid., 118.

108. Ibid., 120.

109. Cavanaugh, *Being Consumed*, 96.

110. Cavanaugh, *Torture and Eucharist*, 240.

111. Cavanaugh, "Dying for the Eucharist," 177–89.

way of life in negative ways. The three beliefs are an inerrant Bible, personal conversion, and the Christian nation. Fitch seeks not to reject these beliefs but to understand them properly and thereby to begin a recovery of an evangelical politics of mission.

Cavanaugh's work comes into play for Fitch in reshaping the third belief, the Christian nation. Fitch explains that Cavanaugh "shows how the Eucharist births a political presence that engages society for redemption and renewal."[112] A politics is born when the church discerns "the body" around the eucharistic table "through the practices of reconciliation, ex-communication, and the mutual participation in receiving Christ's body."[113] This politics enables Christians to resist the politics of violence and isolation, to subvert them, and to draw the world into God's restoration. However, Fitch notes a potential limitation of this approach: "one still wonders whether such a concentric view of the church can do anything more than be subversive."[114] Can such a church see the ways that God's reign is already at work in the world? Is a Eucharistic focus anti-mission?

Fitch turns to Nathan Kerr's *Christ, History, and Apocalyptic*.[115] Kerr contests Cavanaugh's "ecclesiocentrism." By that term, he means a politically concentric understanding of the church in relation to the wider world. Such an understanding implies that the church is concerned so much with its own interior identity that engagement with the world becomes subsidiary.[116] In fact, "Jesus by default becomes domesticated by the church and becomes part of its own ideology. It therefore becomes imperialistic in its engagements with the world."[117] Unlike for Cavanaugh, for Kerr "mission makes the church,' as opposed to de Lubac where 'the Eucharist makes the church.'"[118] Kerr wants a church dispossessed, one without place or center, always scattered in the world: "The church, then, according to Kerr, is the ever open, non-territorial enactment of Jesus' love in the world."[119] In fact,

---

112. Fitch, *End of Evangelicalism?*, 157.

113. Ibid.

114. Ibid.

115. While Kerr does not have Cavanaugh specifically in mind in his work, Fitch applies Kerr's thought to Cavanaugh. This is why I include Fitch and not merely Kerr in this analysis. See also Kerr, *Christ, History and Apocalyptic*, 169–96.

116. Fitch, *End of Evangelicalism?*, 158.

117. Ibid.

118. Ibid., 158–59.

119. Ibid., 159.

it is precisely by way of the reality of and her participation in Christ's apocalyptic historicity that the Christian joins with Israel in *embodying* the coming of God's reign as a mode of apocalyptic hope. For only as it joins Israel in diaspora does the Christian "not yet" become something other than a theological dilemma concerning the "delay" of the *parousia* and become rather the condition for the political cry of "come," a cry for the messianic inbreaking to occur everagain [*sic*], for the Spirit to gather us everanew, in the very contingencies of our own ongoing histories, into the reality of the "already."[120]

In this way, Kerr turns against the model of the church as "counter-*polis*," which he sees as dominant since Barth. This vision is anti-mission because it fails to take into account the diasporic nature of being called out into the world. Thus, Cavanaugh's eucharistic focus is anti-mission.

While Fitch acknowledges the strength of Kerr's critique of the potentially ideological character of the Eucharist, ultimately he rejects it for various reasons. In short, "We need not worry with Kerr that such a politic is inevitably territorial and/or closed off from the world because if the church indeed becomes the very body of Christ in the world à la de Lubac, then it should necessarily embody the very disposition of incarnation in the world in its politic. . . . Its very politic inhabits the posture of a servant to the world."[121] Formed as the body of Christ, the church is not insular but humble, open, vulnerable, and hospitable to the world. The issue at stake is whether a focus on the Eucharist causes a church to be isolated and inwardly focused, and thus unable to effectively serve God in the world. While Kerr argues that the Eucharist causes this problem, Fitch sees in the Eucharist a call to incarnation, to engagement with the world.

With this change of focus, Fitch brings to the conversation one of the ways that I think Conyers can strengthen Cavanaugh's position. Conyers's focus on vocation, along with the way that he fills that out as an imitation of Christ, shifts the eucharistic emphasis in the same direction that Fitch rightly sees is necessary in order to maintain a proper orientation to the world and the church's mission. Vocation helps maintain a focus on mission that prevents the church from becoming too ideological and self-concerned. God constitutes the church through his calling the church to himself, to community, and to God's work in the world.

---

120. Kerr, *Christ, History and Apocalyptic*, 187.

121. Fitch, *End of Evangelicalism?*, 161.

Second, Cavanaugh's eucharistic remedy does not work effectively as a starting point for evangelicals. A Roman Catholic understanding of the Eucharist lies outside of typical evangelical theological imagination. The Eucharist certainly has a place within evangelical political theology, but other theological concepts are more promising starting points. The Eucharist does not immediately serve as an inspiring rallying point for Christian political theology; for evangelicals, it does not immediately inspire the Christian moral vision and imagination that Cavanaugh requires. In short, a doctrine that is as hotly contested as the Eucharist is not a promising starting point when it immediately makes clear the division between different traditions. Conyers's focus on vocation provides a more ecclesially broad entry point, one connected to the "truly catholic vision" that Conyers desires.

A third, smaller limitation in Cavanaugh's remedy emerges as he shifts from Eucharist to various practices. For instance, at the end of *Torture and Eucharist*, Cavanaugh turns to various practices that he believes are accounted for by the Eucharist. Specifically, he points to Chilean practices of excommunication, the Vicariate of Solidarity, and the Sebastián Acevedo Movement against Torture.[122] Two avenues for critique emerge here. First, can the Eucharist really account for all of these practices as Cavanaugh argues? And second, even if the Eucharist can account for them, are there other ways that Christians could move in these directions, ways based on areas of broader agreement, ways more readily understandable?[123] One of the weaknesses of Cavanaugh's work emerges as one gets closer to concrete examples of what his proposals would look like in practice.

It is not that Conyers provides something completely different from Cavanaugh's remedy. Rather, Conyers begins with doctrines that connect a broader spectrum of Christians and therefore are more helpful for evangelical resistance to the formation of the modern nation-state and globalization. Conyers focuses on a multilayered description of the idea of vocation to remedy problems with individualism and universalization present in modernity.[124] One layer combats individualism by focusing on the fact that

122. Cavanaugh, *Torture and Eucharist*, chap. 6.

123. I am not arguing that Cavanaugh thinks the Eucharist is the only way to develop theopolitical vision. He is clear that it is "one privileged site" for such reflection. See Cavanaugh, *Theopolitical Imagination*, 4.

124. First, Conyers turns to what can be called a social trinitarian perspective to argue for a reevaluation of our understanding of power in the modern world. While his treatment is not identical to social trinitarianism, he does make connections between

it is God who calls, not the individual who simply determines via arbitrary will what to do. Another layer combats individualism and universalization by noting that God calls one to specific places and to serve one's community. Thus the local matters, for place is the context of the call. Another layer of Conyer's description of vocation connects vocation to various practice-centered themes, including attention, the practice of toleration, place, rest, and imitation. The multiple layers of vocation serve as an easier entry point for Christians into an alternative theopolitical imagination.

Also, Conyers relies on the doctrine of the incarnation for two important remedies. On one hand, the doctrine of the incarnation encourages the humility that underlies the true practice of toleration, which is absolutely essential for navigating a world of difference. On the other hand, the incarnation serves to tie together the local and the universal: "The 'incarnational' truth of place is that particular places, with their own regional characteristics, and their own kind of community, nevertheless speak of that which is true for all people everywhere, and for all time."[125] The incarnation affirms the importance of local place, since place is "a reflection of the Mystery of the Incarnation. That is, God himself, made himself known, in a particular man, of a particular people, in a particular place. And he did so not in order to lead men to *that* place (as thousands of pilgrims thought), but in order to lead them to their own place—and through that place to the God who made them and *placed them there*."[126] Thus the incarnation begins to combat some of the negative tendencies of the modern nation-state, consumerism, and globalization that Cavanaugh identifies.

Conclusion

Drawing Conyers's work alongside that of Cavanaugh not only shows how Conyers can serve as a bridge for evangelicals to political theology but also demonstrates how Conyers's positions could be strengthened by insights from Cavanaugh. This comparison better situates Conyers's work to serve

---

the Trinity and contemporary social relations, which is a move that has been largely criticized by theologians since Conyers's time of writing. Because of the controversy surrounding the idea of "using" the doctrine of the Trinity for political purposes, it is best to part ways with Conyers at this point. However, his other two concepts provide more promise.

125. Conyers, *Listening Heart*, 150.

126. Ibid., 153.

as a resource and guide for evangelical political theology to develop the social imagination necessary for navigating the modern world. Cavanaugh's work strengthens Conyers's in two main areas: lending more explanatory power to Conyers's treatment of modernity and providing concepts and vocabulary for better guiding praxis.

I have explored how Cavanaugh and Conyers can strengthen one another in ways that harmonize. Much of what they do can be reconciled together into a common position, a common diagnosis of the modern world and a remedy for the future, even if they part ways in particular ecclesial application due to Reformation differences. They both diagnose the modern world as a place of polarization, with large nation-states relating to isolated individuals who are being disciplined and discipled by the state's version of reality. Additionally, market economics has imposed its own disciplinary force, and that force has extended into globalization. Cavanaugh and Conyers both alert Christians to the fact that much of the disciplinary formation, much of the discipleship, that goes on in the modern world leads down roads antithetical to the truths of the Christian gospel. Both point to explicitly Christian concepts—Cavanaugh to the Eucharist and Conyers to vocation—to help identify the modern world's ills and to chart the path forward.

Conyers's treatment of modernity provides aspects that strengthen Cavanaugh's position and arguments in two primary ways. First, Conyers's analysis of the nation-state adds depth to Cavanaugh's treatment by providing a supplemental way of seeing the rise of the nation-state and the shift to an emphasis on the individual and the state at the expense of other groups. Second, Conyers's remedies to the problems of modernity fit with Cavanaugh's focus on the Eucharist to a degree while also serving to broaden the applicability of the remedy to Christians who might not have the same eucharistic understanding as Cavanaugh does. As Cavanaugh himself sees, there are other theological sites for encouraging and developing theopolitical imagination, and Conyers develops some of these sites that are particularly beneficial for Protestant—and even more specifically, evangelical—sensibilities.

This exploration of the work of Cavanaugh has shown that Conyers's work resonates with and contributes to contemporary political theology, especially in the realm of diagnosing modernity and proposing remedies for faithful Christian practice. While Conyers's work is not perfect and can certainly be strengthened, especially by Cavanaugh's careful treatment of the forming power of the nation-state, Conyers's work contributes depth in diagnosing what modernity is and provides an ecclesially broad response.

Conyers's corpus shows signs of constructive potential for a new wave of evangelical political theology that is both more attentive to the concerns of political theology more generally and more faithful in drawing on the evangelical theological tradition to form evangelical theopolitical imagination for navigating modern challenges from an evangelical context. In conclusion, we turn our attention to characterizing an evangelical theopolitical imagination influenced by Conyers.

A Path Forward?

INTRODUCTION

In the past five chapters, we covered a significant amount of ground, seeking to understand A. J. Conyers as a theologian in order to comprehend his diagnosis of modernity and—most importantly—the way he forms an evangelical social imaginary for navigating the modern world in a way that overcomes common weaknesses. We grappled with major intellectual influences, lines of argument, and themes. I now draw on an earlier thesis regarding Conyers's overarching project in order to weave the various threads into a comprehensive understanding of Conyers's work and then to begin to point to the way this work can inform evangelical theopolitical imagination.

In chapters 1 and 2, I argued that Conyers shows a range of influence that provides resources for moving beyond the simple liberal-conservative binary that too often characterizes evangelical theopolitical imagination. His work shows an overarching project and trajectory that connects his earliest scholarly work on Moltmann with his final monographs on the modern world. Now that we have covered the scope of these works, I will try to make this connection clearer. In Conyers's work on Moltmann, he positively draws on Moltmann's insight regarding the importance of eschatology for all of Christian theology. Moltmann moved toward an eschatology of openness because he saw an emphasis on monotheism and the created order as too open to abuse and power. For Moltmann, hierarchy, depending on values in creation or in power, is always abusive. Conyers maintained Moltmann's emphasis on eschatology but criticized his identification of hierarchy and the abuse of power. Conyers turned to the work of Richard Weaver, who argued for the importance of hierarchy and order for structuring human living. For Moltmann, such hierarchy would yield to the abuse of power.

Conyers synthesized these two positions. He used Weaver's emphasis on the hierarchy of the good for providing value and order to critique Moltmann's identification of hierarchy and the abuse of power. However, Conyers did not entirely accept Weaver's position either, for he tied the hierarchy of values not only to a creation order but to the eschatological order; the good is defined by the good toward which God is drawing creation through the redemptive work of Christ. So, through Weaver he corrected Moltmann, and through Moltmann he corrected Weaver. Conyers created a constructive synthesis of the two. Such a constructive synthesis begins to overcome the liberal-conservative binary not by finding a third way between them but by seeking what is true, whatever the sources, and by allowing for nuance rather than drawing us-versus-them binaries.

Three more strands of influence shape Conyers. In thinking about the modern world, Conyers sees an alternative possibility in the work of Johannes Althusius. This alternative vision, which is essentially the belief in the importance of mediating institutions, provides Conyers with the realization that things could be different and with a method to pursue change. Eric Voegelin provides a concept of order that Conyers draws on as well. The third strand I described as Southern Agrarianism, a stream of influence that provides the context for Richard Weaver, played a role in Conyers's reception of Moltmann. The Southern Agrarians provide Conyers with the resources for a different sort of conservatism, both theological and political, within which he is able to draw together moral and economic critiques of the modern world that are uncharacteristic of conservative evangelicals today. Conyers synthesizes the work of Althusius with the concerns of the Southern Agrarian influence to serve as the foundation for his diagnosis of and remedy for the modern world.

This constructive synthesis is vital for understanding Conyers's work on modernity. For Conyers, the essence of modernity is viewing the world not as given but as open: "This change of orientation experienced in modern times is a profound one: moving the human being from the role of receptive discoverer, listener, and responder to the world, to that of shaper, fashioner, even creator of the world."[1] Modernity is fundamentally human-centered. He demonstrates how a change in the use of toleration serves to advance this new conception of the world, to create an isolated individual and a strong, centralized state at the expense of all mediating institutions. The problem of the modern world is that a shift from seeing the world as gift to seeing the world as a project calling for arbitrary force has led to rampant autonomous individualism. Under such conditions, there are no resources for charting a way forward together or for binding communities. All that is left is force.

Conyers responds to this situation. He starts with vocation. While at first this concept may seem arbitrary, he sees it as opposing the self-centeredness of the modern world: where the modern world focuses on the autonomous individual's creation of meaning and reality, Conyers lifts up vocation, being called, responding to Another.[2] The sentiment of vocation provides a path for delivering us from the decay of modernity.[3] Where modernity exalts the autonomous individual, vocation upholds the individual's dignity while rooting the individual in meaningful community. Where modernity calls for choice, vocation calls for faithful response.

For Conyers, vocation is not the final answer but the starting point. Reclaiming vocation reorients one's worldview, shifting it from the self to Another, from self-will to the acceptance of gift. Conyers narrows the choice to a vocational view of life versus an elective view of life.[4] Vocation is a starting point with concrete, particular practices and applications. A person is called in a particular place, among a particular community. She is called toward a destiny, to rest in a transcendent goal. While the modern world provides opportunity for distraction by trying to deny the reality of final causes and purpose, starting with vocation helps promote attention— attention needed to persevere among the suffering that comes in pursuing the good.

Conyers's diagnosis of modernity and his remedy emerge from this creative synthesis, through which he provides a "truly catholic vision" for navigating the modern world. He is more than just the sum of his influences,

---

1. Conyers, "Can Postmodernism Be Used," 295.

2. Here again Conyers connects closely with the concept of piety important in Weaver.

3. Conyers, "Can Postmodernism Be Used," 296.

4. Ibid.

and he uses these influences to correct deficiencies that he sees in each and thus comes to his own constructive, creative stance. His untimely death prevented him from drawing out the full implications of his starting point of vocation and from strengthening various weaknesses. That project is left for others who share his point of view. In what follows, I sketch how an evangelical theopolitical imagination informed by Conyers might look.

Conyers and Evangelical Theopolitical Imagination

In the introduction, I noted four tendencies in evangelical theopolitical imagination. I argued that these tendencies of imagination result from some of the strengths of evangelicalism but in fact weaken evangelical theopolitical imagination. A brief review of these four tendencies will be useful here: first, a tendency to reduce everything to a binary, us-versus-them rhetoric, which stems in part from an evangelical emphasis on conversionism (a focus on conversion contributes to viewing people as being in two opposing camps, which can then fuel an us-versus-them rhetoric). Second, evangelicals embrace certain aspects of the modern world uncritically. This embrace is especially true with regard to democratic and free-market institutions. Evangelicals see such institutions as promising solutions (against problems such as political totalitarianism and poverty) while failing to account adequately for the problems such institutions themselves create.[5] In other words, evangelicals promote how such institutions can cooperate with the advance of the gospel without being as aware of the ways these institutions can be harmful to the gospel. This weakness is related to evangelical activism, and specifically with the desire to leave fundamentalist isolationism behind. Third, in seeking to be biblical, evangelicals sometimes revert to an oversimplified reading of Scripture, despite their commitment to the Bible as authority. This oversimplified reading reduces the text and makes it serve ideological ends, often related to modern institutions. This weakness is a perversion of evangelical biblicism. Fourth, evangelicals often fail to incorporate the theological work of other Christian traditions, even when that work would strengthen evangelical priorities. In the case of po-

5. Here is another example of where Cavanaugh's work helps supplement Conyers's, as Cavanaugh pushes deeper into problems with democratic and free-market institutions, especially regarding their formative power. Asking the sorts of questions that Cavanaugh does helps us overcome binary thinking because it presses beyond questions of conservative or liberal—and modernity or antimodernity—and instead casts the questions in terms of moral formation and imagination.

litical theology, more could be done to connect the thinking of evangelicals to that of other Christians. This weakness correlates (at least in part) with a focus on the Bible as the primary authority. Such a focus can lead to a neglect of other sources for consideration, such as the work of Christians from other traditions.

Each chapter argued in part how Conyers provides resources for overcoming these tendencies of evangelical theopolitical imagination. His work incorporates conservative and liberal influences in a way that moves beyond a simple binary that all too often characterizes evangelical discourse.[6] The conservative sources that influenced him most do not coincide comfortably with contemporary conservatism (for instance, they included an economic critique that today's conservatives do not often echo), and he also utilized eschatological insights from theologians such as Moltmann to emphasize an aspect of openness and hope for the future rather than a mere adherence to the past (as a caricature of conservatism would). Through his work on toleration, he unapologetically takes aim at modern institutions—such as the nation-state and the free-market economy—that many evangelicals either take for granted or actively promote. His foundational idea of vocation serves as a starting point for building a vision that is biblically informed and saturated without resorting to simple proof texting about economics or politics. Finally, his work provides a fruitful avenue for dialogue with Christian political theology more broadly conceived and practiced, as shown through the interaction with the work of William Cavanaugh. Conyers certainly does not solve these weaknesses for evangelicals, but turning to his work points a way forward in beginning to overcome such problems.

But besides overcoming a few perceived weaknesses, what are the primary features of an evangelical theopolitical imagination shaped by Conyers? Conyers identifies three features of a recovery of vocation. First, this sense of divine vocation is communal: "the generosity, benevolence, forgiveness, and mercy of God finds representatives in the community of disciples (imitators of Christ, whose own benevolence is mediated through virtuosos in the community)." Second, "the virtues of generosity, kindness, mercy, forgiveness . . . are more congenial" to a view of life informed by

---

6. Conyers's conservatism was most shaped by "paleoconservatism" and sources such as Johannes Althusius, Eric Voegelin, and Richard Weaver. His continual interest in Moltmann, who would not be considered a conservative, helps him move beyond the simple binary between conservative and liberal. Thus Conyers does not point the way forward on conservative-liberal binaries by creating a new third way but by disarming the spectrum to a degree by acknowledging truth (and problems) wherever he finds it.

divine vocation. Third, distinctions among people that are an embarrassment to a culture shaped by power and the market become points of greater understanding. For "while giving expression to what is temporally divided, we begin together to give witness to what is finally united. For the end of all things is the God who calls us, in whom we find rest, by whose one light we find out separate ways toward that city 'not made with hands, eternal, in heaven.'"[7] In the following, I identify nine additional elements of Conyers's vocational theology that cluster into three groups: method, emphases, and application. Though presented here in condensed form, these elements begin to show what would characterize an evangelical theopolitical imagination informed by Conyers's work.

Method

First, an evangelical theopolitical imagination informed by Conyers holds the Bible as the final standard. While not all of Conyers's works were filled with explicit Scripture citations, he had a reputation among his colleagues for being deeply committed to being biblical. For example, he stated that his final book could be considered a commentary on the apostle James's "What causes wars among you?"[8] If someone drew attention to some element contradicting Scripture, he was always willing to listen.[9] Just because Conyers's writing topics were not explicit expositions of Scripture does not mean that he was not concerned with being faithful to the Bible and allowing it to be the final norm for his theology. Theology can and must have Scripture as its final standard, but that does not mean that interpretation and use can only occur on one level.

Second, Conyers was inspired by the Great Tradition of the Christian faith, and evangelical theopolitical imagination could benefit from a similar priority. This element is evident in Conyers's work on the early Truett Seminary curriculum. It can also be seen as Conyers interacts with a variety of sources throughout his theological work. Princeton scholar Eric Gregory has recognized the need for evangelical political theology to engage more with specific figures from the tradition.[10] Additionally, drawing Conyers and Cavanaugh together shows how evangelicals and Catholics can find

7. Conyers, *Listening Heart*, 191–92.

8. Ibid., 3–4.

9. Robert Sloan, phone conversation with author, August 5, 2013.

10. See Gregory, "Politics," 389–401.

common sources and themes for theopolitical imagination. This cooperation extends beyond partnering on activism based on conclusions about specific issues, such as abortion, to identifying strategies for forming moral imagination. These sources and themes are tied to the Great Tradition while creatively interfacing with issues such as nationalism, consumerism, and globalization. Conyers's focus on the Great Tradition does not neglect contemporary concerns, but as with Cavanaugh he mines the resources of the past for wisdom for the present and the future.

The third methodological element for evangelical theopolitical thought drawn from Conyers is the practice of entering into dialogue with other Christian traditions not only on the level of political issues (abortion, gay marriage, etc.) but also on the level of doctrines and practices that form theopolitical imagination. Conyers was committed to promoting a broadly catholic vision for the world, and such a vision requires interaction not only (or even primarily) at the level of specific issues, but at the level of doctrines such as Eucharist, incarnation, Trinity, and others that inform our being in the world.

Emphases

First and most obviously, an evangelical theopolitical imagination following Conyers's emphases is oriented around a robust notion of vocation. It responds wisely and faithfully to the call of God, recognizing a few important elements. On one hand, Conyers's emphasis on vocation recognizes that God calls individuals, but on the other hand, Conyers does not consider the individual isolated but placed within certain important formative communities (family, church). Also, we must remember that the call of God does not always draw one to prestigious positions, ideas, or places. Instead, as one sees in the Bible, the call is often away from comfort and "importance."

Second, Conyers emphasized that vocation and incarnation lead to a humble acceptance of the diversity that often causes division in the modern world (e.g., race). These differences serve as points of entry for understanding existence in valid but partial ways. This theme will change the tone of evangelical engagement with difference, racial or otherwise. It sets a tone of humble listening to the other.

Third, eschatology is central to any evangelical theopolitical thought inspired by Conyers. Conyers found eschatology central because it made the gospel applicable to any aspect of life. Eschatology makes the gospel central to all of life by showing that life requires a telos and that the future God is calling his people toward serves as that orienting telos. Human life is properly defined, understood, and pursued through an understanding of the future toward which God is calling his creation. Conyers shows in his work how eschatology can provide a helpful balance between created order and redeemed order. While he noticed that Moltmann privileged eschatology to a high degree in order to avoid abuses of power, Conyers turned to concepts of hierarchy and order in the Southern Agrarians, Richard Weaver, and Eric Voegelin to insist that eschatology could remind Christians of the good of what God is calling the world toward without being involved in too radical a critique of the present world, as he felt Moltmann was. Evangelical theopolitical imagination must be formed not only with what is present in the created order but also with an openness to what God is working through the power of the cross of Christ.

Application

Conyers's work also inspires some specific applications to contemporary issues that would direct evangelical theopolitical imagination, especially in light of its tendency to take certain modern institutions for granted. First, Conyers's work leads to questioning the allegiances and the loyalties that the state proposes, because he understands that they can divide true community. Such loyalties can come at the expense of more immediate ones.

Conyers certainly has room for affirming certain good aspects of modernity, but his attention was focused on exposing ignored problems for the sake of Christian living in the world. As Oliver O'Donovan has argued, the relationship of Christianity and modernity can be read in more than one direction. Modernity is a *bene esse*, with the stamp of the church evident in liberalism's four aspects—freedom, mercy, natural right, and openness to free speech; or it is a *pessimum esse*, displaying the emergence of the pseudo-Christ in the last times.[11] Conyers would agree with this assessment, and it shows that an evangelical theopolitical imagination informed by Conyers can be positive about modernity while still taking seriously its nefarious qualities. In fact, Conyers's concern is with Christians who are so interested in the positive aspects of modernity that they neglect the "submodernity" of the oppressed and suffering. Leaving the positive or the negative out leads to an incomplete picture.

11. O'Donovan, *Desire of the Nations*, 283–84.

The line between the two can be difficult to discern, however, and the subsequent judgment of specific policies and states is contested. For instance, evangelical theologian Peter Leithart believes America is a "Babel," an empire offering unity. But he argues that it is not yet a "Beast," by which he means an empire that persecutes God's people.[12] However, Leithart's neat categorization does not stand up to scrutiny. Is physical persecution of Christians the line? This definition should be expanded in some way, perhaps to show that "Americanism" (as Leithart calls it) persecutes faith in other ways and therefore can qualify as a beast. It is helpful to draw a distinction between empires that physically persecute and those that do not, but is it also dangerous in that it is helpful? Could it lead us to accept what America is without being as critical as we as Christians should be of elements like those identified by Conyers? Because of evangelicals' tendency to overaccept the state and free-market economics, a voice like Conyers serves as a helpful corrective in finding a proper balance amidst modern ambiguity.

This first application leads to a second, more specific one: Conyers's work will help evangelicals refuse to let the church be characterized as a voluntary association in line with the state's preferred version of reality and destiny. Putting this view of the church into practice is difficult, but it begins by questioning the state's totalizing impulses and nurturing the sentiment that American Christians are Christians first, and sometimes that makes it very difficult to be American.

Third, Conyers leads evangelical theopolitical thought to understand that Christians need to temper support of the free market's strengths with its weaknesses as well. While we can acknowledge good elements of it, we must be equally attentive to the way that it creates a certain type of slavery and that many suffer because of it. We must be realistic about the dehumanizing, autonomizing form of discipleship that can occur when economic logic extends beyond economic transactions and into other areas of life. Just as we can see modernity itself as a good thing or a terrible thing, free-market economics deserves the same attention to both sides of the issue.

These important elements of method, emphases, and application begin to show how Conyers's influence might shape evangelical theopolitical imagination. In short, Conyers directs evangelicals to take the Bible and tradition seriously while entering into dialogue with Christians more broadly, to focus on vocation, humility, and the centrality of eschatology,

12. Leithart, *Between Babel and Beast.*

and to call into question the way that the state and the free market disciple Christians in ways counter to the way of Jesus.

Conclusion

While the evangelical social imaginary certainly has its weaknesses, evangelical theology does not lack resources for a critical engagement with and navigation of the modern world. Younger evangelicals need not migrate to other traditions in order to be true to a sense of Christ's rule over political and economic life. Following the work of A. J. Conyers, if we begin with a proper sense of who God is and what God calls us to be and do, we can resist the power lust of the modern world and nurture communities and individuals properly oriented toward one another and toward Another. This route leads us toward the "truly catholic vision" that Conyers sought. His final words are mine as well:

> Only when members of a community understand life as a response to a large and generous world, created by a great and merciful Providence, will the possibilities of life together become more fully realized. Otherwise, without this spirit infusing and animating a people, existence is reduced to competing forces, clashing at twilight, grasping whatever is left of power, fame, and fortune, before the darkness descends. For then, while the isolation becomes rooted in every human domain, its end is necessarily found in the dust of death. But with this spirit of vocation, this conviction that we are not, after all, our own, but belong to Another, the world opens up, becomes a place for others, and is illuminated by a spreading and abiding hope.[13]

---

13. Conyers, *Listening Heart*, 193.

Bibliography

Agar, Herbert, and Allen Tate, eds. *Who Owns America? A New Declaration of Independence.* 1936. Reprint, Wilmington, DE: ISI, 1999.

Alexander, Michelle. *The New Jim Crow: Mass Incarceration in the Age of Colorblindness.* New York: New Press, 2010.

Althusius, Johannes. *Politica.* Edited and translated by Frederick S. Carney. Indianapolis: Liberty Fund, 1995.

Anderson, Benedict. *Imagined Communities: Reflections on the Origin and Spread of Nationalism.* Rev. ed. New York: Verso, 2006.

Anderson, Braden P. *Chosen Nation: Scripture, Theopolitics, and the Project of National Identity.* Eugene, OR: Cascade, 2012.

Ayres, Lewis. *Augustine and the Trinity.* New York: Cambridge University Press, 2010.

——. *Nicaea and Its Legacy: An Approach to Fourth-Century Trinitarian Theology.* New York: Oxford University Press, 2004.

Barnes, Michel René. "Augustine in Contemporary Trinitarian Theology." *Theological Studies* 56 (1995) 237–50.

——. "*De Regnon* Reconsidered." *Augustinian Studies* 26 (1995) 51–79.

——. "Rereading Augustine's Theology of the Trinity." In *The Trinity: An Interdisciplinary Symposium on the Trinity,* edited by Stephen T. Davis et al., 145–76. New York: Oxford University Press, 1999.

Bebbington, David. *Evangelicalism in Modern Britain: A History from the 1730s to the 1980s.* Grand Rapids: Baker, 1992.

Beneke, Chris, and Christopher S. Grenda, eds. *The First Prejudice: Religious Tolerance and Intolerance in Early America.* Philadelphia: University of Pennsylvania Press, 2010.

Benoist, Alain de. "The First Federalist: Johannes Althusius." *Telos* 118 (2000) 25–58.

Berry, Wendell. *The Art of the Commonplace: The Agrarian Essays of Wendell Berry.* Edited by Norman Wirzba. Washington, DC: Counterpoint, 2002.

——. *The Unsettling of America: Culture and Agriculture.* New York: Avon, 1977.

Bingham, Emily S., and Thomas A. Underwood, eds. *The Southern Agrarians and the New Deal: Essays after "I'll Take My Stand".* Charlottesville: University Press of Virginia, 2001.

Bishop, Jeffrey P. *The Anticipatory Corpse: Medicine, Power, and the Care of the Dying.* Notre Dame: University of Notre Dame Press, 2011.

Blomberg, Craig L. *Neither Poverty nor Riches: A Biblical Theology of Possessions.* Downers Grove, IL: InterVarsity, 1999.

Blumenberg, Hans. *The Legitimacy of the Modern Age.* Translated by Robert M. Wallace. Cambridge: MIT Press, 1985.

Bradford, M. E. *Remembering Who We Are: Observations of a Southern Conservative.* Athens: University of Georgia Press, 1985.

Brand, Chad. *Flourishing Faith: A Baptist Primer on Work, Economics, and Civic Stewardship.* Grand Rapids: Christian's Library Press, 2012.

Brock, Brian. *Singing the Ethos of God: On the Place of Christian Ethics in Scripture.* Grand Rapids: Eerdmans, 2007.

Budde, Michael L. *The Borders of Baptism: Identities, Allegiances, and the Church.* Eugene, OR: Cascade, 2011.

Budziszewski, J. *Evangelicals in the Public Square.* Grand Rapids: Baker Academic, 2006.

Carney, Frederick S. "Translator's Introduction." In *Politica*, edited and translated by Frederick S. Carney, ix–xxxiii. Indianapolis: Liberty Fund, 1995.

Carson, D. A. *The Intolerance of Tolerance.* Grand Rapids: Eerdmans, 2013.

Castoriadis, Cornelius. *The Imaginary Institution of Society.* Translated by Kathleen Blamey. Cambridge: MIT Press, 1975.

Cavanaugh, William T. "Balthasar, Globalization, and the Problem of the One and the Many." *Communio* 28 (2001) 324–47.

———. *Being Consumed: Economics and Christian Desire.* Grand Rapids: Eerdmans, 2008.

———. "The Body of Christ: The Eucharist and Politics." *Word & World* 22 (2002) 170–77.

———. "Coercion in Augustine and Disney." *New Blackfriars* 80 (1999) 283–90.

———. "Consumer Culture." In *Gathered for the Journey*, edited by David M. McCarthy and M. Therese Lysaught, 241–59. Grand Rapids: Eerdmans, 2007.

———. "Consumption, the Market, and the Eucharist." *Concilium* 41 (2005) 88–95.

———. "Dying for the Eucharist or Being Killed by It? Romero's Challenge to First-World Christians." *Theology Today* 58 (2001) 177–89.

———. "'A Fire Strong Enough to Consume the House': The Wars of Religion and the Rise of the State." *Modern Theology* 11 (1995) 397–420.

———. "From One City to Two: Christian Reimagining of Political Space." *Political Theology* 7 (2006) 299–321.

———. "If You Render unto God What Is God's, What Is Left for Caesar?" *The Review of Politics* 71 (2009) 607–19.

———. "The Invention of Fanaticism." *Modern Theology* 27 (2011) 226–37.

———. "Killing for the Telephone Company: Why the Nation-State Is Not the Keeper of the Common Good." *Modern Theology* 20 (2004) 243–74.

———. "The Liturgies of Church and State." *Liturgy* 20 (2005) 25–30.

———. *Migrations of the Holy: God, State, and the Political Meaning of the Church.* Grand Rapids: Eerdmans, 2011.

———. *The Myth of Religious Violence: Secular Ideology and the Roots of Modern Conflict.* New York: Oxford University Press, 2009.

———. "Separation and Wholeness: Notes on the Unsettling Political Presence of the Body of Christ." In *For the Sake of the World: Swedish Ecclesiology in Dialogue with William T. Cavanaugh*, edited by Jonas Ideström, 7–31. Eugene, OR: Pickwick, 2009.

———. *Theopolitical Imagination: Christian Practices of Space and Time.* New York: T. & T. Clark, 2003.

———. *Torture and Eucharist: Theology, Politics, and the Body of Christ.* Malden, MA: Wiley-Blackwell, 1998.

———. "The Unfreedom of the Free Market." In *Wealth, Poverty, and Human Destiny*, edited by Doug Bandow and David L. Schindler, 103–28. Wilmington, DE: ISI, 2003.

———. "The World in a Wafer: A Geography of the Eucharist as Resistance to Globalization." *Modern Theology* 15 (1999) 181–96.

Cavanaugh, William T., et al. "Introduction." In *An Eerdmans Reader in Contemporary Political Theology*, edited by William T. Cavanaugh et al., xvi–xxiv. Grand Rapids: Eerdmans, 2011.

Cole, David. *The Political Philosophy of Eric Voegelin and His Followers: A Criticism of the Voegelinians.* Lewiston, NY: E. Mellen, 2009.

Collins, Kenneth J. *Power, Politics and the Fragmentation of Evangelicalism: From the Scopes Trial to the Obama Administration.* Downers Grove, IL: IVP Academic, 2012.

Conkin, Paul K. *The Southern Agrarians.* Knoxville: University of Tennessee Press, 1988.

Conyers, A. J. "After the Hurricane." *Christianity Today*, November 9, 1992, 34–36.

———. *A Basic Christian Theology.* Nashville: B&H Academic, 1995.

———. "Beyond Walden Pond: Illusion and Reality in Pursuit of the Simple Life." *Touchstone* 11 (1998) 26–30.

———. "Can Postmodernism Be Used as a Template for Christian Theology?" *Christian Scholar's Review* 33 (2004) 293–309.

———. "The Changing Face of Baptist Theology." *Review and Expositor* 95 (1998) 21–38.

———. "*Christianity Today* Talks to Jürgen Moltmann." *Christianity Today*, March 20, 1987, 67.

———. "Cloning and the Moral Imagination." *Touchstone* 10 (1997) n.p.

———. "Communism's Collapse: The Receding Shadow of Transcendence." *Christian Century* 107 (1990) 466–67.

———. *The Eclipse of Heaven: Rediscovering the Hope of a World Beyond.* Downers Grove, IL: InterVarsity, 1992.

———. *The End: What Jesus Really Said about the Last Things.* Downers Grove, IL: InterVarsity, 1995.

———. "God and Man in the Dialogue with Marxism." *Christianity Today*, July 2, 1971, 914–16.

———. *God, Hope, and History: Jürgen Moltmann and the Christian Concept of History.* Macon, GA: Mercer University Press, 1988.

———. "History as Problem and Hope." *Asbury Theological Journal* 55 (2000) 29–39.

———. *How to Read the Bible.* Downers Grove, IL: InterVarsity, 1986.

———. "Is Patriotism Christian?" *Christian Heritage* (June 1972) 11–12.

———. "James: A Pillar of the Church." *Biblical Illustrator* (Fall 1988) 22–25.

———. "Jürgen Moltmann's Concept of History." PhD diss., The Southern Baptist Theological Seminary, 1979.

———. "Liberation Theology: Whom Does It Liberate?" *Modern Age* 27 (1983) 303–8.

———. *The Listening Heart: Vocation and the Crisis of Modern Culture.* Dallas: Spence, 2006.

———. "Living Under Vacant Skies." *Christian Reflection* (2002) 9–17.

———. *The Long Truce: How Toleration Made the World Safe for Power and Profit.* Dallas: Spence, 2001.

———. "A Profile of Levi." *Biblical Illustrator* (Spring 1995) 20–22.

———. "Protestant Principle, Catholic Substance." *First Things* 67 (1996) 15–17.

———. "The Real Old Time Religion." *Southern Partisan* 23 (2004) 16–20, 26.

———. "Rescuing Tolerance." *First Things* 115 (2001) 43–46.

———. "The Revival of Joachite Apocalyptic Speculation in Contemporary Theology." *Perspectives in Religious Studies* 12 (1985) 197–211.

———. "Simms's Incarnational Theology and the Emerging American Tradition." *Southern Quarterly* 41 (2003) 84–92.

———. "Simms's *Sabbath Lyrics* and the Reclaiming of Sacred Time in the Religious Imagination." *Simms Review* 8 (2000) 15–26.

———. "Teaching the Holocaust: The Role of Theology." *Perspectives in Religious Studies* 8 (1981) 128–42.

———. "Three Sources of the Secular Mind." *Journal of the Evangelical Theological Society* 41 (1998) 313–21.

———. "Vocation and the Liberal Arts." *Modern Age* 45 (2003) 123–31.

———. "Why the Chattahoochee Sings: Notes Towards a Theory of 'Place.'" *Modern Age* 43 (2001) 99–106.

Conyers, Deborah A., and James C. Conyers. "Biography of A. J. 'Chip' Conyers." In *Thriving in Babylon: Essays in Honor of A. J. Conyers*, edited by David B. Capes and J. Daryl Charles, xi–xxxix. Eugene, OR: Pickwick, 2011.

Davis, Ellen F. *Scripture, Culture, and Agriculture: An Agrarian Reading of the Bible*. New York: Cambridge University Press, 2008.

Douglass, Bruce. "A Diminished Gospel: A Critique of Voegelin's Interpretation of Christianity." In *Eric Voegelin's Search for Order in History*, edited by Stephen A. McKnight, 139–54. Baton Rouge: Louisiana State University Press, 1978.

Duncan, Christopher M. *Fugitive Theory: Political Theory, the Southern Agrarians, and America*. Lanham, MD: Lexington, 2000.

Dupre, Louis. *Passage to Modernity: An Essay in the Hermeneutics of Nature and Culture*. New Haven: Yale University Press, 1993.

East, John P. *The American Conservative Movement: The Philosophical Founders*. Chicago: Regnery, 1986.

Elazar, Daniel J. "Althusius' Grand Design for a Federal Commonwealth." In *Politica*, edited and translated by Frederick S. Carney, xxxv–xlvi. Indianapolis: Liberty Fund, 1995.

Elshtain, Jean Bethke. *Sovereignty: God, State, and Self*. New York: Basic Books, 2008.

Embry, Charles R. *The Philosopher and the Storyteller: Eric Voegelin and Twentieth-Century Literature*. Columbia: University of Missouri Press, 2008.

Evans, Rachel Held. "Why Millenials Are Leaving the Church." *CNN Belief Blog*, July 27, 2013. http://religion.blogs.cnn.com/2013/07/27/why-millennials-are-leaving-the-church/.

Federici, Michael P. *Eric Voegelin: The Restoration of Order*. Wilmington, DE: ISI, 2002.

Fitch, David E. *The End of Evangelicalism? Discerning a New Faithfulness for Mission: Towards an Evangelical Political Theology*. Eugene, OR: Cascade, 2011.

Follesdal, Andreas. "Subsidiarity." *Journal of Political Philosophy* 6 (1998) 190–218.

Foucault, Michel. *Discipline and Punish: The Birth of the Prison*. Translated by Alan Sheridan. 2nd ed. New York: Vintage, 1995.

Franke, John R. "God Is Love." In *Trinitarian Theology for the Church: Scripture, Community, Worship*, edited by Daniel J. Treier and David Lauber, 105–19. Downers Grove, IL: IVP Academic, 2009.

Gay, Craig M. *The Way of the (Modern) World: Or, Why It's Tempting to Live as if God Doesn't Exist.* Grand Rapids: Eerdmans, 1998.

Genovese, Eugene. *The Southern Tradition: The Achievement and Limitations of an American Conservatism.* Cambridge: Harvard University Press, 1996.

Gierke, Otto Friedrich von. *Johannes Althusius und die Entwicklung der naturrechtlichen Staatstheorien: zugleich ein Beitrag zur Geschichte der Rechtssystematik.* Breslau: Koebner, 1880.

Gillespie, Michael Allen. *The Theological Origins of Modernity.* Chicago: University of Chicago Press, 2009.

Girard, René. *The Scapegoat.* Translated by Yvonne Freccero. Baltimore: Johns Hopkins University Press, 1986.

Gray, Richard. *Writing the South: Ideas of an American Region.* Baton Rouge: Louisiana State University Press, 1997.

Greggs, Tom. "Beyond the Binary: Forming Evangelical Eschatology." In *New Perspectives for Evangelical Theology: Engaging with God, Scripture and the World*, edited by Tom Greggs, 153–67. New York: Routledge, 2010.

Gregory, Brad S. *The Unintended Reformation: How a Religious Revolution Secularized Society.* Cambridge: Belknap Press of Harvard University Press, 2012.

Gregory, Eric. "Politics." In *The Oxford Handbook of Evangelical Theology*, edited by Gerald McDermott, 389–401. New York: Oxford University Press, 2010.

Grell, Ole Peter, and Bob Scribner, eds. *Tolerance and Intolerance in the European Reformation.* New York: Cambridge University Press, 2002.

Grudem, Wayne. *Politics According to the Bible: A Comprehensive Resource for Understanding Modern Political Issues in Light of Scripture.* Grand Rapids: Zondervan, 2010.

Guilds, John Caldwell. "Introduction." In *The Simms Reader: Selections from the Writings of William Gilmore Simms*, edited by John Caldwell Guilds, 1–35. Charlottesville: University of Virginia Press, 2001.

Gushee, David P. *The Sacredness of Human Life: Why an Ancient Biblical Vision Is Key to the World's Future.* Grand Rapids: Eerdmans, 2013.

Hankins, Barry. *Uneasy in Babylon: Southern Baptist Conservatives and American Culture.* Tuscaloosa: University of Alabama Press, 2003.

Hart, D. G. "Wendell Berry's Unlikely Case for Conservative Christianity." In *The Humane Vision of Wendell Berry*, edited by Mark T. Mitchell and Nathan Schlueter, 124–46. Wilmington, DE: ISI, 2011.

Hauerwas, Stanley. *War and the American Difference: Theological Reflections on Violence and National Identity.* Grand Rapids: Baker Academic, 2011.

Haykin, Michael A. G., and Kenneth J. Stewart, eds. *The Emergence of Evangelicalism: Exploring Historical Continuities.* Nottingham: Apollos, 2008.

Heilke, Thomas W. *Eric Voegelin: In Quest of Reality.* Lanham, MD: Rowman & Littlefield, 1999.

Holmes, Stephen R. "Three Versus One? Some Problems of Social Trinitarianism." *Journal of Reformed Theology* 3 (2009) 77–89.

Hughes, Glenn. "Introduction." In *The Politics of the Soul: Eric Voegelin on Religious Experience*, edited by Glenn Hughes, 1–8. Lanham, MD: Rowman & Littlefield, 1998.

Husbands, Mark. "The Trinity Is Not Our Social Program." In *Trinitarian Theology for the Church: Scripture, Community, Worship*, edited by Daniel J. Treier and David Lauber, 120–41. Downers Grove, IL: IVP Academic, 2009.

Kaplan, Benjamin J. *Divided by Faith: Religious Conflict and the Practice of Toleration in Early Modern Europe*. Cambridge: Harvard University Press, 2010.

Kelly, Robert A. "Public Theology and the Modern Social Imaginary." *Dialog* 50 (2011) 162–73.

Kerr, Nathan R. *Christ, History and Apocalyptic: The Politics of Christian Mission*. Eugene, OR: Cascade, 2008.

Kirk, Russell. "Foreword." In *Visions of Order: The Cultural Crisis of Our Times*, by Richard Weaver, vii–ix. Wilmington, DE: ISI, 1995.

Kirwan, Michael. *Discovering Girard*. London: Darton, Longman and Todd, 2004.

———. *Girard and Theology*. New York: T. & T. Clark, 2009.

Kraynak, Robert. "John Locke: From Absolutism to Toleration." *American Political Science Review* 74 (1980) 53–69.

Labrousse, Elisabeth. *Bayle*. Translated by Denys Potts. New York: Oxford University Press, 1985.

Langdale, John J. III. *Superfluous Southerners: Cultural Conservatism in the South, 1920–1990*. Columbia: University of Missouri Press, 2012.

Larsen, Timothy. "Defining and Locating Evangelicalism." In *The Cambridge Companion to Evangelical Theology*, edited by Timothy Larsen and Daniel J. Treier, 1–14. New York: Cambridge University Press, 2007.

Leftow, Brian. "Anti-Social Trinitarianism." In *The Trinity: An Interdisciplinary Symposium on the Trinity*, edited by Stephen T. Davis et al., 203–50. New York: Oxford University Press, 1999.

Leithart, Peter J. *Between Babel and Beast: America and Empires in Biblical Perspective*. Eugene, OR: Cascade, 2012.

Lilla, Mark. *The Stillborn God: Religion, Politics, and the Modern West*. New York: Knopf, 2007.

Livingston, Donald W. "The Very Idea of Secession." *Social Science and Modern Society* 35 (1998) 38–48.

Lunn, John. "Economics." In *The Oxford Handbook of Evangelical Theology*, edited by Gerald McDermott, 402–17. New York: Oxford University Press, 2010.

Lyon, David. "Being Post-Secular in the Social Sciences: Taylor's Social Imaginaries." *New Blackfriars* 91 (2010) 648–62.

Malvasi, Mark G. "*Ideas Have Consequences* and the Crisis of Modernity." In *Steps Toward Restoration: The Consequences of Richard Weaver's Ideas*, edited by Ted J. Smith III, 59–80. Wilmington, DE: ISI, 1998.

———. *The Unregenerate South: The Agrarian Thought of John Crowe Ransom, Allen Tate, and Donald Davidson*. Baton Rouge: Louisiana State University Press, 1997.

McKnight, Stephen A. "Voegelin's New Science of History." In *Eric Voegelin's Significance for the Modern Mind*, edited by Ellis Sandoz, 46–70. Baton Rouge: Louisiana State University Press, 1991.

McNeill, William H. *The Pursuit of Power: Technology, Armed Force, and Society since A.D. 1000*. Chicago: University of Chicago Press, 1982.

Miner, Robert. *Truth in the Making: Creative Knowledge in Theology and Philosophy*. New York: Routledge, 2004.

Mitchell, Brian Patrick. *Eight Ways to Run the Country: A New and Revealing Look at Left and Right*. Westport, CT: Praeger, 2007.

Moltmann, Jürgen. *The Church in the Power of the Spirit: A Contribution to Messianic Ecclesiology*. Translated by Margaret Kohl. Minneapolis: Fortress, 1993.

———. *The Coming of God: Christian Eschatology.* Translated by Margaret Kohl. Minneapolis: Augsburg, 2004.

———. *The Crucified God: The Cross of Christ as the Foundation and Criticism of Christian Theology.* Translated by R. A. Wilson and John Bowden. Minneapolis: Fortress, 1993.

———. *God for a Secular Society: The Public Relevance of Theology.* Translated by Margaret Kohl. Minneapolis: Fortress, 1999.

———. *God in Creation: An Ecological Doctrine of Creation; the Gifford Lectures, 1984–85.* London: SCM, 1985

———. *Theology of Hope: On the Ground and Implications of Christian Theology.* Translated by James W. Leitch. Minneapolis: Fortress, 1993.

———. *The Trinity and the Kingdom: The Doctrine of God.* Translated by Margaret Kohl. Minneapolis: Fortress, 1993.

Moore, Russell D. *The Kingdom of Christ: The New Evangelical Perspective.* Wheaton, IL: Crossway, 2004.

Morrison, Angus, ed. *Tolerance and Truth: The Spirit of the Age or the Spirit of God?* Edinburgh: Rutherford House, 2007.

Murphy, Paul V. *The Rebuke of History: The Southern Agrarians and American Conservative Thought.* Chapel Hill: University of North Carolina Press, 2001.

Nash, George H. *The Conservative Intellectual Movement in America since 1945.* 2nd ed. Wilmington, DE: ISI, 1996.

———. *Reappraising the Right: The Past and Future of American Conservatism.* Wilmington, DE: ISI, 2009.

Nierman, Brenan Ryan. "The Rhetoric of History and Definition: The Political Thought of Richard M. Weaver." PhD diss., Georgetown University, 1993.

O'Donovan, Oliver. *The Desire of the Nations: Rediscovering the Roots of Political Theology.* New York: Cambridge University Press, 1999.

———. *The Ways of Judgment.* Grand Rapids: Eerdmans, 2008.

Ossewaarde, M. R. R. "Three Rival Versions of Political Enquiry: Althusius and the Concept of Sphere Sovereignty." *Monist* 90 (2007) 106–25.

Pearce, Colin D. "Words Upon a Monument: The Liberalism of Simms's Public Theology." *Simms Review* 16 (2008) 24–30.

Pecknold, C. C. *Christianity and Politics: A Brief Guide to the History.* Eugene, OR: Cascade, 2010.

———. "Migrations of the Host: Fugitive Democracy and the Corpus Mysticum." *Political Theology* 11 (2010) 77–101.

Pinker, Steven. *The Better Angels of Our Nature: Why Violence Has Declined.* New York: Penguin, 2011.

Radner, Ephraim. *A Brutal Unity: The Spiritual Politics of the Christian Church.* Waco, TX: Baylor University Press, 2012.

Rasmusson, Arne. *The Church as Polis: From Political Theology to Theological Politics as Exemplified by Jürgen Moltmann and Stanley Hauerwas.* Notre Dame: University of Notre Dame Press, 1995.

Richards, Jay W. *Money, Greed, and God: Why Capitalism Is the Solution and Not the Problem.* New York: HarperCollins, 2009.

Salmon, J. "The Legacy of Jean Bodin: Absolutism, Populism or Constitutionalism?" *History of Political Thought* 17 (1996) 500–522.

Schindler, David L. *Ordering Love: Liberal Societies and the Memory of God.* Grand Rapids: Eerdmans, 2011.

Scotchie, Joseph. *Barbarians in the Saddle: An Intellectual Biography of Richard M. Weaver.* New Brunswick, NJ: Transaction, 1997.

———, ed. *The Vision of Richard Weaver.* New Brunswick, NJ: Transaction, 1995.

Sheehan, Jonathan. *The Enlightenment Bible: Translation, Scholarship, Culture.* Princeton: Princeton University Press, 2007.

Simms, William Gilmore. *Sabbath Lyrics: Or, Songs from Scripture.* Charleston, SC: The Press of Walker and James, 1849.

———. *Self-Development.* Milledgeville, GA: Thalian Society, 1847.

———. *The Social Principle: The True Source of National Permanence.* Tuscaloosa, AL: The Erosophic Society of the University of Alabama, 1843.

Singal, Daniel Joseph. *The War Within: From Victorian to Modernist Thought in the South, 1919–1945.* Chapel Hill: University of North Carolina Press, 1982.

Skillen, James W. "From Covenant of Grace to Equitable Public Pluralism: The Dutch Calvinist Contribution." *Calvin Theological Journal* 31 (1996) 67–96.

———. "The Political Theory of Johannes Althusius." *Philosophia Reformata* 39 (1974) 170–90.

Smith, Andi. "Evangelicalism and the Political: Recovering the Truth Within." In *New Perspectives for Evangelical Theology: Engaging with God, Scripture and the World,* edited by Tom Greggs, 168–83. New York: Routledge, 2010.

Smith, Christian. *How to Go from Being a Good Evangelical to a Committed Catholic in Ninety-Five Difficult Steps.* Eugene, OR: Cascade, 2011.

Smith, James K. A. *Desiring the Kingdom: Worship, Worldview, and Cultural Formation.* Grand Rapids: Baker, 2009.

———. *Imagining the Kingdom: How Worship Works.* Grand Rapids: Baker Academic, 2013.

Smith, Ted J., III "Introduction." In *In Defense of Tradition: Collected Shorter Writings of Richard M. Weaver, 1929–1963,* edited by Ted J. Smith III, xi–xlviii. Indianapolis: Liberty Fund, 2001.

———, ed. *Steps Toward Restoration: The Consequences of Richard Weaver's Ideas.* Wilmington, DE: ISI, 1998.

Strauss, Claudia. "The Imaginary." *Anthropological Theory* 6 (2006) 322–44.

Tanner, Kathryn. "Trinity." In *The Blackwell Companion to Political Theology,* edited by Peter Scott and William T. Cavanaugh, 319–32. Malden, MA: Blackwell, 2003.

Tate, Allen. *Essays of Four Decades.* Chicago: Swallow Press, 1968.

Taylor, Charles. *Modern Social Imaginaries.* Durham: Duke University Press, 2003.

———. *A Secular Age.* Cambridge: Belknap Press of Harvard University Press, 2007.

Thornbury, Gregory Alan. *Recovering Classic Evangelicalism: Applying the Wisdom and Vision of Carl F. H. Henry.* Wheaton, IL: Crossway, 2013.

Toulmin, Stephen Edelston. *Cosmopolis: The Hidden Agenda of Modernity.* Chicago: University of Chicago Press, 1992.

Treier, Daniel J., and David Lauber. "Introduction." In *Trinitarian Theology for the Church: Scripture, Community, Worship,* edited by Daniel J. Treier and David Lauber, 7–21. Downers Grove, IL: IVP Academic, 2009.

Trepanier, Lee, and Steven F. McGuire. "Introduction." In *Eric Voegelin and the Continental Tradition: Explorations in Modern Political Thought,* edited by Lee Trepanier and Steven F. McGuire, 1–13. 3rd ed. Columbia: University of Missouri Press, 2011.

Twelve Southerners. *I'll Take My Stand: The South and the Agrarian Tradition.* 75th anniv. ed. Baton Rouge: Louisiana State University Press, 2006.

Weaver, Richard. *Ideas Have Consequences*. Chicago: University of Chicago Press, 1984.

———. *The Southern Tradition at Bay: A History of Postbellum Thought*. Washington, DC: Regnery Gateway, 1989.

———. "The Tennessee Agrarians." *Shenandoah* 3 (1952) 3–10.

———. "Two Orators." In *The Southern Essays of Richard M. Weaver*, edited by George M. Curtis III and James J. Thompson Jr., 104–33. Indianapolis: Liberty Fund, 1987.

———. "Two Types of American Individualism." In *The Southern Essays of Richard M. Weaver*, edited by George M. Curtis III and James J. Thompson Jr., 77–103. Indianapolis: Liberty Fund, 1987.

Weinert, Matthew S. "Bridging the Human Rights-Sovereignty Divide: Theoretical Foundations of a Democratic Sovereignty." *Human Rights Review* 8 (2007) 5–32.

Witte, John. "A Demonstrative Theory of Natural Law: The Original Contribution of Johannes Althusius." In *Public Theology for a Global Society: Essays in Honor of Max L. Stackhouse*, edited by Deirdre King Hainsworth and Scott R. Paeth, 21–36. Grand Rapids: Eerdmans, 2009.

Wolin, Sheldon S. *Politics and Vision: Continuity and Innovation in Western Political Thought*. Expanded ed. Princeton: Princeton University Press, 2006.

Young, Fred Douglas. *Richard M. Weaver, 1910–1963: A Life of the Mind*. Columbia: University of Missouri Press, 1995.

Zagorin, Perez. *How the Idea of Religious Toleration Came to the West*. Princeton: Princeton University Press, 2003.

Index

www.ingramcontent.com/pod-product-compliance
Lightning Source LLC
Chambersburg PA
CBHW030824270326
41928CB00007B/884